Gender Issues
and the Library

Gender Issues and the Library

Case Studies of Innovative Programs and Resources

Edited by CAROL SMALLWOOD
and LURA SANBORN

Foreword by Loida Garcia-Febo

McFarland & Company, Inc., Publishers
Jefferson, North Carolina

ISBN (print) 978-1-4766-6473-6 ∞
ISBN (ebook) 978-1-4766-3034-2

LIBRARY OF CONGRESS CATALOGUING DATA ARE AVAILABLE

BRITISH LIBRARY CATALOGUING DATA ARE AVAILABLE

Front cover images © 2017 iStock

Printed in the United States of America

McFarland & Company, Inc., Publishers
Box 611, Jefferson, North Carolina 28640
www.mcfarlandpub.com

Table of Contents

Foreword

BY LOIDA GARCIA-FEBO

In January 2016, the United Nations launched the Sustainable Development Goals (SDGs) as part of their 2030 Agenda for sustainable development the areas of People, Planet, Prosperity, Peace and Partnership. The overall plan is for the 17 SDGs to transform our world. One of the key components to achieve this objective is promoting and supporting inclusive and diverse societies through the promotion of goals and targets.

Goal number five of the SDGs is about "achieving gender equality and empowering all women and girls" (United Nations 2016). It includes target 5.1, "end discrimination against women and girls everywhere," and target 5.6.c, "adopt and strengthen sound policies and enforceable legislation for the promotion of gender equality and the empowerment of all women and girls at all levels."

Goal number four is to "ensure inclusive and equitable quality education and promote lifelong learning opportunities for all." Target 4.5 states that "by 2030, the goal is to eliminate gender disparities in education and ensure equal access to all levels of education."

Target 16.10 is to "ensure public access to information and protect fundamental freedoms, in accordance with national legislation and international agreements."

Having advocated on behalf of libraries and the International Federation of Library Associations and Institutions at the United Nations for the past years, I have sat at many meetings with U.N. country members, non-governmental organizations, civic society, and public and private organizations to share powerful stories about how libraries are essential for democracy and development. My colleagues and I have partnered with allies to place libraries and access to information on global and national development agendas.

Worldwide, libraries support gender equality through programming and outreach. This work reflects statements from UNESCO which "considers gender equality as a fundamental human right, a building block for social justice and an economic necessity" (2016). For instance, libraries in Uganda and Nepal have established initiatives to empower women and girls to acquire life-long learning skills, to "take control of their lives and speak their minds" (IFLA 2015). Libraries in Sweden are providing customized programming to bridge the digital divide, increase literacy, and promote social inclusion and sustainability.

In the United States, school and public libraries in the South Bronx, Los Angeles and Providence are providing inclusive meeting spaces for classes featuring emerging technologies and for insightful dialogues including parents, children and community groups about the right of girls and everyone in the community to participate in programs that were traditionally seen as masculine ones.

The above frame is an indicator that now more than ever we need books like this one, which features case studies and how-to essays about topics such as gender studies, gender and cataloguing, feminist Wikipedia edit-a-thons, herstory, outreach for under-represented groups, silenced voices, activism, collection development and programming, supporting and engaging trans* and LGBT populations, resources to support men and masculine studies, foreign government and international organizations web resources, and U.S. government resources on women and women's issues.

This book is a quality resource for all library workers, library advocates, educators, and decision makers serving our ever-increasing diverse communities. The creativity and innovation reflected in the contributions is remarkable, and these are presented with such clarity that other people should be able to follow them to replicate or model their own. The essays reflect our need to continue reaching out to underserved individuals, documenting our efforts, and sharing these with others to promote equity and inclusiveness to transform our world.

REFERENCES

IFLA. 2015. Access and Opportunity for All: How Libraries Contribute to the United Nations 2030 Agenda. Accessed on December 14, 2016, http://www.ifla.org/files/assets/hq/topics/libraries-development/documents/access-and-opportunity-for-all.pdf.

UNESCO. 2016. Building Peace in the Minds of Men and Women. Accessed on December 15, 2016, http://www.unesco.org/new/en/unesco/themes/gender-equality/.

United Nations, Department of Economic and Social Affairs. 2015. Transforming our World: The 2030 Agenda for Sustainable Development. Accessed on December 14, 2016, https://sustainabledevelopment.un.org/post2015/transformingourworld.

Loida Garcia-Febo, the 2018–2019 president of the American Library Association, is president of Information New Wave and is an international library consultant.

Preface

Gender studies is a part of the curriculum at many colleges. The field is also an area of high interest as popular media and celebrities bring it to the forefront, as has the acknowledged national right for gay marriage. Libraries realize the importance of supporting gender studies but many have difficulty finding resources and programming ideas.

With same-sex marriages and the explosion of LGBTIQ news coverage, gender issues are much in the public eye and of concern to library patrons, and *Gender Issues and the Library* is a book for librarians wanting to know how to deal with changes in cataloging, new terms, and meeting patron needs. The 27 essays are arranged into five subject areas: Research and Library Instruction, History and Herstory, Programming, Collections and Beyond, and Resources.

Lesson Plan for Exploring Gender Roles in Society, Literature and Film

MORNA GERRARD *and* CALLAN WELLS

Introduction

Male emotional expression is documented throughout history, and the canon is dominated by male authors, poets, and playwrights. Yet male emotional expression in modern society is still taboo. With "boys don't cry" a common idiom used in music, film, and art, it is easy to see why many young men do not have access to the words to express themselves emotionally. This essay will describe a lesson plan that challenges 10th to 12th graders to consider masculinity in a very personal way, while, at the same time, they develop skills in literary criticism and writing.

In an interview with "The Good Men Project," Franklin Abbott is described as a "profeminist and poet" (https://goodmenproject.com/man-to-man-interviews/an-inter view-with-poet-franklin-abbott/). His works on men and gender include anthologies like *New Men, New Minds: Breaking Male Tradition* (Crossing, 1987), *Boyhood: Growing up Male* (Crossing, 1993), and *Men and Intimacy: Personal Accounts of the Dilemmas of Modern Male Sexuality* (Crossing, 1993). He has also written two books of poetry, *Mortal Love* (RFD, 1999) and *Pink Zinnia* (AuthorHouse, 2009). In the "Good Men" interview, Franklin, who is gay, describes his coming out in Macon, Georgia, in the 1970s. His coming out coincided with the black liberation movement, the anti-war movement, and the women's liberation movement, and all of those movements became and remained important to him throughout his career. Abbott's work, which is very accessible to male readers, gives an important insight into maleness, expectations, and feminist language.

In 2011, Abbott was interviewed for Georgia State University's Gender and Sexuality Oral History Project. On the same day that he was interviewed, he donated the first installment of what proved to be a sizeable and significant collection of personal materials. That first donation was a box of audiocassettes that document presentations at the 15th Men and Masculinity conference which took place in May of 1990 at Oglethorpe University in Atlanta, Georgia. Presenters included Abbott, James Broughton, bell hooks, Kathleen Carlin and Essex Hemphill, and the tone of the presentations and performances was decidedly feminist. Sessions addressed issues like violence, black gay identity, sex and love. Throughout the following months, Abbott donated many, many more boxes of papers, and today, they are fully processed. Not only are they being used by researchers from across the United States, but they have also been the catalyst for further donations from feminist gay men and organizations. Georgia State University is now the official repository of Gay Spirit Visions (GSV), an organization that holds gatherings for gay men to explore their spirituality and identity in a safe, nurturing, and sacred environment (http://gayspiritvisions.org/). It also houses the papers of individual members of GSV and the Radical Faeries—gay men who consider their sexuality through a spiritual lens, and whose values include feminism (http://www.radfae.org/). It houses an almost complete run of *RFD*, the Radical Faerie Digest, GSV's *Visionary*, the *Short Mountain Goatzette*, and a number of other male-focused feminist publications, like *M.Gentle Men for Gender Justice* and *Brotherbond: Newsletter of the National Organization for Changing Men*. Further, members of GSV are conducting their own oral history project, with guidance of the Women and Gender Collections archivist, and a researcher from Tennessee who is using the collections extensively, has volunteered to interview Faeries for Georgia State University's Gender and Sexuality Oral History Project. This current interest in gay spirituality, masculinity and feminism is also reflected in the teaching and research interests of professors at Georgia State University: At the date of writing, a class on the history of masculinities ("American Men / Local Masculinities") is being taught by history professor Joe Perry; African American Studies professor Jonathan Gayles specializes in black masculinity; and English professor Calvin Thomas has written extensively about masculinity and the male body from a feminist, psychoanalytical perspective. With such an interest and rich and growing resources about masculinities available, it seemed reasonable to create a lesson plan using those materials.

In the unit we designed, *Exploring Gender Roles in Society, Literature, and Film*, we focus on what is expected of men, in their expression and their relationships. Using gender and feminist theory, we also look at gender roles more broadly, and how students relate to those roles. We really wanted to explore feminist concepts through students' own lenses without giving them a prescribed definition of what feminism means. So often, feminism is seen as a movement that is tied to the past, or one that is represented by mobs of angry women who are separate from mainstream society. From the lesson plan's rationale:

> Many facets of feminism transcend gender and work toward creating a society which respects all people. Feminism seeks for all people to have choice and ownership of their own bodies and the space to discuss their thoughts and feelings. Agency and individual choice are the keys to feminist theory.... This curriculum argues for the inclusion of feminist ideals, not only in curriculum but in teaching style. It asks for teachers to respect students in making decisions about their education and their definition of certain concepts. Rather than telling students an encyclopedia definition of feminism, this curriculum asks students to read different primary source pieces on male gender identity and create a new conception of masculinity in possibly feminist terms. Masculinity has long defined the lives and attitudes of men towards themselves and toward women. Boys are taught that "being a man" involves swallowed feelings, macho actions, and certainly no tears. This curriculum seeks to challenge this conception of masculinity as dangerous for boys and the women in their lives [http://research.library. gsu.edu/c.php?g=115900&p=751400].

In creating this lesson plan, we also felt it was very important to include LGBT voices. As is generally the case with women, LGBT figures have been largely excluded from the canon. Exclusion of an entire group is one of the most basic forms of discrimination, however through social justice pedagogy, we have the opportunity to create lesson plans that not only feature LGBT voices, but in fact focus on them. LGBT students and students whose families have LGBT members deserve to feel safe and heard in their learning environments, and heterosexual students will be enriched by the addition of Franklin Abbott and James Broughton's poetry.

Rationale

We created this lesson plan to challenge traditional notions of masculinity, and, more importantly, notions of power. Students are introduced to patriarchy throughout their school years: In particular, history and literature are dominated by male figures. As mentioned, Abbott self-identifies as a feminist. He challenges the very notion of masculinity that is generally accepted. The lesson plan's rationale describes the necessity for understanding power dynamics:

> In her book, *All About Love: New Visions*, bell hooks says, "patriarchal masculinity requires of boys and men not only that they see themselves as more powerful and superior to women but that they do whatever it takes to maintain their controlling position." In this statement, hooks outlines a power dynamic which is seen throughout the world and throughout time. As students progress into more advanced literary studies, power structures will become integral to their understanding and writing about literature. This analytical skill will be extremely beneficial in Advanced Placement and College Entrance essays as well as throughout college.

In designing this lesson plan, we hoped for two major outcomes. First, students would learn the language to discuss their feelings about themselves and their relationships. This involves teaching "grit." Additionally, we imagined students being able to discuss Francesco Petrarch's *The White Doe* using the framework the unit provides, or viewing William Shakespeare's *Romeo and Juliet* through a gender theory lens. The skills required to critically analyze literature using gender and feminist theory will benefit students throughout their academic careers.

Course Outline

Day One

Day one of the lesson begins with a journaling exercise that asks students to define masculinity and femininity. Next students watch a video created by the Representation Project called *The Mask You Live In (http://therepresentationproject.org/film/the-mask-you-live-in/)*. The video shows a series of images of young boys accompanied by male voices telling them "Don't cry. Stop with the tears. Stop with the emotions." While Abbott and Broughton's work will take center stage later in the lesson, we felt it was important to include multiple forms of media throughout the presentation. In today's educational landscape, we have to engage students in cultural literacy and teach them how to read and interpret more than just words.

After the video, students are asked to answer a series of questions. We believe that questioning students on their experience with material rather than feeding them information about that material is a better way to create a sustained connection to the subject matter. Additionally, using questions rather than lecture format for topics like masculinity and feminism ensures that the teacher can avoid the charge of subjectivity and the students are able to develop their own thoughts on the issues.

The following questions are asked of students:

- How is masculinity portrayed in popular culture? Give examples.
- How could this be positive for boys? How could this be negative for boys?
- Are girls and women affected by masculine culture?
- Would you consider gender a binary? Why or why not? [http://research.library.gsu.edu/c.php?g=115900&p=751667].

We are aware of the extremely sensitive subject matter being considered throughout these lessons, and how students may respond to it, especially as it pertains to masculinity and teenagers. Abbott's work, which is steeped in gender questioning language, and the other media being introduced to the students, provide a framework for discussing these complex subjects.

Day Two

For day two, students work in groups as they are introduced to Abbotts's work. The lesson plan requires that each group will have an equal number of boys and girls so that no one feels isolated, underrepresented, afraid to speak, or unheard throughout the discussion. Each group is asked to read one of Abbott's short stories from his book *Boyhood: Growing Up Male*. The men who wrote these stories represent multiple cultures. One story is set in Africa; one is about an abusive father; another is about bullying. After they read the stories in class, students are given a series of questions to discuss. The questions are about the stories specifically, but they begin to bring up questions about masculinity, feminism across cultures and times, and relationships among men and women and men and their families. Thus, we introduce the language of gender theory.

The questions are as follows:

- How was the man in the story affected by cultural expectations of masculinity?
- How was the author's relationship with his family defined by expectations of masculinity?
- How is the author's culture/time different from your culture/time in its representation of masculinity?
- Did the man have a good or bad relationship with women? How were the women in their childhood described?
- How might feminism be viewed differently in the culture of the author?

The questions assume comprehension of the story and ask students to delve deeper than they normally would when working with a textbook. Asking them to analyze relationships with family, women, and themselves pushes students to think of others' motivations. We believe this type of contemplation develops skills in critical analysis and writing that students will need when they face Advanced Placement tests, and later, in college. For homework on the second day, students are asked to look for a childhood photograph or artifact that they can bring to school the following day.

Day Three

Day three begins the more introspective section of the course. Here we acknowledge that the unit has an agenda, which is to confront traditional notions of masculinity, introduce feminist theory, and challenge the gender binary. This section of the lesson will have to be approached delicately by the teacher.

Day three's opening activity is inspired by Abbott's *Boyhood: Growing Up Male.* Students are asked to write a short poem, story, narrative, dialogue, or essay about how gender roles impacted their childhood. After writing it, students get into groups of four and share their essays with the other members of their groups so that they can experience peer criticism and analysis. The essays will be further edited and turned into the teacher as homework.

Students remain in their groups as they plan a creative project that challenges traditional definitions of gender, masculinity and femininity. Projects can include:

- a photo essay about their group peers (including a craft essay);
- a book of poetry about gender by students in their group (including a craft essay);
- an anthology of poetry about gender, with critical analysis about the themes within the poems;
- starting a "Beyond the Binary" campaign to educate their classmates and other teachers about gender, and how gender might be bigger than the binary;
- an analytical essay about a film's representations of gender.

Day Four

Day four's activity focuses on Franklin Abbott's audio recording of "Radio Venezuela," (http://research.library.gsu.edu/c.php?g=115900&p=751532) and specifically on Abbott's introspection throughout the poem. The poem is about Abbott's experience as a gay man traveling through Venezuela and the friends he meets there who are like family to him. In their journals, students engage their comprehension and written analysis skills with the following questions:

- How did Franklin Abbott's friends act like a family? Why might they have needed to act like a family?
- What are some ways you experience privilege? What are some ways you experience oppression?
- How did Abbott experience privilege and oppression?
- Why is it important to learn about Franklin Abbott's experience in Venezuela?

Students then have the opportunity to share their childhood essays with the class. Giving students the opportunity to publish their own work, even if this simply entails reading it aloud to the class, shows them that their work is important and gives them confidence to pursue publishing on a broader scale.

Day Five

Day five of the lesson introduces Franklin Abbott's friend, James Broughton. A member of the San Francisco Renaissance movement, Broughton was also well known as an avant-garde film maker and playwright. His 1953 film, *Pleasure Garden,* won Best Fantastic-Poetic Film at the 1954 Cannes Film Festival.

In their small groups, students read and analyze James Broughton's "The Word for No is Yes: Letter to a Young Poet Contemplating Suicide" (http://research.library.gsu.edu/ld.php?content_id=4075630). The poem speaks directly to the narrator about a brighter time than the narrator can currently imagine. Students are asked to answer the following questions:

- Why is boy in the poem so troubled?
- Where is the place where "heart and mind meet"?
- What does the speaker mean by "the word for No is Yes"?

Students will have the rest of the class period to work on their group projects. Projects are due on Day 6. The goal of the group project is "to engage in an analytical process that furthers the exploration of gender roles as they pertain to literature, art, or film. You have flexibility in the final product, but you will be graded on:

- how you present gender theory;
- how you substantiate your claims with evidence from other scholarly work;
- how you present your final project;
- and how effectively you display an understanding of gender within a larger framework (i.e. literature, art, film, society, the school, your own life)" [http://research. library.gsu.edu/c.php?g=115900&p=751836].

Days Six and Day Seven

Students will present their group projects to the class and the instructor. Specific assignments and rubrics are made available to the instructor on the LibGuide website.

Conclusion

As with the *Silent Voices* lesson plan described (in "Silenced Voices Lesson Plan"), this unit is challenging. Teachers may not want to broach the issues of LGBT identity and inclusion, and they may also find the theory behind the unit intellectually demanding. We feel, however, that this is an important topic that deserves consideration, and for those who want to tackle the topic, the unit provides a useful framework.

Other units that have been created using the Women and Gender collections are a great deal more accessible, and include *The ERA: Oral Histories Curriculum* (http://re search.library.gsu.edu/c.php?g=115860) and *Georgia Women Speak!* (http://research. library.gsu.edu/c.php?g=115912). The *ERA* curriculum, which is designed for 8th to 12th graders, brings together History and English-Language Arts curriculum. It seeks to use the history of the Equal Rights Amendment to educate students about the practice and interpretation of oral histories and analysis of primary sources and contemporary media. The *Georgia Women Speak!* unit, also designed for 8th to 12th graders, utilizes speeches by women in Georgia to teach students about regionally well-known and respected politicians (Georgia state representative and senator Cathey Steinberg and Atlanta Mayor Shirley Franklin), educators (Dean Nell Trotter), and artists (author Pearl Cleage). At the same time, students learn about the fundamentals of rhetoric, as they learn how to write compelling speeches of their own.

One question that arose during the development of the *Exploring Gender Roles* and the *Silenced Voices* units was, "Is it worth spending time and energy to create lesson plans that are not universally accessible?" Our response to that question was an overwhelming, "Yes, it is worth it." If a subject is well-supported with primary sources, if it imparts important lessons for young people, and if it follows Common Core standards, there is very little reason not to create a lesson plan. Further, as a straightforward intellectual and practical exercise, creating these lesson plans is a great proving ground for bright and motivated Graduate Student Assistants. We would certainly encourage future education majors to work on similar projects moving forward, as the experience benefits the students who create them, the students and teachers across the state who use them, and the collections that provide the materials to make them possible. Above all else, these lesson plans require young people to interact with primary sources: students learn what primary sources look like and how they are used; they learn about the challenges connected to working with primary sources, as well as the power that they hold; they learn how to compare and analyze disparate and often competing voices; and throughout the lessons, they learn how to consider their own developing feelings about difficult subjects as they listen openly to the opinions of their peers. Moving forward, archives will be useful and exciting tools in their academic and civic lives, and the students lucky enough to be able to use archival materials as young adults will be more likely to seek them out as they go about their business of changing the world.

REFERENCES

Abbott, Franklin. *Boyhood: Growing Up Male.* Freedom, CA: Crossing, 1993.
Abbott, Franklin. *Men and Intimacy: Personal Accounts of the Dilemmas of Modern Male Sexuality.* Freedom, CA: Crossing, 1993.
Abbott, Franklin. *Mortal Love.* Liberty, TN: RFD, 1999.
Abbott, Franklin. *New Men, New Minds: Breaking Male Tradition.* Freedom, CA: Crossing, 1987.
Abbott, Franklin. *Pink Zinnia.* Bloomington, IN: AuthorHouse, 2009.

"Masculinities: A Feminist Perspective"
A Hybrid Course Built from Scratch

Darcy I. Gervasio, Rebecca Oling
and Patricia Rind

This essay provides three perspectives from each of its co-authors to illustrate the collaborative nature of developing a new course.

Building a Hybrid Course from Scratch (Patricia Rind)

As a professor of gender and women's studies, I've built many courses "from the ground up." The field is always changing, so there's always preparation before a new semester—new literature to read, terms to be learned, and concepts to understand—even when I am teaching a course I have taught many times before. In spring 2015, I was asked to teach a course in the fall that would be entirely new for me: "Masculinities, A Feminist Perspective." A few weeks after I accepted, I was asked if I would teach it as a hybrid— 60 percent online and 40 percent in-class. Although I love the classroom experience, I agreed to do it, figuring it would give me an opportunity to learn about online teaching. The class would meet six times for three hours on a Monday night, spread at intervals throughout the semester. As I had never built an online course, I was faced with the challenge of not only learning new literature and creating a syllabus, but also learning what tools I had at my disposal and how best to use them to create the most effective pedagogical experience for my students.

The Learning Management System at SUNY Purchase is Moodle. I had thus far used it in fairly basic ways—posting files, URLs, and TurnItIn assignments—but I didn't know what other tools embedded within Moodle could help make my course come alive. Periodically, the Teaching, Learning, and Technology Center (TLTC) within the Purchase College Library offers summer workshops for faculty teaching online courses, but, unfortunately, they were not being offered that summer.

Initially, my primary focus for the fall was on learning as much about the masculinities literature as I could. I started researching articles, ordering books, and reading, and I put nuts-and-bolts questions of how the course would be set up on the back burner. In hindsight, that probably wasn't the best way to go about it. By the end of June, I had a list of probable readings, but had only a vague idea of how to set up the online portion of the class and what Moodle tools could help. It was then that I reached out to the TLTC for help. Rebecca Oling, the library instruction coordinator, answered my call.

When Rebecca and I met, we discussed what the course was about, the kinds of assignments I was considering, and how I liked to teach my face-to-face (F2F) classes. We brainstormed assignments, discussed various tools in Moodle I could use, and researched videos that were available for streaming or that she could obtain. Unbeknownst to me before our meeting, Rebecca is also the go-to librarian for streaming video. In my twelve years of working at Purchase, it had never occurred to me that I could reach out to a librarian to help me find such content for my class. With Rebecca's assistance, I was able to provide the students with seven different movies and documentaries to watch on their own throughout the semester, all of which complemented the assigned readings for the respective weeks.

Rebecca and I also talked about creating discussion forums in a manner that would best replicate the kinds of in-class discussions I find so valuable to learning. This was of particular importance to me, as I worried about losing such discussions when I lost two thirds of my classroom time. Rebecca also discussed the usefulness of having a clear rubric for grading students' forum posts, and then found examples of good rubrics and printed them for me. These served as the models for the rubric that I eventually developed. In the end, I set up weekly discussion forums for the weeks we would not meet F2F. The students were required to respond to one or two questions, then reply to one or two responses from their peers.

Rebecca offered two additional suggestions that I ended up using. First, I had a weekly "Contributions from the Real World" module on Moodle. The following were the instructions I provided: "On this page, you can post anything you see, hear, read, etc. that has to do with masculinities, gender, or sexuality. Just a few examples of things you might post would be a music video, a commercial, a conversation you had or overheard, song lyrics, or a comment on a sports talk show. Please post at least one per week. You will be graded only on whether or not you did the assignment, not on its quality."

The second was a "Class Resource Bank" where the students could share resources that they found for their research paper, which would be due at the end of the semester. While weekly "Real World Contributions" were required, the Resource Bank was not, despite the offer of extra credit for contributing to it. Unfortunately, because it was not required, students did not utilize the Resource Bank during the semester at all.

After our meeting, Rebecca and I exchanged emails and met again at the end of July to finalize the online portion of the class. I also met with Keith Landa of the Teaching, Learning, & Technology Center, who helped me set up Gradebook. Having that as an additional tool was enormously helpful and saved a great deal of time.

Around the same time, in early August, Darcy I. Gervasio sent out an email to faculty in gender studies offering her services as liaison librarian. I responded, saying it would be great if she could set up a tailored research guide for my students to use for their research paper. She said she could and also offered to come into the class to do a lesson on research and using the guide. Although I would have loved to have her come in, I was only meeting with the students six times, so I didn't want to "lose" any classroom time.

By mid–August, my class was ready to run (although after classes started, my Moodle page required a bit of cleanup by our go-to Moodle expert, Marie Sciangula). In addition to the assignments described above, students had to write weekly 500-word reaction papers. They also had a midterm and a research paper, all submitted through Moodle.

Overall, the hybrid course went well, but I remained frustrated by the lack of classroom time. While many students had part- or full-time jobs and, thus, liked that we didn't meet each week, they also felt there was too much work. Because in a F2F class, a student can choose to come to class unprepared and sit for the three hours without saying anything, being forced to answer questions online in a thoughtful manner about the readings can feel like more work.

On a final evaluation I created with input from Darcy and Rebecca, many of the students said they liked the discussion forums and found it helpful to read other students' responses both to the initial posting and in reply to what they, themselves, had posted. While clearly a classroom discussion can go both deeper and wider, the Discussion Forums forced everyone to "speak" (if they wanted to get credit) and allowed everyone to see how others reacted to what they had to say. Very often in a classroom, there are several students who speak a great deal and several who do not choose to contribute at all. That dynamic is sometimes established early in the semester and can be difficult to break.

The "Contributions from the Real World" was the easiest portion of the assigned work for the students to complete each week. Not surprisingly, most of the students posted regularly and shared really interesting things. However, since there was no requirement for them to look at one another's postings, it's unlikely they did so very often. To avoid overloading them with more work, it may make sense to rotate this assignment in some way—that is, have a small group of students post on a given week, while the rest of the students are required to view what has been posted and comment on it.

The students seemed to enjoy the majority of the readings and videos. In classroom discussions and forums, it was clear that they got a great deal from the videos. Perhaps not surprisingly, if they were to do only a portion of the work for that week, they would opt to watch the video rather than do the reading. Since the videos were all interesting and informative, as well as entertaining, I was very glad to have them as a teaching tool.

Although I had certainly worked with librarians over the years, this was the most I had ever collaborated with them. I found it enormously helpful on many levels. In particular, when I first came to Rebecca I was unclear as to how I was going to make the online portion of my class work. Our meetings and email correspondence both provided me with practical tools and the knowledge of how to find videos and helped me to focus on ways to engage the students online that would be pedagogically effective.

Helping with Moodle and Instructional Design (Rebecca Oling)

As the coordinator of instruction, I responded to professor Patricia Rind's inquiry in summer 2015 to address some seemingly simple questions about Moodle. Often, these interactions begin with technical concerns but transform into conversations about instructional design and library resources. As a librarian, I welcome these conversations with faculty and treat them as an informal needs assessment, allowing us to discover how library collections might bolster class assignments and help students reach the stated objectives of the course.

As is often the case, Pat's inquiries about Moodle and online teaching led to a conversation about finding appropriate streaming content. We discussed the pros and cons of choosing films for students to watch versus asking them to choose titles themselves from our collection to suggest to the other participants in the course. While the latter involves more "active learning," the choice hinges on how much time the instructor has and how much control she is willing to relinquish over the course content. In this case, Pat needed to ensure certain concepts were covered in the content she shared. As this course was a hybrid, with only a few F2F meetings, we focused on culling materials that best fit her objectives and that students could digest on their own.

We spent some time searching the library's streaming content together, discussing what might work and why. Pat was looking for films and documentaries that illustrate the broad strokes of what it means to be "masculine" or to interpret "masculinity"—not something that overtly depicted or focused on a subset of stereotypes. This give-and-take is aptly described by Campbell et al. (2015, 47): "[T]here is a reciprocal relationship between design and conversation: conversation is design, and design emerges through conversation." With a better understanding of what Pat needed, we were able to more effectively sift through the Library's streaming collections.

Ultimately, the films *Boyhood, I Am a Man: Black Masculinity in America, The Bro Code,* and *Guyland* were chosen as the main streaming titles. Typically, when I work with faculty of F2F courses, I ask them to think carefully about which titles must be used outside of class and therefore accessed via streaming or placed on physical reserve. Faculty need to determine which titles demand immediate feedback and discussion, while balancing class time with adequate opportunities for students to react to the materials. Students can benefit from the ability to re-watch and review, to think and percolate before writing their reflections. Or, as in this case, external circumstances may require streaming. This is often true of hybrid classes where F2F time is precious. For "Masculinities," the titles were all viewed outside the F2F experience.

As this exploration and selection took place, Pat and I brainstormed different ways for students to interact with streaming media, including:

- Masculinity on Film: Before watching documentaries or movies for the course, ask students to define masculinity or masculine stereotypes. Use a Q&A discussion forum to ask students to share a movie or scene they have seen on their own and explain briefly how that selection reinforces or resists the idea of "masculinity."
- Mr. Mom Project: Have students find examples of "text" (movie, video, article, book, etc.) about a "Mr. Mom" and examine how this is characterized and reinforces or pushes against our ideals of masculinity.
- Have students post lyrics or clips from their favorite musicians and identify patterns and symbols they see that relate to masculinity. How might their peers see them? Ask students to re-examine their own playlists.
- Have students share examples of "masculine" or "hypermasculinity" messaging that they encounter this week (radio, advertising, music, film, TV, internet, interpersonal, observation, etc.). If they don't come across any, why do they think that is?

There were many other ideas, but I've provided just a few to illustrate how offering a long menu of suggestions to faculty reduces the pressure on them to adopt any one assignment. I explained to Pat that these were merely nuggets and she could choose to adapt, combine, or ignore them as she saw fit within the confines of the course goals. Additionally, it became clear that Pat would need to coordinate with the subject librarian,

Darcy I. Gervasio, who is much more knowledgeable about gender studies and the latest resources available in the discipline.

Tailored Course Guides for Collection Development and Outreach (Darcy I. Gervasio)

As the subject liaison librarian for gender studies, I make it a habit each semester to email faculty teaching courses on gender and women's studies to offer my instruction services and solicit suggestions for the library's collections. Professor Patricia Rind responded to my offer in August 2015. Her new course, "Masculinities: A Feminist Perspective," was a hybrid with limited F2F meetings, but she still wanted to provide her students with some library instruction to prepare them for their final research paper. Much like Rebecca's "menu" of potential learning activities, my standard outreach email suggested alternatives to traditional in-class instruction, including creating customized course LibGuides. Pat expressed interest in this option, and I jumped at the chance to create a course research guide for "Masculinities," in large part because I was eager to learn more about the subject area.

I always find creating LibGuides to be a great way to familiarize myself with a collection, and the "Masculinities" guide was no exception. By forcing myself to thoroughly explore the library's catalog, ebooks, databases, online encyclopedias, and streaming resources, I not only put together a research guide tailored to the needs of this specific class, but I became an expert on an important subset of our gender studies collection. Through the process of creating the "Masculinities" LibGuide, I learned that Purchase College Library already owned a surprising number of books discussing men's studies and masculinity, many of which were quite current. On the LibGuide, I highlighted books, ebooks, and reference works from our collections that represented the breadth of the Library's holdings in masculinity studies. I also featured textbooks Pat had placed on course reserve to show students how their assigned readings intersect with the larger library collections.

I also find the tangibility and serendipity of walking through the stacks very enlightening.In addition to physically exploring monographs in the HQ section (the Library of Congress classification for gender and women's studies), I combed through our e-journals for men's studies titles, which included, among others: *Culture, Society & Masculinities, Journal of Men, Masculinities & Spirituality, Journal of Men's Studies, Men and Masculinities,* and *Sex Roles.* I also explored subject headings in WorldCat and library databases, many of which were surprisingly specific, such as: "househusbands," "male friendship," "machismo," and "butch lesbians." By including these subject headings on the course guide, I pointed students to relevant resources and deepened my own understanding of masculinity studies research.

Creating this LibGuide fed directly into collection development. Each year, I focus my collection development efforts—and allocate my limited acquisitions budget for gender studies—on a different subtopic. In the past, I've updated the library's holdings on same-sex marriage, transgender rights, rape culture, and sexual assault on college campuses. Inspired by the "Masculinities" course and my examination of our holdings, I used my 2015–2016 gender studies budget to supplement our men's studies and masculinities collections.

Using LibGuides as a collection development tool was not new for me, but creating a course-specific LibGuide that served a more instructional purpose was a fresh experience. After discussing the tight schedule and hybrid nature of the "Masculinities" class with Pat, I understood the course LibGuide would need to be self-explanatory and independent of F2F instruction. The course-specific LibGuides I'd created in the past were typically designed to accompany in-person library workshops and serve as a gateway to resources, not as an instructional tool. To that end, I structured the "Masculinities" LibGuide more like a tutorial, with how-to instructions and research tips on the first page. I embedded video tutorials on conducting database research into the LibGuide. Finally, I took advantage of LibGuides 2.0 features like tabbed boxes and customized search boxes (for ProQuest, Credo Reference, and the library catalog), to make the guide more streamlined, visually appealing, and intuitive. The LibGuide can be viewed at http://purchase.libguides.com/masculinities.

Last but not least, I became embedded in the "Masculinities" Moodle as a "course librarian." This role allowed me to link to the LibGuide and other resources, including video tutorials about library services, within the online course. From Moodle, I sent several course announcements throughout the semester reminding students about the LibGuide and inviting them to contact me for research help. I also received email notifications from Moodle, allowing me to send timely reminders about library resources relevant to current assignments or discussions. All in all, I sent about one reminder via Moodle per month.

One of the more frustrating aspects for a librarian liaising with an online course is not knowing whether the resources and guidance you provide are being used. After all this effort, how useful did students find the LibGuide? The results are inconclusive. Only one student scheduled a research appointment with me in-person. According to Moodle user access data, the LibGuide link from within Moodle received only 26 hits. However, LibGuides user statistics show 124 views for the "Masculinities" guide, with spikes of activity on or shortly after the days email reminders were sent out. There was a final flurry of activity in the last week of fall semester, indicating many students waited to consult the LibGuide until just before their final paper was due. This reinforces what I already suspected about library outreach for online courses: (1) reminding students repeatedly about resources throughout the semester will increase usage, and (2) students are unlikely to complete an online activity/tool unless it is explicitly required. These findings mirror what Purchase College librarians learned from "flipping the classroom" and assigning video tutorials as homework prior to one-shot instruction sessions with freshman writing courses: students need repeated reminders to complete an online activity, and they need to feel it is part of their grade (Oling and Sciangula 2011, 10).

Despite students' less-than-stellar usage of the LibGuide and my liaison services, Pat found the quality of their research papers to be satisfactory. On the evaluations we created, most students reported feeling comfortable finding appropriate library research for their assignments. If "Masculinities" is offered as a hybrid in the future, I would work with Pat to schedule a mini-library session, create a required online assignment that involves interacting with the LibGuide or video tutorials, and introduce myself to the class in a more personal way—perhaps with a video profile—to make online students more comfortable approaching a librarian for in-person help.

Recommendations and Conclusions

Based on our experiences creating and supporting a hybrid "Masculinities" course, we offer the following recommendations to librarians, faculty, and instructional designers:

- We suggest instructors begin from an instructional design/pedagogy perspective, rather than wait until the last minute to address these concerns. Immersing yourself in new literature must go hand-in-hand with cultivating readings, course content, and learning activities that help students understand the key concepts of the course.
- Librarians and faculty can work together and help each other learn more about a subject area through conversations and knowledge-sharing. These conversations help instructors find resources—whether streaming films, texts, or ebooks—that will best serve their students and also help librarians with collection development.
- Embedding resources into a learning management system or a customized LibGuide is a great way to share them. Creating a course-specific LibGuide is just as useful for the librarian as for students and faculty, helping all parties familiarize themselves with resources in a new subject area.

    Engaging students in an online or hybrid environment can be challenging. Students may be surprised that an online course, while more flexible, requires additional, more proactive participation. To increase student engagement, we suggest the following:

- Use discussion forums. Discussion forums are key to fostering students' understanding and interactions in an online environment. We found detailed, specific question prompts were more successful than open-ended ones in generating discussions. Next time, we will have students create their own discussion forum prompts, perhaps rotating the responsibility amongst small groups from week to week, in order to engage students in more critical thinking.
- Make it required. As in any class, students are less likely to avail themselves of resources or complete activities that are not graded. Require students to engage with library online resources by having them watch a library tutorial and take a quiz for a grade, or by creating an assignment where students use the course LibGuide to complete preliminary research tasks. This ensures more engagement with library resources while also scaffolding the final research assignment.
- Have a library session. We all concluded that, despite the limited F2F meetings of a hybrid course, it is worth it to make time for a mini library session or a personal introduction to the librarian. For purely online courses, alternatives to a library research session could be offered via live chat or video conferencing software.
- Flip the classroom. Remember that many of the same online resources—streaming videos, discussion forums, assignments, course LibGuides—can be used to enhance traditional F2F classes as well. For example, instructors can load a streaming film onto Moodle and have students watch it at home, using class-time for discussion. F2F students can post their "Contributions from the Real World" online or contribute to a discussion forum as homework. Students can watch a library tutorial before class to prepare them for a hands-on library session.

All three of us found the collaborative nature of developing this class to be quite fruitful, and we intend to build on that collaboration in the future. In fact, we have already begun to plan an in-class library session for next semester when "Masculinities: A Feminist Perspective" will be offered as a face-to-face course. Just as students are hesitant to "bother" library staff with their questions, faculty are often unaware of what can be gained from contacting library staff as they develop their courses. This is why it's so important for librarians to continue their faculty outreach efforts, specifically touting their instructional design services and the advantages of a collaborative approach.

REFERENCES

Campbell, Katy K., Richard A. Schwier, and Richard F. Kenny. 2015. "Conversation as Inquiry: A Conversation with Instructional Designers." *Journal of Learning Design*. 8(3): 46–65.

Oling, Rebecca, and Marie Sciangula. 2011. "Learning to Leverage: Using Moodle to Enhance F2F Interaction in One-Shots." *LOEX Quarterly*. 38(3): 8–10.

Cataloging and Gender Studies

Linda Garrison

"Representation of the world, like the world itself, is the work of men; they describe it from their own point of view, which they confuse with the absolute truth."

—Simone de Beauvoir (Beauvoir 1989, 143)

Libraries are transitioning to newer, more robust and flexible technologies. However, Library of Congress authorized classification systems are still dependent on archaic tools that are steeped in gender bias. This essay explains how the intellectual construct and application of these tools marginalizes women. I begin by describing how canonical reference works legitimized the masculinization of technology. This is followed by a brief historical treatment of how bias has been successfully addressed in the past. I then address how specific library classification tools continue to prescribe human interaction through invisible knowledge infrastructures, and finally, I discuss an experiment I conducted in my own school library in which I made a seemingly innocuous decision to re-categorize babysitting books.

The Masculinization of Technology

Professor and gender theorist Ruth Oldenziel asserts that while "there is nothing inherently or naturally masculine about technology," it has historically been defined in such a way as to exclude both those technologies which women invented and those which are primarily used by women (Oldenziel 1999, 10). Beginning in the post industrial revolution era, society recognized an increased differentiation in women's and men's work, including a physical separation of home and work spaces, a segregation of technology use, and a new emphasis on payment as a definition of "work" (Durack 1997, 103). The result of this devaluation of women's work, i.e., "home" work, was a critical moment in defining the term *technology*: by the mid–20th century, technology had become something that men do.

Economist and anthropologist Thorstein Veblen reinforced this paradigmatic shift when he classified engineers as the sole producers of technical knowledge, i.e., technology (Veblen 2012, Oldenziel 1999, 44). This connotation of technology as the province of men was secured in 1978 when the *Encyclopaedia Britannica,* under the entry "Technology," defined man as a technologist because he is a "toolmaker"; and while the definition of the word "technology" does not make it the exclusive domain of men, when knowledge structures such as archives, dictionaries, and encyclopedias omit women's work and inventions, they define by default who and what are important to society (Oldenziel 1999, 182–183). Therefore, Oldenziel asserts, canonical reference works which claim inclusivity and objectivity—such as the *Encyclopaedia Britannica* and the Library of Congress Subject Headings (LCSH) and Library of Congress Classifications (LCC)—have the power to shape the dominant discourse of their times. As the LCSH is the dominant tool that catalogers around the world use to assign subject headings, it can be considered a canonical work, a standard to which others look as the ultimate authority.

The term *technology* encompasses not only tools, but also action and knowledge (Durack 1997, 107). This definition allows all aspects of library cataloging to be defined as a technology: the process of cataloging, the tools it employs, and the knowledge work which creates its structure. While theorists such as Laura Beckwith, Sherry Turkle, Jennifer Rode and others have made arguments that software (such as the Online Public Access Catalog, commonly referred to as the OPAC) itself can also be a gendered technology, that discussion is beyond the purview of this essay. The tools I will be discussing in this essay are the Library of Congress Subject Headings and Library of Congress Classifications, including the LOC authorized Dewey Decimal Classification system (DDC), and the knowledge practices supporting them.

Classification Equals Marginalization

Charles Cutter wrote one of the earliest sets of American cataloging standards, the 1876 *Rules for a Printed Dictionary Catalog*, while he was librarian for the Boston Athenaeum. He had just spent years correcting that library's original error-filled, nearly unintelligible catalog (Sheola 2010). It is important to understand Cutter's experience with free-form cataloging by unskilled workers because it allows one to understand why library catalogs have henceforth been created by trained librarians who adhere to strict rules: they give authority and create order where there was once chaos. Cutter, however, saw rules as guidelines, explicitly advising librarians to alter catalog cards by writing on the card itself if the subject headings clashed "with the public's habitual way of looking at things" (Cutter 1904, 6). Unfortunately, not all librarians took this admonition to heart. Authority records and controlled vocabularies have become unwieldy and unresponsive, lacking the appropriate and intuitive language needed by users to create successful searches (Roberto 2008, 3). These finding tools, designed to enhance access to material, in fact deny access to anyone who is not perceived by the cataloger as the normative user of the tool.

The foundation of all library classification work is the critical concept that an object cannot be found within a classification schema if it does not exist within that scheme. While this concept seems to be so basic it does not need discussion, no classification schema is innocent and arbitrary; it is instead a direct reflection of political power (Star 1998). History itself has, until recently, been the story of agency: those who had the power to tell the story got to choose whose stories were deemed significant; hence, the stories were about men, told to or by men, and recorded by men, with tools invented, built and controlled by men, who then presented them as the universal human story (Durack 1997,

37). Not surprisingly, the agency of women and other minority groups was ignored. Women's work, and by extension their tools, did not warrant notice and therefore were not recorded for the basic reason that it was women's work (Durack 1997, 37, 39).

The original LOC tools were developed by American/Western European, Christian, white, heterosexual males who built their inherent biases into their work (Beveridge 2011). This meant that women and other minorities rarely rated subject heading status in the LCSH. Further, if a woman created something deemed technologically worthy, it was often misclassified, trivialized, or attributed to men (Durack 1997, 37). When catalogers did acknowledge women or other minorities, they simply placed gender and race identifying terms in front of the original term, such as "women as inventors" and "Black inventors"; this modification of the term "inventor" pushed both of these groups outside of the dominant white, male catalog classification norm, ensuring that material on either topic—women or black engineers—would not be shelved alongside mainstream materials on inventors (Olson and Schlegl 2001).

Library Classification Tools as Invisible Knowledge Infrastructures

Cataloging as a technology can be viewed through multiple theoretical lenses or perspectives. I use the feminist lens, placing gender at the center of my critique, specifically as it applies to the exclusionary policies of LOC authority records. While I use the term "feminist" to describe my approach, and I focus on women's issues, their voices, and their lived experiences, I also acknowledge that feminist topics often overlap those of other marginalized communities (Hesse-Biber 2014, 3). In the 1960s, women, African Americans, gays, and Hispanics, unhappy with their representation within the LCSH system, demanded that their voice be heard. Since then, librarians such as Sanford Berman, Barbara Gittings, Joan Marshall, Ellen Greenblatt, Hope Olson, K.R. Roberto, Amber Billey, Emily Drabinski, and countless others, have challenged subsuming cataloging technologies. Their work confronted the traditional empirical underpinnings of knowledge which led to them being replaced with a much broader way of knowing.

The LCSH and LCC, as is the case with all information classification entities, are not just content but also a methodology that takes place within various communities of practice (Bowker and Star 2000, 157). These seemingly innocuous tools actually prescribe human interaction through their invisible knowledge infrastructure. It is critical to explain that those who function comfortably within a system or community will never see that system as oppressive. In her classic book *The Violence of Literacy*, Elspeth Stuckey explains that systems are designed by those who lead "comfortable lives," and it is only those people who are *un*comfortable within a system who actually see that violence (Selfe and Selfe 2009, 54). The creators of the LCSH and LCC did not recognize their complicity in creating exclusionary authority records and it is possible that we will not see how some of our decisions will create new problems. Nevertheless, we must address issues as we encounter them.

As the subjective cataloging process determines an item's usefulness, it is understandable that most critics focus their energies on omissions and racist, sexist, xenophobic labels in the subject headings. While it is easy to confuse them, the Library of Congress Subject Headings is not the same as the Library of Congress Classification (LCC). Catalogers use the LCSH to assign subject headings so that users can identify material which is pertinent to their search; catalogers originally used the LCC to organize and arrange book collections on the library shelves. Charles Cutter designed his system to work as a gathering function, to find commonalities among works so that they could be grouped together for ease of access (Olson and Schlegl 2001). Because this structure was based on identifying/excluding members of a group or collection, it is a classic example of a binary system and Cutter's standards, while efficient and well-intended, ultimately marginalized anything outside of the mainstream (Olson and Schlegl 2001). While the new bibliographic conceptual model and its accompanying set of implementation rules known as FRBR/RDA (Functional Requirements for Bibliographic Records/Resource Description and Access) (Library of Congress 2012) has alleviated some of the syndetic issues, the juxtapositions or hierarchical placement of topics within descriptive classification lists such as the LCC or DDC still represent a serious threat to marginalized populations (Olson and Schlegl 2001). Because it is often overlooked as a source of bias, the authority of the classification list may not be as seriously questioned by librarians as the LCSH. But, as language supports cultural norms, it is the subtle nuances within language systems which enforce gender limitations; therefore a classification tool that places a bibliographic record outside of its proper context can grossly misrepresent a non-normative subject (Olson 2000). Classification systems are powerful instruments, and as such, must be gender-sensitive (Aleksander 2013, 31, 41).

As libraries increasingly embrace digital tools and information seekers use Google-type search engines which employ folksonomies and tagging, one may think that traditional classification schemes have become less important. There is one space, however, where they are still potent teaching tools: the school library. Libraries are a place (physical or virtual) in which the user can share and collectively produce knowledge (de Jong and Wieringa 2013, 14). As an elementary school librarian, I watch students help each other at the shelves and I see firsthand this sharing and production of knowledge. Yes, libraries can be empowering spaces for marginalized subjects but, conversely, they can also be destabilizing spaces because of how they position the "repressed other" (Koevoets 2013, 142, 148). Elementary age students may not consider browsing the shelves as anything more than looking for a good book, but in fact, what material they find and *where that material is located*, influences their understanding of, and their place in, society and the world at large. If a child does not see their community represented fairly in the stacks, they will either abandon the library as non-representative, or worse, accept the disenfranchisement that the library offered them.

Gender Bias in the Stacks: Reclassifying Babysitting Books

As is typical with most school librarians, I do not create original bibliographic records, but import records that have been created by someone else. Additionally, my OPAC software system is not FRBR/RDA friendly, so I am still constrained by outdated cataloging tools. I do, however, make items more accessible to young students by simplifying subject headings and I assign all of the call numbers. As a school librarian, I am "allowed" to deviate from the strict rules to which public or academic librarian must adhere. If I think a book is not being utilized, I move it to a section where I think it is more likely to be discovered (I like to think is in line with Cutter's original plan, as discussed).

I rarely deviate from the classic DDC because I want the students to be comfortable navigating their local public library. But one day, several students asked a question that gave me considerable pause. They had been looking in the 300 section for babysitting books but could not find them. I directed them to the 640s and went about my business. But throughout the day I revisited that encounter with the students. Their seemingly simple question had made me rethink my beloved Dewey system so I spent time exploring the 300 and 640 sections of my library and my local public libraries. We all classified babysitting books as 649.1, subsumed under 640—Home & Family Management—649 Child Rearing & Home Care of Persons. We also placed career books (with some variation, typically medical, music, and veterinary) in the Social Science section. In my library I found the following books (note: because of the small size of my library, I tend to use very broad classifications):

- 331.7–Labor Economics: *Cool Jobs for Kids Who Like Kids: Ways to Make Money Working with Children*
- 363 Social problems & social services: *I Want to Be a Police Officer; I Want to Be a Firefighter*
- 381 Commerce (Trade): *Make Money! Have a Lemonade Stand*

I think it is important to distinguish that these students were preparing for a summer job, not looking for information about how to care for a younger sibling. Therefore it would have made sense for the students to look in the Economics or Commerce sections, where I place most books about money making ventures. While an argument can be made that I incorrectly assigned these particular call numbers and that the books should have been assigned altogether different numbers, I believe I followed typical school cataloging practices.

Professional catalogers take great pride in their jobs, and consider multiple issues, ambiguities, and dual provisions when assigning numbers (Behrens 2014). They must interpret the item's intellectual content and place the item within complex, predetermined classification schemes. The guiding principle of the DDC is that a work is classed in the discipline for which it is intended—that is the nature of classification. But, every subject heading and/or classification decision elevates one point of view and silences another. Authority records and classification systems were created specifically to reflect what the cataloger assumed to be the searcher's perspective, and that searcher, as discussed above, was, historically, assumed to be white, heterosexual, and male. Child care has traditionally been considered "women's work," i.e., unpaid labor which did not impact the economics of society but belonged in the domain of the household. Placing babysitting books under "Home and Family Management" rather than "Economics" continues the narrative that child care is not a societal issue but a family issue. I must ask: What does this say to children—particularly young women—that the career of caring professionally for children is not given the same classification as those traditionally masculine fields of societal care such as police officers, and fire firefighters, or fields which deal with the economics of society, such as entrepreneurs and economists? What does this say to young men who may want to care for children? That child care belongs in the home and is not a viable career?

There are profound challenges where intersecting theories of difference collide. Does reclassifying a babysitting book to the Economics section make me complicit in denigrating home care activities, or "women's work"? Unfortunately, at this point in time, homemaking is not a high-status position in our society, despite the increasingly important conversation of the economics of care. This is one simple example of how even well-meaning cataloging decisions must consider multiple perspectives; reclassifying may disrupt the discourse of the invisible, masculinized hierarchy of authorized tools, but that same decision may also unknowingly denigrate the moral agenda for those who participate in unpaid care duties.

This experiment was surprisingly emotional. First and foremost, I learned that one of my most cherished tools is actually a classic example of a masculinized technology. I use LCSH and the DDC every day in my work as a librarian, not only as a guide for placing books on the shelf but also as a teaching tool. My students expect me to give them an equal opportunity world. The Library of Congress authority records, which I had always admired for creating order out of potential chaos (not only in my small library but also across the Anglo world), are still steeped in gender bias.

Conclusion

Modern-day library discovery tools—the LCSH, the LCC, and the DDC—despite decades of restructuring, still articulate a narrow definition of gender. Users and librarians still view cataloging tools as androcentric and marginalizing; further, the LOC only acts to correct any perceived shortcomings when pressured by power-wielding individuals or groups (Aleksander 2013, Hoffman 2005). Is moving a book from one section in the library to another going to solve our gender equality issues? Probably not, because every decision valorizes one position and silences another. There is no perfect answer, and each librarian must approach classification as a holistic process, in consideration of *all* of their population. As academic disciplines, including library science, increasingly embrace feminist awareness, old systems of knowledge will continue to be challenged (Aleksander 2013, 45). New theories will emerge which acknowledge other marginalized communities, and we will continue to question epistemic privilege as we embrace multiple standpoints. As librarians, we must recognize the social consequences of our classification systems and continue to question their place in the narrative production of gender on our library shelves.

References

Aleksander, Karin. "Parallels in the History of Women's/Gender Studies and Its Special Libraries." In *Teaching Gender with Libraries and Archives: The Power of Information*, edited by Sara de Jong and Sanne Koevoets, 31–48. New York: Central European University Press, 2013.

Beauvoir, Simone de. *The Second Sex*. Edited and translated by H.M. Parshley. New York: Vintage, 1989.

Behrens, Mark A. 2014. "The Work of a Classifier in the Dewey Section of the Library of Congress." *LCCN*, April 15.

Beveridge, Andrew A., Susan Weber, and Sydney Beveridge. 2011. "Librarians in the United States from 1880–2009." Oxford University Press's Academic Insights for the Thinking World. *Oxford University Press*. Nov. 9.

Bowker, Geoffrey C. and Susan Leigh Star. *Sorting Things Out: Classification and Its Consequences*. Cambridge: MIT Press, 2000.

Cutter, Charles A. *Rules for a Dictionary Catalog*. 4th ed. Washington, D.C.: U.S. Government Printing Office, 1904. Google Books 2008. archive.org/details/rulesforadictio06cuttgoog

De Jong, Sara, and Saskia Wieringa. "The Library as Knowledge Broker." In *Teaching Gender with Libraries and Archives: The Power of Information*, edited by Sara de Jong and Sanne Koevoets, 13–30. New York: Central European University Press, 2013.

Durack, Katherine. 1997. "Gender, Technology, and the History of Technical Communication." *Technical Communication Quarterly*. 6(3): 249–60.

Hesse-Biber, Sharlene. "A Re-Invitation to Feminist Research." In *Feminist Research Practice: A Primer*, ed. Sharlene Nagy Hesse-Biber. 2d ed. Los Angeles: SAGE, 2014.

Hoffman, Gretchen. 2005. "Cataloging's Power Players," *Social Consequences of Cataloging* (blog). March 2. catalogingconsequences.blogspot.com.

Koevoets, Sanne. "Beyond the Bun-Lady: Towards New Feminist Figurations of Librarianship." In *Teaching Gender with Libraries and Archives: The Power of Information*, edited by Sara de Jong and Sanne Koevets, 142–163. New York: Central European University Press, 2013.

Library of Congress. 2012. "FRBR: Fundamental Concepts." *Cooperative and Instructional Programs Division, Library of Congress.* September.

Oldenziel, Ruth. "Making Technology Masculine: Men, Women and Modern Machines in America 1870–1945." Amsterdam: Amsterdam University Press, 1999. Print.

Olson, Hope A. 2000. "Difference, Culture and Change: the Untapped Potential of LCSH." Cataloging & Classification Quarterly. 30(1): 53–71.

Olson, Hope A. and Schlegl, Rose. 2001. "Standardization, Objectivity, and User Focus: A Meta-Analysis of Subject Access Critiques." *Cataloging & Classification Quarterly.* 32(2): 61–80.

Roberto, K.R., ed. "Preface: What Does 'Radical Cataloging' Mean, Anyway?" *Radical Cataloging: Essays at the Front.* Jefferson, NC: McFarland, 2008.

Selfe, Cynthia L. and Richard J. Selfe. "The Politics of the Interface: Power and Its Exercise in Electronic Contact Zones." In *Rhetorically Rethinking Usability: Theories, Practices and Methodologies*, edited by Susan K. Miller-Cochran and Rochelle L. Rodrigo. Cresskill, NJ: Hampton, 2009. 39–65.

Sheola, Noah. 2010. "Charles Ammi Cutter." *Boston Athenaeum.* June. www.bostonathenaeum.org/library/book-recommendations/athenaeum-authors/charles-ammi-cutter.

Star, Susan Leigh. 1998. "Grounded Classification: Grounded Theory and Faceted Classification." *Library Trends* 47(2).

Veblen, Thorsten. *The Engineers and the Price System.* 1920. Reprint, Eastford, CT: Martino, 2012.

Breaking the Glass Screens
A Case Study in Feminist Wikipedia Edit-a-Thons

Kendall Larson *and* Stewart Van Cleve

On December 17, 2015, ABC released the first episode of *American Crime*'s second season. The anthology brought viewers to Indianapolis, where a high school student accuses peers in a private school basketball team of raping him and sharing video of the incident online. Dealing with class, gender, homophobia, race, and the failures of education administrations, *American Crime* built upon increased national attention to "campus rape culture" and the complex social problems that undergird the exponential increase in reported rape among teenagers and young adults within the American educational system.

Without having seen the show, a reader may reasonably be expected to find basic information about it through Wikipedia, the world's largest and most popular source of reference information. On the page for *American Crime*, one will find a semester's worth of attention, critical thought, careful writing, and challenges—the focus of a cohort of students from a rural college in Southeast Minnesota. In fall 2016, students of Winona State University (WSU) in Winona, Minnesota, summarized the story of each episode of *American Crime*'s second season and, in the process, confronted campus rape culture and a sexist environment that has seized the most influential source of collaborative information production on the planet.

Inspired by the 2015–2016 theme at Winona State University (WSU), "Our Digital Humanity," we collaborated with Dr. Tamara Berg, a professor in the Women's, Gender, & Sexuality Studies (WGSS) program, to sponsor a student Wikipedia "Edit-a-thon" as part of "Understanding & Changing 'Rape Culture' on College Campuses," a humanities topics course. "Edit-a-thons" are special events that focus participants' attention on a missing or problematic section within Wikipedia; the events include a party atmosphere and instruction on the mechanics of Wikipedia editing. Participants take advantage of Wikipedia's free editing structure to create, modify, or even remove articles in order to improve the representation of women and other underrepresented demographics. Edit-a-thons can have open enrollment or closed participant structure. For the *American Crime* Edit-a-thon, students in Dr. Berg's course organized into teams that were each responsible for writing about one of the ten episodes in the second season. Their articles included a summary of the plot, the episode's perspective on campus rape culture, and other relevant information. In the process, students learned that Wikipedia's global team of anonymous editors enforces content standards that support a male-centered worldview.

This essay discusses how information literacy education can support faculty curriculum planning around gender studies and the structure of student learning sessions through Wikipedia Edit-a-thons. After a brief review of current literature on feminist interventions in Wikipedia, we share our strategies for the inspiration and preparation for our Edit-a-thon assignment, developing a logistical timeline for the Edit-a-thon, handling potential challenges, and overcoming those challenges. Last, our conclusion offers "lessons learned" that help other potential Edit-a-thon planners prepare for success.

Feminism and Wikipedia

It is important to stress that the *American Crime* Edit-a-thon was one component of an entire course that focused on campus rape culture. Strengthened by Dr. Berg's instruction and reading selections, students developed a critical eye for identifying and critiquing rape culture. In addition to teaching students how to write and edit articles in Wikipedia, we taught students how to "watch" their Wikipedia article and justify their work in a critical online environment. Thus, the project forged fundamental learning objectives that are typically housed in different academic spheres: information appraisal and research skills in the library, and critical thought and writing in the classroom. By merging these objectives and applying them to a practical and tangible resource that students were already familiar with, the project offered an innovative approach to confronting the new sexism that lurks in online reference infrastructure.

As observed by Klein and Konieczny (2015), Wikipedia's status as a platform for disproportionate male authorship is not a new phenomenon in popular reference texts; the *Encyclopædia Britannica* had disseminated majority-male reference writing on a global scale before widespread Internet use (Israel and Thomas 1992; Reagle and Rhue 2011). Wikipedia's ascending dominance with respect to other reference sources, traditional library services, and structured means of knowledge production has exacerbated the effect on ever-larger audiences in more concrete ways. Its overall accessibility allows real time content modification, communication, and coordination among readers and editors, which can lead to men creating hostile online environments that make it difficult for women to find interest as both initiators and sustainers of content (Yanisky-Ravid and Mittelman 2015).

A landmark 2010 survey of Wikipedia users supported by the United Nations University-Maastricht Economic and Social Research Institute on Innovation and Technology (UNU-MERIT) revealed the tangible effect of such a hostile environment. Of the 53,888 respondents who identified themselves as "contributors," or individuals who either actively added new articles or modified existing ones, only 12.64 percent identified as women (Glott, Schmidt, Gosh 2010, 7). The study inspired global attention from news media, and this attention sparked furious responses from some Wikipedia enthusiasts and vocal members of the reading public who focused sexist anger on feminist activists with an active online presence (Eckert and Steiner 2013). Further, a 2016 psychological study of women Wikipedia users found that lack of confidence in personal expertise, discomfort with editing another's work, and negative experiences with receiving feedback from other editors made participation a remarkably different experience for male and female Wikipedia editors (Bear and Collier 2016).

Personal attitudes toward Wikipedia and media reporting of the website's gender imbalance each work to exclude feminist perspectives in a majority of content. In the past few years, a growing number of groups have begun addressing these content deficiencies. Scholars and users alike have documented the limited article coverage on women's biographies, feminist issues, and other gender-related topics of interest. Around the world, groups are using Wikipedia Edit-a-thons to correct this disparity, including Art+Feminism, which has coordinated popular Edit-a-thons since 2014. Art+Feminism is a great place to find inspiration, a wealth of promotional ideas, and support for new organizers (Art+Feminism, 2016).

Inspiration and Preparation for the Assignment

The Edit-a-thon assignment began when the Women's and Gender Studies Advisory Committee at Winona State discussed the possibility of using Wikipedia for a creative project. We narrowed possibilities to three options: write new Wikipedia articles, identify and improve short articles intended for expansion called "stubs," or improve existing articles. Authoring a new article or improving stub articles each required identifying topic areas not covered in Wikipedia. Plenty of existing articles were candidates for disrupting dominant cultural perspectives, yet editing existing articles required unequal amounts of editing time that would have posed workload inconsistencies among the groups. After consideration, we chose to have students write new articles, and then we discussed how to create an equitable assignment.

We determined that a focus on a television show, *American Crime*, provided an excellent structure for an Edit-a-thon. In particular, *American Crime*'s popularity and unsparing look into campus rape culture made it a timely and appropriate selection. Many television series have some form of representation on Wikipedia, but most are only described by articles that focus on the entire series, rather than on individual episodes. Only "significant" series, such a *Buffy the Vampire Slayer*, have articles for each episode, yet Wikipedia does not have clear metrics for what makes a television show "significant." Before the Edit-a-thon, *American Crime*'s Wikipedia presence only included an article at the series level, and did not have episode descriptions at all. This absence created the justification for an ideal assignment that could be integrated into other course content. As part of the course requirements, all students were expected to watch the entire second season of *American Crime*.

We crafted an episode template for *American Crime* based on other significant Wikipedia television series episode articles. The template had two purposes. First, it provided a uniform structure for the writing assignment. Second, although each student group had dramatically different parts of the TV series story to work with, the standard template ensured that each student group had equal expectations and workloads.

In summer 2016, we sat down together with the course syllabus and our schedules to prepare for the project in the fall. The Wikipedia Education Foundation (WEF) was essential to this preparation. In its own words, "The Wiki Education Foundation connects higher education to the publishing power of Wikipedia. Bridging Wikipedia and academia creates opportunities for any learner to contribute to, and access, open knowledge" (Wiki Education Foundation, 2016). WEF offers a user friendly platform which connects instructors to options for assignments including customized timelines for those assignments, training modules for students and instructors, and a coordinated way for an instructor to connect with their students' Wikipedia articles.

The WEF's toolkit of resources included tutorials for Wikipedia editing basics, article evaluation, plagiarism avoidance, and "the TeaHouse," a social area for new instructors to meet and ask questions. For each course, the WEF assigns two trained staff to provide guidance. We consulted WEF staff on how to approach our student assignment with regards to our topic and the expectation of neutrality for Wikipedia articles. The WEF also provides helpful suggestions for advertising an Edit-a-thon, technology requirements, logistic considerations, and metrics for assessing the event. It enhanced our development as librarians and Wikipedia skill training for our students. Wikipedia also provides a general wiki for Edit-a-thons that recommends having a purpose and a list of tasks associated with every stage of the event, from preparation to assessment (Wikipedia: How to Run an Edit-a-thon, 2016). In addition, it provides reference pages on the topics of neutrality, writing one's first article (Wikipedia: Your First Article, 2016), and how to edit and format a Wikipedia article to using talk pages and citing your sources (Wikipedia: Tutorial, 2016). We strongly recommend new Edit-a-thon organizers review these resources before they begin arranging the logistics of an event.

Logistical Timeline

After the consulting the WEF and Wikipedia resources, we scheduled three class sessions dedicated to the Wikipedia assignment. We also made sure to communicate approximately every two weeks with Dr. Berg to ensure that our schedule continued to work for her and her students. Our first session took place during the second week of the class. We provided an overview of Wikipedia's purpose and history and then introduced students to the demographics of Wikipedia's largely male editors and how their disproportionate participation shapes the variety, perspective, and content of all Wikipedia articles.

- After the first class, we realized a discussion would have created a more active experience with the addition of a reading.
- A reading assigned before this class would give students context for the Wikipedia introduction and history.
- An article such as "Wikipedia: Systemic Bias," (2016) and the sections "The Nature of Wikipedia's Bias, Why It Matters, and What Can You Do," would have given students more context.

We next shared our outline of the Wikipedia assignment, including clear expectations. We avoided giving students too much detail at this early stage in the project; it was important to consider the intimidation that our students faced with this a brand-new technology. We concluded the class by answering questions about the assignment and discussed the strengths and weaknesses of Wikipedia as a world's largest participatory resource.

In our second class session with students, we used our Wikipedia Assignment LibGuide to outline Wikipedia and link to key resources. It also linked to the assignment template that we created, which included the uniform content fields and the Wikipedia code for article authoring. This template provided a uniform start for each new article students would create. In the main portion of the class, we had students create individual logins to Wikipedia and then walked them through transforming the code template into a live Wikipedia page step-by-step. Though we prepared for the account creation portion of the class, Wikipedia blocked new accounts after about two-thirds of our students succeeded in creating new accounts. We provide advice on how planners can avoid new account creation problems later in this essay.

In our final session, which took place in an event space carved from a former bowling alley at WSU's student center, we worked with students to craft their articles in their personal accounts "sandbox" space, which were safer from aggressive deletion or editing by anonymous third-party editors and could be easily restored in the event of a surprise deletion. At that final session, we brought pizza, snacks, and beverages, and played an episode from *American Crime* on a large projected screen. Each of our students had a laptop, so computer access was not an issue, but we do recommend that planners ensure each participant has access to a laptop computer. We contacted our Information Technology Department to confirm wireless access, and that our infrastructure could handle heavier web traffic in the event space. We walked between each of the ten groups and offered our advice and assistance as they needed it; for the first half of the session, students primarily needed technical coding assistance from us; in the second half, they needed writing and content help from Dr. Berg.

Challenges

One of the major challenges in this project hinged on the actual mechanics of Wikipedia editing. Loosely based off of HTML code, Wikipedia coding has its own set of standards with a steep learning curve. In addition, Wikipedia uses a different citation style than those students encounter when writing papers. While we had taken careful steps to create most of the article template coding for students ahead of time, some students struggled to understand the process at all, while others—presumably those with technology experience, had few problems or learned how to resolve issues on their own. Considering this, Edit-a-thon planners may want to include a quick, anonymous technology skills assessment of participants before an Edit-a-thon, in order to provide extra assistance to unfamiliar users before they are expected to perform editing tasks. Novice users would most benefit from the excellent Wikipedia editing tutorials provided by the WEF that we identified earlier in this essay.

Before adding new content to Wikipedia, students need to create individual Wikipedia accounts. To avoid account creation errors, we recommend Edit-a-thon planners:

- Contact Wikipedia programmers a month or more before an Edit-a-thon event;
- Ask participants to register for accounts weeks before the Edit-a-thon, as Wikipedia only allows six new accounts within a 24-hour time period for local IP ranges. Additional accounts get blocked to prevent fraud.

We prepared for this issue by sending a request to Wikimedia's "bug tracker" by making a "Wikimedia-Site-request ("Mass Account Creation," 2016). Our request was quickly implemented, but we experienced a technical problem during our second session and Wikipedia began to block new accounts after approximately two-thirds of our students had created them. We adapted quickly by encouraging those students who had successfully created accounts to partner with those who were not successful (and who created their accounts the next day).

After each group had successfully posted their article templates, Wikipedia editors began to aggressively delete the new articles, which had barely existed for an hour. Students received contributor comments that complained the new articles did not meet standards of Wikipedia's episode naming conventions and other formatting guidelines (Wikipedia: Naming Conventions (Television), 2016). We assumed that student could save their articles with only skeletal templates and return to them later, but the editing community was quick to delete them for not having enough content to justify their presence.

Some editors were more helpful than others. Wikipedia's Etiquette policy offers guidance for communication amongst editors than can be helpful reference material when interacting with them (Wikipedia: Etiquette, 2016). Some editors, who can come across as rude or disrespectful, decisively addressed perceived violations. We had both terse comments and helpful advice from editors who provided links to guidelines and additional suggestions. In particular, the "neutral point of view" standard is challenging when addressing topics that do not frequently appear in Wikipedia. The focus on a rape victim's perspective and trauma-informed writing can be perceived as a bias; for *American Crime*, these views are essential to component the story.

A few students were understandably frustrated at different points of this assignment. We saw these moments as excellent teaching opportunities. The experience underscored the problems that surround Wikipedia's gender dynamic and the control editors have over the content. Students in the class, a majority of whom were young women with no Wikipedia editing experience, had their voices silenced in a system created by a majority of men who cited vague and conflicting standards. Following this experience, and prior to our final session, we decided to have students use their own "sandboxes," which are safe spaces to create new content, before adding them to live Wikipedia articles. The WEF also offers to review articles and give constructive suggestions to improve them.

Writing articles on contentious topics using a participatory platform is, of course, an inherent challenge. Our assignment's focus on the story of victims and their trauma challenged both our and other users' understanding of a "neutral" perspective. The focus of our assignment definitely fit the prescription for our student's articles to be challenged, yet it appropriately fit the course goals to examine the social construction of rape culture and disrupt the dominant culture.

We learned that any course assignment featuring Wikipedia editing—let alone an organized Edit-a-thon event—requires a considerable investment of preparation time and continuing follow-up through the event timeline. Despite our previous experience with Wikipedia, albeit many years ago, we quickly realized we were essentially Wikipedia editing novices. While we believed we had planned for the event sufficiently, we discovered that additional communication with Wikipedia via talk pages, requesting feedback, utilizing the WEF TeaHouse, and developing our own experiences with Wikipedia would have helped us minimize our moments of surprise and frustration. We planned for ample time to acquaint ourselves with Wikipedia and to request feedback, yet we recommend anyone planning an assignment should build into your schedule time to:

- Extensively read about Wikipedia and the editing process.
- Research any relevant guidelines, conventions, or standards.

- Go through the process of editing or adding new content, essentially a test run to experience the full process before leading students through it.

We were fortunate to turn our experiences into positive learning opportunities, but we encourage readers to learn from our experiences for future Edit-a-thons.

Conclusion

Our Wikipedia assignment had two outcomes: each group developed an article that described an episode of *American Crime* and each student examined the problems of Wikipedia's male-dominated environment. In addition to teaching students how to write and edit articles on Wikipedia, we taught students how to "watch" and support their Wikipedia articles and justify their work in an intensely critical online environment. Thus, the assignment forged fundamental learning objectives that are typically housed in different locations: information appraisal and research skills in the library, and critical thought and writing in the classroom. By merging these objectives and applying them to a practical and tangible resource that students were already familiar with, the project offered an innovative approach to confronting the new sexism that lurks in this online reference infrastructure.

Perhaps without noticing it initially, students at Winona State University encountered the problems of this landscape immediately upon visiting the article for *American Crime*. Unlike other Wikipedia articles on popular television episodes (such as *Buffy the Vampire Slayer*), which can feature the addition of plot synopses and editorial revisions within hours of a new episodes' broadcast, the episode descriptions for *American Crime* were noticeably absent. The topic of sexual assault is receiving attention in not only higher education, but at all levels of our society. In the case of *American Crime,* instead of giving readers basic information about how each episode furthers the plot, Wikipedia only offered information about the episode's title, director, writer, air date, and estimated viewership. While there are undoubtedly multiple reasons for the absence of such information, it is important to note that discomfort with the topic of teenage male rape likely played a role.

Overall, the experience gave students insight into the realities of Wikipedia, it addressed the challenges to its reliability, and it illustrated how an individual author's perspective affects the shape, tone, and content of published work. Such awareness has become increasingly crucial as information production, classification, dissemination, and revision has become increasingly democratic. By sharing our Wikipedia editing experiences with the greater community, we hope to build a base of students and faculty for future work. Growing a community of Wikipedia editors at Winona State, we seek to change the disproportionate composition of Wikipedia editors and the content they create.

REFERENCES

"About Us." *Wiki Education Foundation,* accessed October 15, 2016, https://wikiedu.org/.
"Art+Feminism Is a Rhizomatic Campaign to Improve Coverage of Women & the Arts on Wikipedia, & to Encourage Female Editorship." *Art+Feminism*, last modified March 4, 2016, http://art.plusfeminism.org/.
Bear, Julia B., and Benjamin Collier. "Where Are the Women in Wikipedia? Understanding the Different Psychological Experiences of Men and Women in Wikipedia." *Sex Roles* 74, no. 5–6 (2016): 254–65, doi:10.1007/s11199–015–0573–y.

Eckert, Stine, and Linda Steiner. "(Re) Triggering Backlash: Responses to News About Wikipedia's Gender Gap." *Journal of Communication Inquiry* 37, no. 4 (2013): 284–303.

Glott, Ruediger, Philipp Schmidt, and Rishab Ghosh. "Wikipedia Survey–Overview of Results." *United Nations University: Collaborative Creativity Group.* 2010, accessed October 2016, http://www.ris.org/uploadi/editor/1305050082Wikipedia_Overview_15March2010-FINAL.pdf.

Israel, Kali, and Gillian Thomas. *A Position to Command Respect: Women and the Eleventh Britannica."* 1995 JSTOR. http://www.jstor.org/stable/3829182.

Klein, Maximilian, and Piotr Konieczny. "Gender Gap Through Time and Space: A Journey Through Wikipedia Biographies and the 'WIGI' Index." 2015, accessed November 11, 2016, http://arxiv.org/abs/1502.03086.

"Mass Account Creation." *Wikimedia Meta-Wiki,* last updated July 17, 2016, https://meta.wikimedia.org/wiki/Mass_account_creation.

Reagle, Joseph, and Lauren Rhue. "Gender Bias in Wikipedia and Britannica." *International Journal of Communication* 5, no. 21 (2011), 1138–1158.

"Wikipedia: Etiquette." *Wikipedia the Free Encyclopedia,* last modified July 29, 2016, https://en.Wikipedia.org/wiki/Wikipedia:Etiquette.

"Wikipedia: How to Run an Edit-a-thon." Wikipedia: The Free Encyclopedia, accessed October 15, 2016. https://en.Wikipedia.org/wiki/Wikipedia:How_to_run_an_Edit-a-thon.

"Wikipedia: Meetup/ArtAndFeminism." *Wikipedia Art+Feminism,* last modified September 13, 2016, https://en.Wikipedia.org/wiki/Wikipedia:Meetup/ArtAndFeminism.

"Wikipedia: Naming Conventions (Television)." *Wikipedia the Free Encyclopedia,* last modified August 3, 2016, https://en.Wikipedia.org/wiki/Wikipedia:Naming_conventions_(television).

"Wikipedia: Neutral Point of View." *Wikipedia the Free Encyclopedia,* last modified September 17, 2016, https://en.Wikipedia.org/wiki/Wikipedia:Neutral_point_of_view.

"Wikipedia: Systemic Bias." *Wikipedia the Free Encyclopedia,* last modified November 6, 2016, https://en.Wikipedia.org/wiki/Wikipedia:Systemic_bias.

"Wikipedia: Tutorial." *Wikipedia the Free Encyclopedia,* last modified November 9, 2016, https://en.Wikipedia.org/wiki/Wikipedia:Tutorial.

"Wikipedia: Your First Article." *Wikipedia the Free Encyclopedia,* last modified November 5, 2016.

Yanisky-Ravid, Shlomit, and Amy Mittelman. "Gender Biases in Cyberspace: A Two-Stage Model, the New Arena of Wikipedia and Other Websites." *Fordham Intellectual Property, Media & Entertainment Law Journal* 26, no. 381 (2015), 378–416.

Silenced Voices Lesson Plan

Morna Gerrard *and* Callan Wells

The Women and Gender Collections in Georgia State University's Library's Special Collections document women and LGBTQ-centered activities in Georgia and the South. The focus of the collections is overwhelmingly progressive and the subject matter is regularly controversial. Major topics include reproductive justice, domestic violence, LGBTQ rights, politics, and environmentalism. The collection's archivist, Morna Gerrard, had been keen to use these collections to teach young people about challenging subjects, and in 2012, she saw an opportunity to make that happen when she hired Callan Wells, a graduate student working on her masters of arts in teaching. Over two years, we created four lesson plans for students from 8th to 12th grade. This essay will detail the first lesson plan, Silenced Voices: Understanding Domestic Violence through Primary Sources.

Wells was the first graduate research assistant hired specifically to create lesson plans using materials from the Women and Gender Collections. She was given a great deal of freedom to consider the collections and to select topics for lesson plans that she personally felt spoke to her. Very quickly, we focused on the sources relating to domestic violence (DV), and we were particularly struck by a letter from an imprisoned woman who had killed her batterer. We felt strongly that the letter and associated documents spoke clearly to the realities of DV and the legal system. Once the theme was selected, we spent a number of months selecting and dissecting the content of documents, while creating a framework for the lesson plan. Throughout this time, we met very regularly together, and with Wells' advisor Dr. Alyssa Dunn. Dr. Dunn's input was very important as we had to ensure that the finished unit would be age-appropriate and abide by Georgia's Common Core standards. A LibGuide was created for the lesson plan, and content was added (http://research.library.gsu.edu/c.php?g=115814).

Unit Objectives, Goals, and Rationale

The objectives and goals for the Silenced Voices unit relate primarily to reading and analyzing primary sources, understanding policy, and creating persuasive arguments for policy makers. While the underlying goal of the unit is to promote empathy, the goals and objectives provide teachers with a foundation in academics.

Character education, also known as teaching "grit" (http://www.theatlantic.com/magazine/archive/2016/06/how-kids-really-succeed/480744/) or "moral intelligence" (http://micheleborba.com) encompasses the ideal that schools and teachers should take a part in shaping a student's moral fiber. This ideal is central to the Silenced Voices lesson plan as it asks students to empathize as they interact with the primary sources presented to them. The objectives for the course are as follows:

- Read letters from and critically analyze the perspective of survivors of domestic violence;
- Discuss preconceived notions about domestic violence and then evaluate if and how these notions have changed after reading primary sources. Also discuss how these primary source texts function differently than secondary texts;
- Understand and evaluate the effectiveness of policy about domestic violence and analyze how effective this policy is based on primary sources written by domestic violence survivors;
- Develop and present a research based argument regarding policy change in a persuasive letter to community leaders, and effectively cite primary sources and research papers in an argumentative essay [http://research.library.gsu.edu/c.php?g=115814&p=751145].

The ten-day unit covers the gamut, from critical analysis of primary sources, to evaluation of policy, to finally developing and presenting a well thought out and researched argument. The lesson is thoroughly based in practical applications of government, literature, and history while incorporating a social justice focus that satisfies those teachers who crave moral intelligence in the classroom.

A course's "rationale" seeks to explain the reasoning for a course, using an academic framework. With the rationale, which students do not typically see, we wanted to discuss some of the larger dynamics at play in this unit, namely power. To quote from the rationale:

> We believe this unit is not just about domestic violence but also about power. Much of modern literary criticism centers on power structures; postcolonial, feminist, and postmodern criticism are examples of this. Giving students a foundation for how to discuss power structures through this unit will prepare them for literary theory in later scholastic discussion. One power structure that is pervasive through all cultures is that of men and women. Men have had power throughout most of history, and the structure persists into modern day. Students should be given the opportunity to see this on a local level—in intimate relationships—in an effort to understand the broader social implications of a pervasive power structure. As Linda Christensen says in her book *Reading, Writing, Rising Up*, "Our society's culture industry colonizes [the students'] minds and teaches them how to act, live, and dream" (40) (http://research.library.gsu.edu/c.php?g=115814&p=751790). She wants "students to wrestle with the social text of novels, news, or history books, they need the tools to critique media that encourage or legitimate social inequality" (41). The lessons learned in this unit will provide students with those tools and allow them to question the "loving" relationships in such famous novels as *Farewell to Arms* and *In the Lake of the Woods*—providing them a framework to understand underlying violence and control that is not written about explicitly.

Power dynamics are the underpinning of nearly every literary criticism students will encounter in a college setting. Developing the ability and terminology to discuss power with attention to nuance will benefit them throughout their academic careers and beyond.

A non-academic aspect of the rational is the matter of teen dating violence. According to the CDC, "23 percent of females and 14 percent of males who ever experienced rape, physical violence, or stalking by an intimate partner, first experienced some form of partner violence between 11 and 17 years of age (http://www.cdc.gov/violencepreven tion/intimatepartnerviolence/teen_dating_violence.html). The 2013 national Youth Risk Behavior Survey found approximately 10 percent of high school students reported physical victimization and 10 percent reported sexual victimization from a dating partner in the 12 months before they were surveyed." Educators are in a unique position to reach students during this critical time, to teach them not only the warning signs and how to leave an abusive relationship, but more importantly, to reach young, would-be abusers and begin instilling in them the important message that violence to an intimate partner is wrong.

While ethics may not be recognized in any Common Core standards, one cannot deny that schools play an important part in shaping society. Many educators feel it is their imperative to guide young people to ethical behavior.

The Primary Sources

The primary sources used in this unit include a child's drawing, letters from DV survivors, police reports, and academic articles about the impact of DV. We began the search for primary sources by combing through hundreds of documents, in much the same way that we look for exhibit materials. This was a harrowing experience. As she now works with domestic violence survivors as part of her career, Wells can affirm that nothing is more powerful at making real the DV experience than hearing from survivors themselves. We knew that the letters from survivors would be incredibly important tools to teach students exactly how terrifying, deadly, and universal DV can be. Consider this quote from an imprisoned woman who had killed her batterer: "Being helpless became easier than seeking help when after a while, I began to believe that the police, my family, and even God didn't understand what I was enduring. It was easier for me to quit trying to understand the violence too. It was easier for me to carry the onus ... and I did and still am" (http://131.96.12.97/cdm/ref/collection/arwg/id/3).

While any teacher can discuss a character in a book or an historical figure, nothing quite expresses the alienation experienced at the center of a violent relationship than the person speaking from within that relationship. This woman's letter shows the lack of response from law enforcement and the stigma victims feel from outside their relationships. She writes from jail, imprisoned for murdering her abuser. Overall, this is a complex situation, with a central character who does not neatly fit into a victim/abuser category. Students are forced to parse out details in her letter and challenge their own assumptions about domestic violence.

Another primary source included in the plan is a copy of a Temporary Protective Order (TPO) (http://131.96.12.97/cdm/ref/collection/arwg/id/1). While creating this lesson plan, we realized that students learn very little about how the law actually works. We learn to call 911 in the case of an emergency but often neglect what happens after that call. How do laws really keep us safe? TPO is not a commonly known abbreviation / term to those outside of the law enforcement or domestic violence advocacy communities. How many students have the opportunity to see a TPO, learn what it might take to get one, learn how they are enforced?

Additional resources made available to students include government documents and research papers, which provide good examples of well-researched, objective writing.

Jody Raphael's "Prisoners of Abuse: Domestic Violence and Welfare Receipt," is one of those papers. Students will evaluate the veracity and effectiveness of each of the documents presented to them as they move forward with the lesson.

Unit Activities

This unit is comprised of four activities that cover four main skills: thoughtful dialogue with the "Think, Pair, Share" activity, understanding and presenting in the "Jigsaw" presentation, persuasion and policy analysis in the "Letter to Community Leaders," and finally creativity and advocacy in the "Clothesline Project."

The "Think Pair Share" activity takes place on the first day of the unit and intends for students to first assess their own thoughts and feelings about domestic violence, then share with their classmates and engage in a dialogue about those thoughts and feelings. Two questions are asked: "When a woman is abused (physically or verbally) by her partner, what should she do?" and "If you see a friend/stranger/family member abusing or getting abused, what should you do?" This activity is carefully mediated, and students are encouraged to talk about what they appreciated, learned, agreed with or disagreed with as their peers shared their thoughts. Because of the sensitive nature of the subject matter, it is important for the teacher to be an active participant in the groups, while still recognizing that students are discovering as they go. We anticipate that as students read through the primary materials, their views on these topics may change, so the teacher's role is facilitator and thought-provoker: they should try not to insert any ideas of their own.

Through the use of a structured dialogue, students are given a model for healthy discussion. Taking time to speak and listen illustrates the importance of each person's opinion in a conversational setting. It is hoped that this model will serve students both in and out of class.

For the "Jigsaw Presentation," students are in the same groups as the "Think, Pair, Share" activity and are given a grouping of primary source documents that includes a letter from a survivor, a court document, a scholarly essay, and other supporting materials. As a group they answer the following questions about each document:

- What happened in the primary source document?
- Who is the author and why did they write it?
- Is the primary source document reliable? Credible?

Aside from the factual data about the primary source document, students are also asked to discuss their own feelings after reading the document and track the changes in their feelings. Each group shares these details about their primary source document packets to the class.

We encourage teachers to challenge students to think about how the legal system can serve in these situations. The primary sources show that many survivors do not feel protected by the law enforcement that they encounter. Letters to judges and elected officials with brief responses show the difficulty survivors have in asserting a voice. Throughout the lesson, the primary sources speak for themselves, giving the teacher a pathway to paradigm shifts. This is where discussions from the "Think, Pair, Share" activity can come into play. Without making a student feel wrong, teachers can show students that allowing new information to shape their thinking is a sign of growth and strength.

The goal of the "Letters to Community Leaders" activity is to teach policy advocacy and to demonstrate civics in action. Students are asked to research community leaders in their city and prepare a persuasive letter advocating for a specific policy change to better protect domestic violence victims. Each student is required to reference three primary sources that they have encountered.

We feel a lesson like this one is important in several ways. First, giving students the opportunity to take action empowers them to play a role in civics, a lesson that is not taught in textbooks. Second, students are expected to learn who their civic leaders are. Elected officials often do not look like the population they serve and when students discover this on their own, the effect can be powerful. Imagine writing about domestic violence to a group that is comprised of entirely of men. Lastly, giving students the agency to make their own decisions about what to recommend shows them that they are powerful; at the same time, requiring them to reference the thoughts of others teaches them humility. The experiences they are examining may not be theirs, but they have the tools and capacity to listen and work on behalf of others.

The "Clothesline Project" activity is based on the activities of the national Clothesline Project, which was established in 1990. The Project, created by survivors of violence and those in support of survivors and victims, encourages communities to display decorated t-shirts, hung on clotheslines in public spaces, as a testimony to the reality of violence and the strength of survivors. (Power of Women pamphlet). The catalyst for the Project was the discovery of a set of statistics: 58,000 soldiers died during the Vietnam War; during that same period, 51,000 women were killed by intimate partners (http://www.clotheslineproject.org/history.htm). The goal of this project is to create a visual representation of statistics. For the project, students decorate a t-shirt with images or words that represent the emotions experienced or expressed throughout the unit. The shirts can contain words, images, or symbols. Students are given the opportunity to publish their work through a Clothesline gallery to which they will formally invite members of their family, school, and community. The T-shirts will be hung around the room for all to observe silently. If students choose, they can include written descriptions of their finished products. After the observation, a dialogue is opened for the students and their guests. After many discussions throughout the unit, students should be able to lead the dialogues with their community. Encouraging students to go back to their families, friends, and local leaders with what they have learned gives further voice to the primary sources presented, bolsters a student's sense of civic duty, and creates a catalyst for sustained focus on an important issue.

Conclusion

This lesson plan aims to encompass the many moving parts that make up a comprehensive social justice education. First, the unit allows for all learning types, with listening, reading, speaking, writing, and opportunities for creativity. The lesson values the voice of the law, the voice of the victim, and the voice of the student. It aims to teach students empathy and empower them to take action on their own. It uses primary sources to inform and gives a venue for the important documents in Georgia State University's Archives for Research on Women and Gender.

There is no doubt that domestic violence is a difficult issue for young people to consider. In fact, most adults prefer to avoid thinking too deeply about it. As a society, we may feel badly for victims and survivors, but we are content to let the professionals deal with the issues head on. Throughout their academic lives, students are traditionally given lessons in civics from a third hand perspective. What this lesson plan does is remove the barriers and immerse the students in real and raw experiences. At the same time, it encourages them not to just think, but also to feel and evaluate feelings as they learn about the world around them. Primary sources can be incredibly powerful—even without the structure and careful guidance presented in this unit. In the back rooms of Special Collections, students processing DV materials, though carefully mentored, rarely complete a project without experiencing rage, grief, and/or a new-found desire to change the world.

Not every school district will embrace such emotionally charged subject matter, but some schools will encourage the opportunity to challenge their students. It is for that reason that other lesson plans like this one should be developed. Additional difficult subjects are currently being tackled in primary-source exercises within Special Collections at Georgia State University: reproductive rights, sex education, racism, and inequities in access to public health are regularly considered by students as they learn how to think critically while they develop skills in archival literacy. With these topics, students are required to listen with open, objective, academic minds as they and their classmates evaluate and report on materials that document starkly opposing views. Classes do not debate; instead they consider language, audience, methodology, and historical context. They compare the words of the people who wrote or spoke them first hand, and not through a mediated lens. We tell the students that they are the interpreters and that there are no wrong answers. It is a truly empowering experience to hold in your hands the original thoughts or writings of a person or an organization, and to consider those thoughts and writings for yourself, without the interference of politicians, parents, community, or the media. It is also revealing to understand that your own interpretation and appreciation of those materials is inevitably colored by your own life experiences and beliefs. If you understand that about yourself, it is easier to understand that about your fellow classmates, as well as fellow men and women generally. Knowing our university's students find such value in primary sources, we believe that younger students, with thoughtful guidance, should have access to these powerful documents. Without a doubt primary sources are significant tools for teaching empathy, and as such, should be an integral part of student learning.

REFERENCES

Power of Women pamphlet. Power of Women Clothesline Project Records (W057), Archives for the Research on Women and Gender, Special Collections and Archives, Georgia State University Library, Atlanta.

The Implications of "High Scatter" for Women's Studies Journals and Collection Development

Stephanie H. Wical

While some college and university libraries have explicitly stated which areas in the Library of Congress classification scheme are important to women's studies, most would have a difficult time completely ignoring other LC classes because issues that are relevant to women's studies are almost everywhere. "Women's studies" is an authority file (HQ 1180- HQ 1186), but there are many useful items that are outside of this LC classification. The problem becomes one of what do we do with these "outsiders"? In other words, who is responsible for collecting these materials? Many of the collection development policies in *Women's Studies Collection Development Policies* also include evaluations of their collection levels for particular subjects important to the scholarly study of women. Ohio State University's Women's Studies Library, for example, stated which subjects are excluded from its collection: "Materials merely by or about women that do not contribute to the academic study of gender are excluded from the women's studies collection" (*WSCDP* 1992, 6). The Collection Development and Bibliography Committee of the Association of College and Research Libraries' Women's Studies Section published *Women's Studies Collection Development Policies* in 1992 to help librarians by presenting a collection of sixteen different women's studies collection development policies as examples.

One of the problems with adhering to a rigid collection development policy in which selectors only choose by LC class is that materials, while they may have multiple subject headings, can only have one call number. "In the case of interdisciplinary materials, this determination may result in assignment of overly broad subject headings," according to Kristin Gerhard, Mila Su and Charlotte Rubens, and this broadness prevents "meaningful searching" (1998, 130). The interdisciplinarity of women's studies is one of its greatest strengths, but it also presented challenges to collection development as it had evolved in college and university libraries. Lynn Westbrook's offers the following definition: "Interdiciplinarity is the purposeful weaving together of two or more disciplines that are usually considered to be quite unconnected in order to create a new understanding, create a new academic end product, or advance research on a particular question" (Westbrook 1999, 26).

The assignment of a permanent place to library materials can be at the expense of whatever value these works may have to the discipline outside of what the original classifiers deemed central to the works. One example is the scholarly writing of Michel Foucault. Although not considered feminist or given a "women's studies" subject heading, Foucault's writing is valuable to feminist scholars because of its theoretical perspective and framework. As Lynn Westbrook notes, "Representing the framework or theoretical perspective of a work is an even more delicate task than assigning topical indexing terms" (1999, 37).

Because materials of interest to women's studies scholars are dispersed throughout the whole LC system and because women's studies scholars often find useful information in alleged non-women's studies materials, women's studies is what Lynn Westbrook calls a "high scatter field." High scatter fields will affect service decisions in a way that their more rigid, "low scatter" counterparts do not. Unable to rely on adequately indexed journals, a consistent nomenclature, and consistent use of controlled vocabulary (Spanner 2001), information seekers in high scatter fields such as women's studies need more research help. This is further complicated by some of the methods of information seeking. Westbrook notes that feminist scholars rely on both "semantic clues," such as subject headings and titles, and "non-semantic clues," such as layouts and illustrations (1999, 37). Denda observes, "In order to support their research, librarians need to create a mechanism that concatenates disparate terms and concepts from different disciplines and place them in a specific context or structure of knowledge" (2005, 268).

In "Collection Development as a Social Process" Hur-Li Lee observes that Lynn Westbrook's study of women's studies scholars "revealed no information about the characteristics of browsing behavior engaged by participants: how did they browse?" (2003, 28). Lee further notes that "specific questions regarding browsing and collection use are also lacking in general research on interdisciplinary information seeking" (2003, 28). Research into the browsing habits of women's studies scholars would likely reveal the wide variance in the "depth of indexing and level of specificity in discipline-specific" bibliographic tools (Spanner 2001, 358).

As women's studies programs came into existence, older, more established departments were "unwilling to see their own collections and resources reduced" to create a women's studies collection or library (Lee 2003, 29). Lee observes that "women's studies' lack of departmental status and faculty lines created a situation in the library system where women's studies was more of an afterthought than a priority subject area" (Lee 2003, 29). Jean-Pierre V. M. Herubel asserts that "for librarians attempting to hone collections, the disciplinary orientations of university presses are crucial to an understanding of scholarly communication" (2007, 53). Knowledge organization remains important and, for Rick Szostak, we need a knowledge organization system "that not only guides users to information they know to look for but to related information for which they might not have searched" (2014, 39).

Studying women's studies (WS) programs presents some challenges because of the "amorphous" nature of the study's population (Westbrook 2003, 194). As Westbrook notes, "although WS scholars exemplify many aspects of interdisciplinary scholarship, they do not represent all interdisciplinary scholars" (2003, 195). Don Spanner observes that "there is no consensus within the literature about how best to meet the collection needs of [interdisciplinary] scholars" and further states "this very problem illuminates some very serious flows in how libraries approach collection development" (2001, 358).

Alan Porter, David Roessner and Anne Heberger assert that interdisciplinary research "requires *integration* of knowledge" (2008, 276, emphasis theirs). They suggest that the examination of citations in research papers is worthwhile because "citations contained in a single paper arguably reflect some degree of integration by the paper's author(s) of knowledge drawn from the references cited" (Porter et al. 2008, 274). This approach is preferable to the frequently used approach that considers co-authorship as a way to discern interdisciplinarity because "tallying the educational backgrounds of co-authors, or their departmental affiliations, is not efficacious, in part because department affiliations are useful for teaching but may be less relevant for research activities" (Porter et al. 2008, 276).

How should we as librarians go about supporting the research of women's studies scholars? One place to start is by looking at the Core List of Journals for Women and Gender Studies, compiled by the Association of College and Research Libraries Women and Gender Studies Section (http://libr.org/wgss/projects/serial.html). In May of 2015, I looked at how many of the titles on the core list of journals were available at the University of Wisconsin—Eau Claire (UWEC), a regional, liberal education-focused university with an FTE of 9,576, ninety miles from the Twin Cities. UWEC has current access to 57.14 percent of the 35 publications on this core list of women's studies journals. We provide at least a little bit of access to 94.29 percent of the titles on the list (see Table 1.1). Subscribing to a core list of journals is not something that is realistic in this current economic climate in which there is widespread disinvestment in public higher education. Leaner and meaner times call for new approaches and the resource environment has shifted dramatically since the early creations of collection development policies for women's studies. The proliferation of electronic resources and the mass acquisitions of Big Deal packages by research universities have created a new landscape for evaluating women's studies collections. The widespread adoption of COUNTER Usage Reports now allow us to see how frequently articles are downloaded, making use of resources a data point in the decision to renew resources. Citation analyses have provided useful information to scholars about local needs and combination approaches can help discern what is truly necessary.

Table 1.1: University of Wisconsin—Eau Claire Access to Journals on the WGSS Core List of Journals

Coverage of Journal Title	*Number of Journals*
Current Access	20
12 Month Embargo	6
18 Month Embargo	1
Complete Run but Ceased Publication	1
Older Coverage, but Not Current	5
No Access	2

Todd Vandenbark and I completed a study in which we combined usage data and citation data for the publications of faculty in four departments at the University of Wisconsin-Eau Claire (Wical and Vandenbark 2015). Would the approach we used for four lower-scatter disciplines—nursing, mathematics, chemistry and biology—also work for women's studies? In this current study I looked at ten years of Peer-Reviewed Publications in Women's Studies listed under Women's Studies in the University of Wisconsin—Eau Claire Office of Research and Sponsored Programs (ORSP) reports. This resulted in only four peer-reviewed publications from the following journals: *Journal of Child Custody, Journal of Lesbian Studies, Literature Compass* and *Journal of Feminist*

Family Psychology. Of these four titles, only one is on the Core List of Women and Gender Studies Journals—*Journal of Lesbian Studies*. These four articles cited 43 different articles in 41 different journals. Among the 41 journals cited, only four titles were on the Core List of Women and Gender Studies Journals: *Journal of Lesbian Studies, Psychology of Women Quarterly, Tulsa Studies in Women's Literature* and *Women and Therapy*. Relying on self-reported women's studies publications does not produce a large enough sample for this unmodified approach to work. Adding keywords allowed me to come up with 48 journals of interest (where faculty published). I searched for the following keywords in the most recent 10 ORSP reports: "female," "sex," "woman," "women," "gender," and "feminist." In reviewing the citations to make sure that they were appropriate for women's studies, I found an additional two titles by just browsing, so I had 50 different peer-reviewed journals where UWEC faculty members published women's studies scholarship. I then looked to see what kind of access we had to the 50 titles (see Table 1.2). Table 1.3 presents a breakdown of which publishers provide current access to the 22 of the 50 titles. Relying solely on keywords will result in titles that are worthy of inclusion being missed. This highlights the importance of browsing and subject expert knowledge.

Table 1.2: UWEC Access to 50 Titles

Coverage of the Journal Title	Number of Journals
Current Access	22
12 Month Embargo	5
18 Month Embargo	7
Older Coverage, but Not Current	5
No Access	11

Table 1.3: Current Access Specifics (N = 22)

Publisher/Database	Number of Journal Titles
Sage Journal Subscription	5
Wiley Journal Subscription	3
Elsevier Journal Subscription	2
Database Coverage or Direct Subscription	12

Table 1.4: Total Usage of Sage Titles at UWEC (N = 742)

Year	Total Full Text	HTML Full Text	PDF Full Text
2014	23877	1986	21891
2013	18955	1470	17485
2012	18909	758	18151
2011	15291	287	15004

Table 1.5: Average Usage of Sage Titles at UWEC

Year	Total Full Text Average	PDF Full Text Average
2014	32.18	29.50
2013	25.55	23.56
2012	25.48	24.46
2011	20.61	20.22

I chose to focus on two different subsets of journals where faculty published: Sage Journals and journals where Women's Studies Faculty published which were featured in the ORSP reports. The Sage journals Where Faculty Published were *Journal of Developing Societies, Journal of Macromarketing, Journal of Social and Personal Relationships, Psychology of Women Quarterly,* and *Review of Radical Political Economics*. Because we

Table 1.6: Usage for *Psychology of Women Quarterly*

Year	Total Full Text Retrievals	PDF Full Text Retrievals
2014	236	187
2013	202	200
2012	123	97
2011	22	17

subscribe to a Sage Big Deal package at UWEC, we can see look at COUNTER reports to see if these journals are used more than the average Sage journal. Table 1.4 shows the total usage for Sage journals from 2011 to 2014 and Table 1.5 shows the average use of journals in the Sage package from 2011 to 2014. I looked more closely at measures for two of the Sage journals: *Psychology of Women Quarterly*, as it is on the core list of journals, and *Review of Radical Political Economics* as this journal published an article by one of UWEC's women's studies affiliates. Table 1.6 shows the total usage for *Psychology of Women Quarterly* from 2011 to 2014. The article published in *Psychology of Women Quarterly* was co-authored by a world renowned expert in Non-Suicidal Self Injury, Jennifer Muehlenkamp, who is in the psychology department, does research that is feminist, but is not a women's studies affiliate at UWEC:

> Peat, Christine M. and Jennifer Muehlenkamp. 2011. "Self-Objectification, Disordered Eating, and Depression: A Test of Meditational Pathways." Psychology of Women Quarterly 35 (3): 441–450.

UWEC has access to 27 of the 31 peer reviewed journals cited by this article, and 20 of these titles have current access coverage.

The second Sage journal for which I looked more closely at measures was Review of Radical Political Economics, which published the following article by a UWEC women's studies affiliated:

> Chaudhuri, Sanjukta. 2012. "Female Infant Mortality Disadvantage in India: A Regional Analysis." *Review of Radical Political Economics* 44 (3): 321–326.

Table 1.7 shows that this journal was not accessed nearly as much as Psychology of Women Quarterly (see Table 1.5) or as much as the average Sage journal (see Table 1.4). UWEC Library has access to three of the five peer reviewed journals cited in this article. The three journals that we have current access to are: *Development and Change* (through our Wiley journal package); *Oxford Review of Economic Policy* (through our Oxford University Press journal package); and *Population and Development Review* (through our Wiley Package). All three of these titles have coverage in one or more EBSCO databases but each one of the titles has a one-year embargo in the EBSCO databases.

Table 1.7: Usage for *Review of Radical Political Economics*

Year	Total Full Text Retrievals
2014	8
2013	9
2012	35
2011	14

The library has current access to three out of five of the journals, however, two journals were cited twice by Dr. Chaudhuri's article and one journal was cited three times by her article. It may be the case that you would want to calculate the results in terms of this. If we were to calculate the measures so that recurring journal citations are counted, then we would provide current access not to 60 percent of the journals, but to 66.67 percent of the journals.

By looking at the Sage journal package—or any journal package—in this way, we can see which titles support women's studies scholarship. This is a very useful approach if you need to determine the stakeholders for any Big Deal package. Scholars themselves may not be aware of their dependence on some of the publishers' packages, but finding out usage and relative importance to any discipline can help inform a universities collection decisions.

Returning to the four articles of the explicitly described "women's studies" journal publications—the sample size that was determined to be too small—the following publications were from the UWEC ORSP reports on women's studies publications for the most recent 10 years:

> Kieffer, Laurel, and Susan C. Turell. 2011. "Child Custody and Safe Exchange/Visitation: An Assessment of Marginalized Battered Parents' Needs." *Journal of Child Custody* 8 (4): 301–322.
> Turell, Susan, and Molly Herrmann. 2008. "'Family' Support for Family Violence: Exploring Community Support Systems for Lesbian and Bisexual Women Who Have Experienced Abuse." *Journal of Lesbian Studies* 12(2–3): 207–220.
> Turell, Susan, Leslye Mize and Jo Meier. 2004 "Sexual Orientation and the Sister Relationship: Conversations and Opportunities." *Journal of Feminist Family Psychology* 16.4 (2004): 1–19.
> Theresa D. Kemp. "Women's Patronage Seeking as Familial Enterprise: Aemilia Lanyer, Esther Inglis, and Mary Wroth." *Literature Compass* 4.2 (2007): 384–406.

Laurel Kieffer and Susan Turell (2011) cite 12 peer reviewed journals and the UWEC library has current access to all of them. One could say that the scholarship of current women's studies Affiliate Kieffer and former women's studies affiliate Turell is well supported at UWEC. However, looking at the article Turell published with Molly Herrmann (2008) shows a different situation entirely. This later articles also cites twelve peer-reviewed journals, but the UWEC library only has current access to four of them. Perhaps co-author Herrmann had better access to the eight titles UWEC does not have current access to. This work was published seven years ago and UWEC journal and database holdings looked different then. Databases lose access to journal titles and we librarians often do not know about the loss until a problem with access is reported. There is no easy way to recreate past journal holdings that include all modes of access. Turell also published an article with Leslye Mize and Jo Meier (2004) and the UWEC library has current access to 66.67 percent of the titles cited in the article. Theresa Kemp's article cites seven peer reviewed journals and the UWEC library has current access to three of them. *Journal of Family Psychology* and *Journal of Homosexuality* were cited by two of the four women's studies articles so the list of citations was de-duped so we had a list of 41 titles. Additional analyses could be performed to determine if current subscriptions are warranted for the titles with embargoes or the titles where we have no access (see Table 1.8).

Table 1.8: UWEC Access to Articles Cited in the Four Women's Studies Articles

Coverage of the Journal Title	*Number of Journals (N = 41)*
Current Access	26

Coverage of the Journal Title	Number of Journals (N = 41)
12 Month Embargo	2
18 Month Embargo	3
Older Coverage, but Not Current	4
No Access	6

Looking at the Sage journals and their citations next to those of the "women's studies" journals which UWEC Faculty cited and seeing how many of these titles are current subscriptions at UWEC provide an interesting way to look at the collection of scholarly journals supporting local women's studies scholarship. Questions to ask include: "Is it more important to collection titles where authors publish or titles they cite in their publications?" and "Will finding overlap change the priority status of a journal title?" Figure 1 shows the overlap between the three subsets: Journals that women's studies scholars cite; Journals where women's studies scholars publish; and Journals on the Women and Gender Studies Section Core List of Journals. Journal of Lesbian Studies is one title that appeared where the three circles meet in the Venn Diagram. Sadly, UWEC have access to this core women's studies title that a UWEC faculty member published in, that this same faculty member cited.

The methodology my colleague and I used in an earlier (Wical and Vandenbark 2015) study could not be applied as easily to women's studies scholarship at The University of Wisconsin—Eau Claire in part because women's studies is a high scatter discipline and because women's studies is a small program that draws extensively on affiliates who have tenure homes in other departments. This current study focused solely on women's

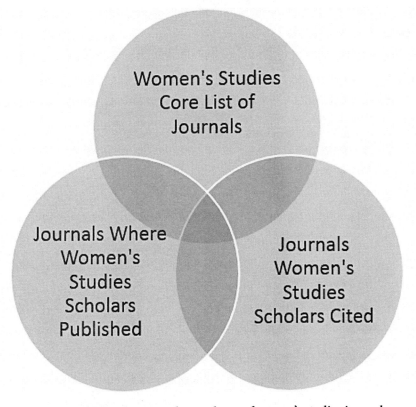

Figure 1. Overlap between three subsets of women's studies journals.

studies collections at the University of Wisconsin–Eau Claire so we cannot generalize the findings. Additionally, the ORSP reports rely on faculty self-reporting their scholarship and may not contain all publications that could be counted. What is counted as women's studies or feminist scholarship may not reflect what could be counted. This approach could be applied to larger universities or pared down for smaller colleges: You may only need to examine a few years of women's studies faculty publications; You may want to eliminate tracking the publications of women's studies faculty members who have left so that any findings can inform current needs; and You may want to only look at the most recent three years of usage statistics for electronic journals and databases because usage patterns change.

Is a core list of journals even valuable? For women's studies, a core list of journals may not be as important as a core list of books or essays. It really depends on the program and the university culture. For many, it may no longer be necessary as it developed when the print format was the norm. While you can scale this approach up or down, you can also decide how much importance you are going to attach to collecting titles where faculty members publish and to collecting titles that faculty member cite. Who is counted as a women's studies scholar: Core faculty; Affiliates who have tenure homes in other departments; Scholars who do what can be considered feminist scholarship although they may not explicitly identify with a women's studies program or department? Priorities of research intensive universities are very different from the priorities of teaching colleges and universities and so it is important to figure out what works best for any given academic library.

Another possible further inquiry could include looking at the articles cited in the 50 different journals where UWEC faculty published women's studies scholarship. This would provide additional data points. Looking at the Women's Studies publications of several colleges and universities could yield some useful information. The results could inform what individual women's studies departments and programs should do. The core list of journals could be updated and/or modified to reflect local research needs because I believe important to build any collection recommendations around the teaching and research needs of current faculty.

Faculty members who are not affiliated with the UWEC women's studies program are doing feminist scholarship, so we need to rethink how we measure and what we count as feminist scholarship. In addition to the applying to subject matter in a collection, the concept of scatter could also apply to the fact that our sisters and brothers in the struggle are dispersed throughout the university. So the question becomes how do we reunite everyone from this political and intellectual diaspora? Looking at where scholars publish, what journals they cite as well as looking at how many full-text articles are retrieved at a university provide valid measures of the value of the women's studies collection. How this is statistically presented to stakeholders could be intentional and strategic.

References

Collection Development and Bibliography Committee, Women's Studies Section, Association of College and Research Libraries. 1992. *Women's Studies Collection Development Policies.* Chicago: American Library Association.

Denda, Kayo. 2005. "Beyond Subject Headings: A Structured Information Retrieval Tool for Interdisciplinary Fields." *LRTS* 49 (4): 266–275.

Gerhard, Kristin H., Mila C. Su and Charlotte C. Rubens. 1998. "An Empirical Examination of Subject Headings for Women's Studies Core Materials." *College and Research Libraries* 59 (2): 129–137.

Herubel, Jean-Pierre V. M. 2007. "Musing on Disciplinary Morphology and Nomenclature in the Humanities and Social Sciences: Implications for Book Selection." *Journal of Scholarly Publishing* 39 (1):54–62.

Lee, Hur-Li. 2003. "Collection Development as a Social Process." *The Journal of Academic Librarianship* 29 (1): 23–31.

Porter, Alan L., J. David Roessner and Anne E. Heberger. 2008. "How Interdisciplinary Is a Given Body of Research?" *Research Evaluation* 17(4): 273–282.

Spanner, Don. 2001. "Border Crossings: Understanding the Cultural and Informational Dilemmas of Interdisciplinary Scholars." *The Journal of Academic Librarianship* 27(5): 352–360.

Szostak, Rick. 2014. "The Importance of Knowledge Organization: Economics of Knowledge Organization Systems." *Bulletin of the Association for Information Science and Technology* 40(4): 37–42.

Westbrook, Lynn. 1999. *Interdisciplinary Information Seeking in Women's Studies.* Jefferson, NC: McFarland.

Westbrook, Lynn. 2001. "Reference Support for Interdisciplinary Scholars: Resources for Working with Women's Studies Faculty," *Proceedings of the Association of College and Research Libraries 10th National Conference, March 15–18, 2001, Denver, Colorado.* Hugh Thompson, editor. Chicago, IL: Association of College and Research Libraries, 265–270.

Westbrook, Lynn. 2003. "Information Needs and Experiences of Scholars in Women's Studies: Problems and Solutions." *College and Research Libraries* 64.(3): 192–209

Wical, Stephanie H. and Todd Vandenbark. 2015. "Combining Citation Studies and Usage Statistics to Build a Stronger Collection," *Library Resources and Technical Services* 59 (1): 33–42.

Women and Gender Studies Section of ACRL. Core List of Journals for Women and Gender Studies. http://libr.org/wgss/projects/serial.htmlChin

Documenting Women's Labor History
A Case Study in Improving Access and Outreach for Underrepresented Groups

KRISTEN L. CHINERY *and* ELIZABETH CLEMENS

Despite underrepresentation within traditionally male dominated collections, research related to women workers grows exponentially each year. Undeniably, the histories of labor and women's rights are intertwined. However, reaching the material that documents that intertwined history is sometimes difficult; often the richest resources for women's labor history are found in unprocessed or non-manuscript materials. In order to reach a greater audience and more fully utilize the breadth of formats that document previously underrepresented subjects, staff at the Walter P. Reuther Library, Wayne State University in Detroit, Michigan developed an outreach strategy using image galleries, blog articles, and digital collections, as well as collaborative social media like Historypin and Pinterest.

The Walter P. Reuther Library of Labor and Urban Affairs was established as the Labor History Archives at Wayne State University in 1960, with the goal of collecting and preserving original source materials relating to the development of the American labor movement. In addition to being the largest labor archives in North America, its collection strengths extend to the political and community life of urban and metropolitan Detroit, the civil rights movement in Michigan and nationally, and women's struggles in the workplace. The Reuther Library is also home to the Wayne State University Archives.

Visitors to the Reuther's Reading Room include a variety of patrons, everyone from faculty to union members to documentary filmmakers, with the majority of on-site researchers being graduate students. Phone and email reference requests come from an even more diverse group of patrons, including media outlets, museums, publishing houses, advertising agencies, and film producers. One of the fastest growing areas of research at the Reuther has been the role of women in the labor movement. Recent topics include pay equity, sexual harassment in the workplace, women defense workers, women in union leadership, labor activism as it relates to the Black Power Movement and the role of black women, and the influence of labor unions on women's reproductive health legislation. Although the increase in requests related to women and labor is statistically documented (see Table 1), providing the same level of access to remote and in-person patrons presents an ongoing challenge. In particular, it is difficult to capture all relevant

50

collections for thematic research when those collections contain multiple formats or have not been fully described.

Table 1: Reference Statistics

Reading Room Requests

	2014–2015	2015–2016	Increase
All Collections	1478	1736	17.5%
Women's Collections	174	265	52.3%

Remote Reference Requests

	2014–2015	2015–2016	Increase
All Collections	1160	1350	16.4%
Women's Collections	160	235	46.9%

Source: Chinery and Clemens 2016, 2–3.

The increase in the number of researchers requesting material about women both remotely and in the Reading Room over the past two years (April 2014–April 2016) is substantial, averaging 50 percent. When analyzing individual requests, it was evident that for most women's history subjects researched at the Reuther, there are not a finite number of go-to manuscript collections but pieces of many. For example, a review of data related to two of the Reuther's most heavily researched women's topics, pay equity and women defense workers, showed that patrons accessed 13 and 11 different collections, respectively. This example highlights the need for pulling content together across collections and formats. One of the Reuther's strategies to accomplish this is to use its website as both an outreach tool and access point. The website is home to the Reuther's digital content, which includes finding aids, images, audio files, transcripts, publications, and links to external digital collections, and it allows users to do a broad search across all content types. Large subsets of the collections, however, are unprocessed and thus not searchable using the website. Audiovisual materials are particularly affected.

The Reuther's audiovisual collections include over 2 million still images and negatives, over 15,000 audio and video recordings (1-inch tape, Beta, U-matic, VHS, reel-to-reel), approximately 5,000 films, and countless linear feet of artifacts, textiles, artwork, and assorted graphic materials. The Reuther employs a number of cost effective tools to bring hidden objects within the audiovisual holdings to light, including digital and artificial collections, blog articles, and interactive social media. In order to launch these projects, staff first had to develop policies for the selection of materials, digitization standards, and copyright. Digitization was identified as a priority early in the process as only 5 percent of the audiovisual holdings have been captured. Budget and staff constraints prevent mass digitization efforts at this time, so staff outlined a number of smaller initiatives that focus on important aspects of the Reuther's collecting scope. A series of projects recently completed highlight the role of women in organized labor.

Selection and Digitization

There are numerous elements to evaluate when creating a digital project. Research potential is often the primary driving factor, which is determined by analyzing trends among patrons as well as the wider academic community. In addition, when selecting photographs, it is helpful to consider 4 W's that establish unique characteristics: Who is in it? What is depicted that makes it unique? Where was it taken? Why is the event or person significant? Though most archival material is by definition unique, you should determine if a particular person or topic has extensive representation elsewhere, either in your collections or in the collections of other institutions or organizations, before committing resources.

The physical condition of materials also plays an important role in the selection process. Older or damaged pieces are often digitally captured for access purposes; patrons use the digital derivative in order to spare further handling of the original. The same approach applies to fragile formats, such as nitrate film negatives and reel-to-reel magnetic tape recordings, many of which have reached the point in their life span where signs of degradation are evident. For these fragile format materials, the Reuther established a policy of digitization on demand. Any time a researcher wishes to listen to older magnetic tape stock, for example, an archivist digitizes it as the researcher listens to the recording.

The standards for digitization follow archival best practices. Photos are scanned as 600dpi uncompressed TIFF files with the output equaling 10 inches (6,000 pixels) on the longest axis (Smithsonian Institution Archives, n.d.). The original is scanned without correction, then adjustments are made on a duplicate file to try and bring the image back to what the photographer may have intended. All patron requests are scanned at a preservation level in an effort to reduce the number of times an image is handled. The Reuther does not currently have the capacity to transfer film or video to a preservation output, so staff members create access copies with the equipment available. The Audiovisual Department also established a policy for researchers who are interested in having material professionally transferred in exchange for waiving all licensing fees. In most cases, this agreement is less expensive for the filmmakers and future patrons will benefit from a preserved copy.

Copyright

The final step in developing digital projects is verifying copyright. Clearing copyright is one of the more time consuming aspects of the process, but it is an important one, as the rights of the owner need to be respected. Section 107 of the U.S. Copyright Act allows for the "fair use" of copyrighted works for teaching and research (Crews 2012, 152), which greatly benefits archives and libraries. The *Code of Best Practices for Fair Use in the Visual Arts*, created by the College Art Association, contains easy-to-understand information about fair use. The potential for infringement when fair use does not apply should inform choices when making selections for digitization, as reproducing an image for educational purposes differs from licensing an image to a third party for use in a book or documentary. In such cases, there are three things to consider in terms of copyright: ownership, allowable uses, and personality rights.

Determining who owns a particular image can be difficult, especially when collections have different types of ownership. Some donors transfer copyright outright, others retain it but allow for the archive to act as a proxy and distribute their material for educational projects. To determine ownership, the easiest place to start is with its age. Material that pre-dates copyright law, or had its copyright expire, will likely be in the public domain. If the item is not in the public domain, the task is more complicated. Thankfully, there are a number of tools to assist in assessing copyright status. The slider tool available at http://librarycopyright.net/resources, for example, allows you to input information and provides calculations about where the material falls under public domain.

One of the biggest copyright challenges is dealing with orphan works, a term used when the owner cannot be identified. Most archives and libraries have large amounts of orphaned material. At the Reuther, archivists weigh the potential research value against the possible risk of infringement. In these cases, it is important to practice due diligence in looking for the owner(s), clearly document your search, and include a notation on the record that ownership is unknown. Another challenge is identifying works made for hire. When dealing with copyright for organizational records, you have to consider whether an employee of the donor created the work, or whether they were under contract; this is especially significant for photographers. If a photographer was under contract, the donor owns copyright of anything produced while in their employ. If the photographer retained intellectual ownership, he or she determines where and when the images may be distributed.

The term "allowable uses" references restricted use parameters set up by either the institution housing the material or the copyright owner. Often these materials are of a more sensitive nature. For example, a donor could place restrictions on an oral history so that it can be accessed for research purposes but it cannot be used for publication. Some donors restrict how their works can be used in advertising or political campaigns. Whatever the case, make sure you are standing on the right side of your donor agreements.

Finally, there is the question of rights of publicity, commonly known as personality rights. Personality rights refer to "an individual's right to prevent others from commercially exploiting his or her identity without permission" (Boisineau 2013, 66). Individual states rather than the federal government regulate this right, typically as either the right to privacy or property rights (Rufo 2016, par.3), but it varies widely from state to state. To prevent potential legal challenges, it is necessary to verify whether the responsible parties require permission of use.

Image Galleries and Artificial Collections

Once materials are selected, digitized, and cleared for copyright, you can move forward with a project. In the Reuther's case, archivists developed a gallery system on the website for audio recordings, images, transcripts, exhibits, blogs, and publications, all of which are formatted for ease of use. Image galleries are the most frequently accessed of these resources. They contain content specific to an organization, event, or topic, and link to one of the Reuther's three historical collecting areas: organized labor, urban affairs, or the history of Wayne State University. The number of images in each gallery varies greatly, but there is a target minimum of 40 to 50 images. Each record will display the existing metadata for the individual image, which typically includes content type, photographer, date, unique numeric identifier, description, and a title. Taxonomy, a series of descriptors drawn from names and subjects that frequently appear in the Reuther's collections and Library of Congress subjects, is also applied.

In order to draw content together according to a specific subject, archivists create an artificial collection. Content is pulled from across multiple collections and formats to provide easy access to like materials that are physically scattered throughout the holdings. It significantly cuts down on the research time for patrons doing thematic research, and allows for easier browsing. A recently completed labor-related artificial collection showcases the role of women in the Industrial Workers of the World (IWW). The IWW was one of the first industrial unions to adopt the concept of gender equality and extend its membership to women. It viewed women as activists and equal partners in the struggle rather than simply auxiliary support, and women played important roles in some of the larger textile strikes such as Lawrence and Paterson. In terms of labor history, the IWW had two incredibly influential women in its ranks: Mother Jones and Elizabeth Gurley Flynn.

There is broad appeal for research within the IWW collections because of the wealth of information they contain, which features documentation about feminism, free speech, socialism, immigration, communism, pacifism, and the establishment of the eight-hour workday. Outside of popular subjects like well-known strikes and people like Elizabeth Gurley Flynn, most of the images, which were donated to the Reuther as the IWW's official repository, have been out of circulation for nearly 100 years. The majority of these images are not represented anywhere else in the United States due to the fact that many of the IWW's images did not survive numerous government raids during World War I (Walter P. Reuther Library 1984, 2). In addition to images, the IWW artificial collection includes one-of-a-kind artifacts, such as beaded banners and purses made by imprisoned IWW members and makeshift clubs used during textile strikes. These objects have accessibility issues built into them, as they are delicate and very valuable. The digital derivatives allow researchers to easily access the items while bypassing security concerns. The materials in this artificial collection were drawn from both personal papers and organizational records of various IWW branches.

Artificial collections are incredibly useful, yet there are some drawbacks with respect to the varying format types. Audio files remain separate due to the architecture of the Reuther's website, and fully digitized manuscript collections are too unwieldy to host due to their size. Website architecture is also a challenge for the Reuther's moving images as there is no simple way to protect the material from being directly downloaded by a user, which is a problem if you do not own the copyright for all of your moving image materials. Currently, Reuther staff members are sandboxing with the Fedora platform as a solution to these issues. Fedora is a digital repository that preserves and provides access to digitized archival material. From Fedora, collections will be shared with the Digital Public Library of America (DPLA), a portal and platform that aggregates content from museums, libraries, and archives from across the United States. In the meantime, blog articles are used to bring the disparate sources of material together in an easy to digest narrative form.

Blog Articles

In 2008, the Reuther created a blog area on its website to host resource guides, collection spotlights, and event notices. For purposes of access, the blog articles serve as a narrative subject guide, much like a pathfinder. All subject focus or collection spotlight blogs begin with a general introduction to the topic and end with a list of relevant collections, often with brief descriptions, in order to assist patrons in further developing their research. The articles contain links that lead to collection abstracts and finding aids, photographs, audio files, transcripts, or other graphic material. The narrative structure of the articles allows for pieces to be easily reused and repurposed, serving as an efficient way to provide content to other websites and media outlets, and for K-12 educational materials. They are also easily pushed out into social media systems, where they are widely read and shared. Subject focus blog articles are often scheduled to coincide with the launch of a newly digitized collection, which requires advanced planning.

Collaborative Social Media

In an effort to reach more individuals than those traditionally interested in labor research, the Reuther developed a Historypin program in the spring of 2015. Historypin is a popular, interactive social media platform that uses geotagging to link historical photographs to modern mapping systems. These "pins" of content can be grouped together in a tour or collection, each allowing for the individual user to explore historical topics or locations. The first project selected mapped out Detroit's 1937 Sit-Down Strikes. The topic was deliberately chosen as it is popular with researchers, particularly younger students. More importantly, it offered an opportunity to highlight the role of women in that historic year, which is significant because women carried the majority of strikes outside of Detroit's auto factories in hotels, restaurants, dime stores, bakeries, department stores, and cigar plants. While the more famous autoworkers' strikes are featured, the majority of images from the tour deal with women's efforts to organize, a focus that is seldom represented in the historical context of the 1937 strikes. Reaction to the Historypin tours has been overwhelmingly positive, and they are frequently shared by other organizations with similar interests. Educators, at both the K-12 and university level, find the tours to be fun and engaging tools to use within their curricula.

Another social media platform to utilize is Pinterest, a visual bookmarking tool that allows people to organize materials they find around the web into thematic boards. It works similarly to Facebook, in that you have "friends" whose activities show up in your feed. Pinterest's strength is that content is easily shared between people who have like interests, as the platform's algorithms choose content to share in "feeds." Users don't necessarily have to search out a particular board; they are associated by exhibiting a general interest in the topic. The Reuther turned to Pinterest as an access point for collections in the fall of 2015. "Women in the Labor Movement" is second in terms of overall popularity, coming in after a board on Prohibition in the 1920s. An average of 1,275 people interact with the boards each month, the majority of them from the United States, Canada, Great Britain, Germany, and Mexico. It is a great tool for reaching a broad audience with very little effort, since you are typically using material that has already been scanned, described, and uploaded to the web. As Pinterest is indexed through Google, and returns often show up high on search results pages, you have the opportunity to reach an audience outside of the Pinterest community.

Conclusion

The Reuther provides greater access to underrepresented groups and hidden subjects by utilizing a variety of tools, all of which are underscored by careful curation of materials.

Projects that make use of galleries, blogs, digital collections, and interactive social media are easily adaptable, and can serve as a blueprint for improving both access and outreach for underrepresented groups. Once created, take advantage of Facebook and Twitter to push out content to specific communities and to keep constituents engaged. Ultimately, the goal in all of these endeavors is to create broader access to materials, in particular, the stories of those whose voices have not always been heard.

REFERENCES

American Library Association Office for Information Technology Policy. 2012. *Public Domain Slider.* http://librarycopyright.net/resources/digitalslider/.

Boisineau. Lynne M.J. 2013. "Intellectual Property Law: The Right of Publicity and the Social Media Revolution." *GP Solo* 30 (3): 66–67.

Chinery, Kristen, and Elizabeth Clemens. "Documenting Women's Labor History: A Path for Improving Outreach and Access for Underrepresented Groups." Paper presented at the Association of Canadian Archivists Annual Conference, Montreal, Quebec, June 2016.

College Art Association. 2015. *Best Practices in Fair Use for the Visual Arts.* http://www.collegeart.org/pdf/fair-use/best-practices-fair-use-visual-arts.pdf.

Crews, Kenneth D. 2012. *Copyright Law for Librarians and Educators: Creative Strategies and Practical Solutions.* Chicago: American Library Association.

Rufo, Anthony. 2016. *Celebrity Trademark Watch: Who Owns Marilyn Monroe's Image?—Right of Publicity vs. Trademark Rights.*
http://www.trademarkandcopyrightlawblog.com/2016/01/celebrity-trademark-watch-who-owns-marilyn-monroes-image-right-of-publicity-vs-trademark-rights/.

Smithsonian Institution Archives. "Digitization." Accessed July 14, 2016. http://siarchives.si.edu/services/digitization.

Walter P. Reuther Library. 1984. *Guide to the Industrial Workers of the World Collection.* http://www.reuther.wayne.edu/node/3156.

Performing Women's History in the Public Library

Jamie L. Huber

As a former university women's center coordinator and women's and gender studies instructor who now works in a public library setting, gender-focused programming and Women's History Month programming holds a special place in my heart, which led me to create the "Women's History Comes Alive: The U.S. Women's Suffrage Movement" program. As an instructor, I have come across many college students who have extremely limited knowledge of the suffrage movement, which I believe is a very important piece of U.S. history, and I suspect the general public also has limited knowledge about the suffrage movement. Still, I recognize many people are not necessarily interested in attending a lecture or reading a book about the suffrage movement. My goal with this program was to make it interactive and engaging, so I incorporated a performative aspect, with performers performing speeches given by and works written by notable U.S. suffragists.

Selecting Performers and Performance Pieces

To find performers, I utilized academic and community connections, touching base with faculty in local college-level women's and gender studies programs, English departments, and theatre departments, as well as individuals who work in community theatre. Potential performers met with me to do a brief reading and discuss what their preferences might be regarding the pieces they would perform. For this event, all interested performers who had compatible schedules were invited to participate, creating a "cast" of five performers.

After establishing the number performers and having knowledge of the attributes they would bring to their performances, I allowed that knowledge to guide me while moving forward with selecting the texts for the performance. When creating the program, I sought to include pieces spanning the entire suffrage movement, as well as those representing a variety of suffragists' backgrounds. However, particularly as a first time event, I believed it important to include suffragists who would also have more name recognition, with the possibility of creating sequential programming focused on lesser known suffragists. I also wanted to ensure performance selections could be performed in riveting and impactful ways, so I took care to find pieces that had particular emotional appeal.

For this event, I took selections from the following works: Elizabeth Cady Stanton's "Declaration of Sentiments," Susan B. Anthony's "A Constitutional Argument," Inez Milholland's " Appeal to the Women Voters of the West," and both Alice Paul's and Rose Winslow's "Letters from Jail." I found these selections in Doris Steven's *Jailed for Freedom* and Karlyn Kohrs Campbell's *Man Cannot Speak for Her: Key Texts of the Early Feminists, Volume II*, as well as on Robert P. J. Cooney, Jr.'s website *Remembering Inez: The Last Campaign of Inez Milholland, Suffrage Martyr*. After selecting these pieces, I wove them into a narrative journey that highlighted key moments in the suffrage movement, beginning with Elizabeth Cady Stanton and Lucretia Mott's plans to begin a women's movement at the 1840 World Anti-Slavery Convention and ending with the passage of the 19th amendment in 1920. In this narration I also included biographical information about the original author or speaker of each performative piece that was woven into the program.

Other Planning Details

To move forward with the planning, performers rehearsed their pieces individually and in consultation with me, and performers arrived at the library venue 45 minutes before the event to go over staging and last minute details. I made several decisions to keep the event low-stress and low-cost. Rather than having all pieces memorized, performers did performative readings, which allowed them to utilize black binders with their texts/scripts. Performers also dressed simply in white tops and black bottoms rather than period dress (though they did wear period-style hats). Both of these choices are common for basic oral interpretation performances. To add period authenticity to the event, a library colleague helped me coordinate with a local suffrage reenactment group. Members of this group attended the event in early 20th century suffrage dress and greeted attendees as they entered the event. I also created a visual slideshow to accompany the narration of the suffrage movement.

To provide attendees with further information about the suffrage movement, I created a handout of selected resources they could keep as a take-a-way. The handout included books, films, websites, and travel destinations focused on the U.S. suffrage movement. I also chose to provide snacks for the event, including cupcakes iced with the purple and gold (or yellow) colors that visually marked the suffrage movement in its later years.

Program Reception and Assessment

Overall, I considered the program a success. The performances and narrative presentation was followed by a very lively open discussion, and, though no formal assessment was conducted, all attendees verbally indicated that they enjoyed the program and learned something new. As one attendee shared, "The performance was thought-provoking, but I enjoyed the discussion afterwards even more! I think a couple pairs of eyes were opened!" A library staff member in attendance also commented "Thank you for bringing this fun, informative program to our patrons." In retrospect, I believe I should have conducted a brief but more formalized assessment, asking attendees questions such as what they liked about the program, what they would suggest improving, if they would attend a similar program in the future or recommend the program to a friend, and how they found out about the program.

Twelve attendees were at the program, which leads me to believe more could have been done with marketing the event. No additional marketing or publicity was done for this event outside of the steps taken for all library events (appearing in the library district program, monthly email blasts, and calendars), with the exception that it was grouped in a larger Women's History Month category that received some promotion through social media. Some library patrons expressed the sentiment that too many Women's History Month programs were taking place, causing the attendance to be more dispersed. *The Suffragette* (2015), for example, was shown at the same library branch the preceding week. I also believe more efforts promoting the program among community groups interested performances, high schools, and local colleges and universities might have yielded better attendance. This issue, however, is also linked to ongoing changes and developments in the library district's marketing strategies.

Moving Forward to the Next Event

This initial program has given us an opportunity to conceptualize and implement similar types of programs in our library district. Another event that is currently in the works is a film screening of *Iron Jawed Angels* (2004) on Women's Equality Day (August 26), with a discussion to follow, to commemorate the suffrage amendment. Since this event will be held during a presidential election year, we are partnering with a local chapter of the League of Women Voters to hold voter registration at the event, and we are also inviting the suffrage reenactment group back to participate. We have learned that many of the League of Women Voters members who will be facilitating the voter registration will also be donning suffrage-era dress.

By connecting this event to a current event and the broader theme of civic engagement, we hope to increase participant turnout. We also hope that we might increase attendance by holding the program outside of Women's History Month and the jam-packed schedule of women-focused events. That being said, we will also undertake more targeted marketing in addition to the general, overall marketing that the district does for all programs.

The first part of our targeted marketing efforts involves connecting with local women's organizations and personally inviting them not only to attend but also help spread the word about our event. Organizations we are reaching out to include not only the League of Women Voters chapter and suffrage reenactment group we are working with, but also local chapters of the American Association of University Women, the local National Organization for Women chapter, the local Zonta chapter, and the local Junior League Association. These are organizations whose memberships are likely to have a vested interest in the type of programming we are creating and promoting for Women's Equality Day.

The next step of our targeted marketing is focused on reaching out to academic departments/programs and student organizations at nearby colleges and universities. Departments and programs we particularly plan to focus on are women's/gender studies programs, history programs, and political science programs. Since our programming will take place at the end of August when schools are just beginning the fall semester, these institutions are less likely to have "competing" programs than they might have during Women's History Month. While the timing could also make it difficult to reach some students, college and university faculty and staff will oftentimes have email lists of majors, minors, student organization leaders, etc., so students who are likely to be interested in this type of event and who are in the area can be contacted.

While making connections with these community organizations and educational institutions in itself can help draw in more attendees, former more solid partnerships with them can also be a way to encourage them to have a more vested interest in the event and engaged approach to promoting the event. Some ways in which we might create these partnerships are allowing groups to bring information about their own missions and events, perhaps in the format of an information fair. Since the organizations we are targeted have historic links to the suffrage movement and/or women's equality, this format makes sense in many ways. Also, by inviting select faculty or students to participate alongside the League of Women Voters and suffrage reenactors as greeters for the event, we are likely to increase attendance and engagement from this demographic.

When connecting with these groups, we will take a personalized approach, first reaching out to those in leadership positions (organization presidents, department/program chairs, etc.). We will describe our event and why it might be of particular interest to them and their membership/colleagues/students. We will also gauge their interest in taking on more of a partner role in the event. Finally, we will provide them with promotional materials (flyers, press releases, sample tweets and Facebook posts, etc.) geared towards the groups we would like them to focus on when promoting the event. Materials for the American Association of University Women, for instance, might focus on a lifelong learning component and the connection with the organization mission while materials for students might focus on seeing what they are learning about in class being presented in new and exciting ways. If the timing works out, we might have a library representative involved with the event attend some organization meetings or classes to promote the event and answer questions in person.

Another group we are interested in targeting for our event marketing is educators. While I already discussed reaching out to post-secondary faculty, middle school and high school teachers in many ways are ideal attendees for this event, particularly if there is follow-up discussion or event that is specifically designed to discuss utilizing segments or themes from *Iron Jawed Angels* into curriculum development. Such a discussion can incorporate resources from online sources such as Teach with Movies, Beavercreek City School District, Middle Tennessee State University, *Time*, and more that have shared pre-developed teaching and learning guides for the film. Having space specifically for educators will allow for a dialogue focused on the benefits and challenges of using a film like *Iron Jawed Angels* in the classroom at various age levels to teach about the suffrage movement.

Finally, we would like to do more promotional outreach with area women's social groups and book clubs. While these groups might not be as easy to locate, online networking tools like Meetup provide a great place to start looking for these groups, and promoting an event can be as simple as sending a pre-created invited to a group organizer. This might be a productive way to reach potential attendees who otherwise might have been unaware of the program.

By utilizing some of these more targeted marketing approaches in addition to our general district marketing, we hope to really build on our groundwork from the "Women's

History Comes Alive" program and enhance attendance at the Women's Equality Day event. We also hope to begin fostering relationships with area organizations and institutional that will be beneficial when planning future events. As an entity that is heavily invested in creating community, public libraries can be very well-served by connecting with existent communities and working with them to engage them and meet their needs.

Future Events

While I have touched on a couple of events, the possibilities for building upon these types of event are endless. The events I previously mentioned are geared towards adults. For tween/teen/young adult programs, similar tactics with a more engaged and creative focus can be used. For instance, program participants could spend some time researching suffragists, or a particular suffragist, and then, based on their research, create individual or group skits or creative works that can be performed or displayed in the library setting. Programming of this type might require multiple sessions, but can be very beneficial. It will not only enhance participants' understanding of a specific subject matter, but also increase their overall information literacy skills and provide them with a creative outlet.

Working with community theatre groups and historical reenactment groups can also create some fun possibilities, such as a suffrage-era fashion show followed by an informational session on how to create your own suffrage-era costume. When I met some members of our local suffrage reenactment group, they talked about how they go on thrift store shopping sprees to make their costumes. A program like this would also provide an opportunity to partner with local thrift stores, allowing the stores to display some of their merchandise while giving the audience examples of how to find their authentic-looking suffrage getup. This is a program that could be provided as a standalone program, or in conjunction with a program like the one I suggested for tweens/teens/young adults in which participants will create their own performance piece. By pairing these programs together, attendees will have both their performance piece and costume prepared. Incorporating a performative or creative writing aspect to the programming can also create opportunities to apply for grant funding from some state-based arts and humanities councils. As I move forward with this type of programming in my library district, I am keeping these possibilities at the forefront of my mind.

Program Timing

In some ways, Women's History Month provides an ideal time to hold this type of programming. However, as I mentioned, the jam-packed nature of programming for this month can create an oversaturation. Moreover, other community groups or institutions might also be sponsoring Women's History Month programming, enhancing this oversaturation effect. As an academic, Women's History Month programming was always a challenge due to Spring Break generally occurring in the middle of the month. While this might not be as much of a concern outside of the college or university system, it can still be a deterrent if looking to partner with or engage individuals who are at a postsecondary institution. Furthermore, many high schools also have spring break in March, meaning many families and K-12 teachers will use the opportunity for a brief vacation.

So although this type of programming fits exceptionally well with Women's History Month, the timing is not without its challenges.

Women's Equality Day also provides a great opportunity for this type of programming, as do the birthdates of well-known suffragists. Black History Month can provide a great opportunity to highlight suffragists of color and explore the intersections of the abolition and early civil rights movements with the suffrage movement, including both the tensions and collaborations between the movements. And, while these specific dates and time periods create great opportunities to incorporate women's history-focused programming into the calendar, the reality is that this type of programming can take place on any date, at any time. Part of the idea behind women's and gender studies is the notion of integrating women's history into the general curriculum. This same concept applies to programming. These programs might "fit" with these days or time periods, and marketing them as Women's History Month programs or Women's Equality Day programs could have promotional benefits, but they are also part of general U.S. history, and can be learned about at any time. So any one who is deciding to hold this type of programming needs to consider the individual setting and context, and schedule the program for whenever makes the most sense given that context.

Conclusion

Overall the "Women's History Comes Alive: The U.S. Women's Suffrage Movement" event was a successful program for the library district, and with more enhanced and targeted marketing could be an even greater success. Applying performative and oral interpretation techniques to educational and historical programming provides libraries with more tools to present information in enticing and engaging ways, allowing for more varied ways of making programming more appealing to broader populations. Media-based programming such as our upcoming showing of *Iron Jawed Angels* can provide the same opportunities. By engaging community groups and local educational institutions in the programming, public libraries can also create broad-based collaborative efforts that not only produce great programs, but also build positive ongoing relationships.

REFERENCES

Beavercreek City School District. "*Iron Jawed Angels*: Lead, Follow, or Get Out of the Way." Accessed April 30, 2016.
Campbell, Karly Kohrs. 1989. *Man Cannot Speak for Her: Key Texts of the Early Feminists,* vol II. Santa Barbara: Praeger.
Cooney, Robert P. J. "Remembering Inez: The Last Campaign of Inez Milholland, Suffrage Martyr." Accessed March 30, 2016.
Iron Jawed Angels. 2004. Directed by Katja von Garnier. New York: HBO Films. DVD.
Stevens, Doris. 1995. *Jailed for Freedom,* edited by Carol O'Hare. Troutdale, OR: New Sage.
Teach with Movies. "*Iron Jawed Angels*." Teachwithmovies.org. Accessed April 30, 2016.
Teaching with Primary Sources—Middle Tennessee State University. "Civil Disobedience and the National Woman's Party." Accessed April 30, 2016.
The Suffragette. 2015. Directed by Sarah Gavron. Los Angeles: Focus Features. DVD.
Time Learning Ventures. "Teacher's Guide to Accompany HBO Films' *Iron Jawed Angels*." Time.com. Accessed April 30, 2016.

Finding Women's History in Archives and Special Collections
Basic to Advanced Ideas for Outreach and Instruction

Michael Taylor *and* Tara Zachary Laver

It is hard to think of a historical event in which women did not play at least a supporting role. Though historical records may not always reflect this in as much depth and detail as we would like, open any box or pull any book off the shelf in an archive or special collections library and you are bound to find something that relates to women's history in some way, even if it has to be teased out with a little creative thinking. That said, relatively few repositories regard themselves as women's history archives.

For librarians involved in outreach and instruction, this situation presents both a challenge and an opportunity. Even where women's history has not been a primary—or, we would say, conscious—focus of collecting, there are often rich veins of material waiting to be mined if you know where to look. This essay will summarize efforts at the Louisiana State University Libraries to raise awareness of "hidden" women's history materials and incorporate them into a growing primary-source-based instruction program in a way that not only addresses and enriches course content, but also introduces students to the challenges inherent in researching women's history. Progressing from basic to advanced, this approach is suitable for virtually any repository, large or small.

Getting Started

In December 2013, the LSU Libraries' Special Collections launched a program designed to engage the public with the university's collections of rare books and manuscripts. Titled Afternoon in the Archives, this monthly series combines the features of an exhibition with those of a class or reading room environment. Each two- to three-hour event is organized around a theme. Instead of displaying materials in an exhibit case, they are placed on tables, allowing visitors to explore each item in depth. Library staff are on hand to monitor use of materials and talk with visitors about their interests. Intended as an auxiliary to exhibits rather than a substitute, one goal of the series has been to provide an option for maximizing staff effort when a large group of materials of interest to the general public has already been identified and retrieved for another event, such as a class visit. Moreover, since item labels do not need to be written or exhibition supports made, the events are easy to schedule on the fly.

That's what the library did in 2014 when a visit by students in a course on the history of sexuality coincided with Women's History Month. Additional materials were added to the list of what had been shown to the class. The selections were then set out for the public to view in an Afternoon in the Archives. Though the LSU Libraries' Special Collections does collect women's history, the full scope of our collections in this area may not be immediately apparent, as much of the material is located in manuscript collections named after men or organizations.

Scratch beneath the surface, however, and women inevitably appear: wives, mothers, and daughters; female servants, slaves, and business partners; students, constituents, and congregants—the list goes on. The same is true of published materials. For example, a nineteenth-century city directory, a copy of "Punch" magazine, a medieval music manuscript facsimile or Renaissance herbal, and old university handbooks may not appear on the surface to have much to do with women's history. But in fact they are excellent sources. Scheduling an event like the LSU Libraries' Afternoon in the Archives can be a way of encouraging users to see your repository and its holdings in a new light and think carefully about the question of categorization.

Inability to see research materials at more than face value is a problem instruction librarians, especially those with experience in teaching primary source literacy, will be familiar with. Novice researchers, for instance, might assume that only musicians would be interested in a piece of popular sheet music from the early twentieth century. In reality, its illustrated cover, lyrics, or place of performance, if it can be identified, might be used by researchers in any number of disciplines, including women's history. Blindness to the multipurpose nature of primary sources often leads to frustration with searching the library catalog, whether in regard to entering an initial search term or deciding what to select from the list of results.

Partly as a fun, visible way of helping users see the advantages of thinking broadly and creatively when searching for primary sources, the LSU Libraries' Special Collections has employed social media. Two series of Facebook posts—"Finding Women's History" and "Why Rare Books Matter"—were introduced in 2015. The first series features materials that do not have an immediately obvious connection to women's history but show how primary sources can almost always be used to tell multiple stories. A good example from the series is a nineteenth-century block map. Twenty small wooden cubes each contain a portion of a map of the world, which a child would have studied and pieced together like a puzzle. Though it has to be deduced, maps like these were used by mothers, governesses, and schoolteachers tasked with instructing students in basic geography. Other materials to consider including in a social media series like this are works by women printers, publishers, and translators; eighteenth- and nineteenth-century illustrated natural history books, which were often hand-colored by women; cookbooks, children's books, housekeeping manuals, or any other book intended for women's use; and books containing evidence of having been owned and read by women. You may want to tailor your selections to an area of special interest at your institution or something region-specific (one post in LSU's series, for example, was on women newspaper publishers in Louisiana). Anything will work as long as it shows how women's history is ever-present but can sometimes only be found by giving extra thought to the search process and not relying solely on the library catalog.

LSU's second social media initiative, "Why Rare Books Matter," is more general but provides an additional outlet for highlighting women's history. This Facebook series explores how a book's design or "packaging," evidence of previous readers, and other copy-specific information can expand our understanding of textual content. (As Harvard professor Leah Price neatly summarizes this concept, "Words are only one of the channels through which a book conveys information") (Price 2015). One book from the series that relates to "hidden" women's history is a copy of *Camilla: A Picture of Youth*, by the eighteenth-century English novelist Fanny Burney. Examining the subscriber list found in the first edition of *Camilla*, published in London in 1796, would give the impression that Burney's readership was limited to upper-class English men and women. However, a copy of the 1797 New York edition now at LSU adds to the story. According to inscriptions and bookplates, it was originally owned by a woman in frontier Ohio, who, around 1810, married and moved to Baton Rouge, at that time a remote village in the Spanish colony of Florida. She took the five-volume book with her. Interpreted as a unique historical artifact rather than merely another copy of an easily obtainable text (either physically, electronically, or in a modern edition), this book reveals that Fanny Burney, one of the first women to make a career out writing, was being read not just by the English elite, but also by women on the edge of the American wilderness. From it, we gain a deeper understanding of Burney's popularity and accomplishment, as well as the ability of people far from the centers of literary production to acquire good things to read. Keep an eye out for books in your own collection that have a one-of-a-kind story to tell. Apart from their interest to scholars, you can use them as teaching aids for advanced primary source literacy classes. They are also great talking points for conversations about why brick-and-mortar rare book collections are worth supporting at a time when all eyes are focused on digital resources.

Women's History and Primary Source Literacy: Basic Ideas for Instruction

The more mileage you can get out of a social media initiative, the better. An obvious downside to things like Facebook posts is their ephemerality. Though good for creating a "buzz," they are here one minute and gone the next. Thus, you might want your social media plan to include ways to convert the information you have taken the time to pull together into something more permanent and weighty. At LSU, we have done this by folding material originally featured in our "Finding Women's History" and "Why Rare Books Matter" Facebook series into various class-based activities.

One of these activities is "Primary Source Match Game."

Its goal is to help students get better at finding primary sources relevant to their research. As mentioned above, many students have trouble seeing how a source can be used other than in the most obvious way. This adds to the difficulty they already have in searching the library catalog. The "Match Game" activity helps students visualize why they need to put extra effort into planning a search strategy. It also shows the advantages of being more resourceful and flexible, for after completing the activity, they will have seen why it sometimes pays to use what's at hand and adapt your research topic accordingly rather than struggling to find the perfect source.

You can easily customize this activity to whatever kinds of women's history materials your library holds. Start by locating examples of all the major kinds of primary sources. Be sure to include at least one book, letter, diary, serial publication, newspaper, photograph, map, music score, and piece of ephemera. Look for things that do not have an immediately obvious connection to women's studies and could be used to research many different topics. For example, you might select a travel narrative that describes women in a particular city, but, in another section, discusses African Americans. For a serial publication, pick something like an early nineteenth-century medical journal with articles on both women's health and "scientific" racism. Sanborn fire insurance maps are great choices. You could find one that shows businesses owned by women and also segregated city spaces.

After identifying a group of items, spread them out on a large table. Have your students spend a few minutes forming initial impressions of what they think the materials are and how they could be used. Then ask the students to identify which primary sources seem best suited to studying women's history. Repeat this step with one or more additional topics, such as black history or whatever you chose to demonstrate the materials' multipurpose nature. Remember to select topics that could be researched using any and all of the items on the table, keeping in mind that the goal of the activity is to show students that primary sources rarely tell just one story. As a follow-up, have your students locate the catalog records or finding aids for a few of the sources you identified. Quiz them about whether the topics they matched with a source are mentioned in the record or finding aid for that source. Then open the floor to discussion about the challenges of research and how historians locate primary source material.

Taking It Further: Intermediate Primary-Source-Based Instruction

The following is an example of a two-tiered, intermediate-level activity based on women's history materials that you could adapt to primary sources available in your library. It requires students to interrogate sources and complete a series of written assignments based on them.

In an LSU course on the history of sexuality in the United States, students read Alecia Long's The Great Southern Babylon: Sex, Race, and Respectability in New Orleans, 1865–1920. Various materials cited in Long's book, as well as others related to the course topic, were set up for the class to view, with a document analysis worksheet placed beside each source.

Students rotated from station to station, spending about fifteen minutes discussing the worksheet questions. This assignment was especially effective for showing students how the secondary source they read as a homework assignment had been constructed using primary sources.

The students then returned individually to the library to analyze a different document set of a more general nature, placed on reserve. They completed a short writing assignment in which they addressed prompts such as:

- Identify the type of document, its author, date, purpose, and audience.
- Describe physical features that stand out.
- Summarize the contents and what you learned from reading the source; provide three direct quotes.

- List two things you learned about life in the United States at the time the source was written.
- Write a question to the author that the document leaves unanswered.
- Describe your experience reading the source and any emotional response it elicited.
- Describe any challenges you faced (difficulty reading the handwriting, style of language used, physical condition, etc.).

These activities were later repeated in a course on U.S. women's history. Prior to that visit, students briefly researched the women or organizations represented in the documents they viewed during the in-class exercise. The students also used the visit to identify two sources they would later write a short essay about, addressing the following points and questions:

- Explain what the source is, when it was written, who wrote it, and why.
- Include some brief, contextual information about the organization or individual.
- What can you learn based on the source? What does it reveal about life in the United States at the time it was written?
- What does the source not tell you? What are you left wanting to know more about?
- List a few things that stand out to you as surprising or noteworthy.
- If you could ask the source author one question, what would it be?

"Senator for a Day": An Advanced Instruction Activity

A third primary-source-based assignment that the LSU Libraries have developed using women's history materials is suitable for upper-level undergraduates or graduate students. As we have reiterated throughout this essay, women's history is lying in wait nearly everywhere we look, whether or not it is something your repository makes a conscious effort to collect. An especially good place to look for it is in political papers. Politicians, at least in theory, represent all of their constituents regardless of gender. If you can find materials in your collection that relate to a political leader who was in office at an important moment in women's history, chances are good you will be able to use those materials for instructional activities centered on women's history.

The suffrage movement of the early twentieth century generated a prolonged debate and abundant documentary material, and thus lends itself well to primary source literacy instruction. Consider looking for the papers of a senator or representative from your state, or any political leader who might have had to weigh in on the women's suffrage debate. At LSU, for example, we located an extensive group of materials in the papers of Louisiana senator Edward J. Gay, who served from 1918 to 1921 and had to decide whether to vote for or against the proposed 19th Amendment. Gay's constituents as well as people outside of Louisiana sent him hundreds of letters, petitions, flyers, and essays, trying to sway his opinion on the suffrage vote. Today, these documents allow us to catch a glimpse of the complexity and intensity of the suffrage debates of the 1910s.

In an assignment titled "Senator for a Day," students review three dozen documents from the Edward J. Gay Congressional File. The documents represent the full range of viewpoints that Gay had to consider. Students are asked to read at least ten of the documents and then synthesize them in a short essay or class presentation, answering questions such as:

- What reasons did people give for granting or denying women the right to vote?
- What were the simplistic views for or against giving women the vote? What were the more complex ones?
- How do ideas about woman's proper place or proper role inform either or both sides of the debate? How does nativism and/or racism do the same?
- What issues mattered the most to men, women, Southerners, etc.?
- How did party politics and the First World War come into play?
- What parallels (if any) exist between this situation and politics today?

Regardless of the precise materials you choose if you decide to adapt this activity, it will achieve several learning objectives outlined in the American Library Association's "Information Literacy Guidelines for Undergraduate History Students." These include the need for students to be able to synthesize information from a wide range of sources, formats, and viewpoints; contextualize primary sources; acknowledge evidence that runs counter to an argument; and determine authors' intent (American Library Association 2013). From a more holistic standpoint, such activities contribute to fulfilling an even larger goal: not only do they improve students' analytical, research, and writing abilities, but also their verbal communication, collaboration, and time-management skills. We suggest crafting activities—whether basic, intermediate, or advanced—in a way that gives students an opportunity to develop and showcase the kinds of skills that will be useful in their future studies, employment, and lives.

"Curate a Case"

Like the outreach and instruction activities described above, this advanced exercise is one that works well even if your collections are not particularly rich in women's history sources. Using either your physical holdings or digitized content from elsewhere, students pretend to be a curator, identifying and interpreting materials for one display case in an exhibit on women's history. The exhibition can be real or fictional—in other words, it does not actually have to be set up for public viewing for this activity to work. The topic can be one of the student's own choosing or selected by the instructor and/or librarian. After settling on an exhibit topic, ask your students to use the catalog and other discovery tools to identify relevant materials from the library's collections. Next, have them select a number of items, write a brief introduction, and create captions for each document that tie it back to the larger topic. In so doing, students will develop their research skills, learn how to navigate archival collections, and gain experience telling stories and supporting arguments based on primary sources. In addition, this activity will help students understand how the telling of history is shaped by available sources and choices made by the person doing the telling.

Participants could present their findings in an in-house or online exhibit. The latter work especially well for several reasons. Through the use of digital images, multiple pages from the same book or manuscript can be displayed, as opposed to only one page in a physical exhibit. Online projects also have a much wider audience and stick around indefinitely, making them something the students will be able to point to when applying to graduate school, jobs, or other future endeavors.

"Multiple Hats"

In 2013, four Harvard University Teaching Fellows created a short video titled "This Is Not a Chair" for the online course "Tangible Things," taught by historian Laurel Thatcher Ulrich (Ulrich 2015). The video discusses several historical American chairs, observing that they are not simply pieces of furniture, but portals to different historical time periods and topics. What story they tell depends on how we look at them. In other words, re-imagining objects in relation to various contexts or areas of inquiry can raise new questions and insights.

This video inspired a second "you-be-the-curator" activity at the LSU Libraries that is easily adaptable to women's history materials. In "Multiple Hats," students are prompted to treat books and archival documents like artifacts in a museum, thinking once again about the question of categorization, somewhat like they did in the "Primary Source Match Game" described above. Students are given a primary source from the library's collection and asked to pretend they are a museum curator. How would they write an interpretive label for the source if they were planning to include it in an exhibition in a museum of natural science? A costume museum? A museum of women's history? For example, an illustration of an egret from John James Audubon's Birds of America, if displayed in a natural history museum, would likely be discussed in the context of a particular ecosystem or family of birds. If displayed in a costume museum, however, it would probably be used to tell the story of how egrets were hunted to the verge of extinction in the late nineteenth century to provide feathers for ladies' hats. A museum of women's history, alternatively, might use the picture to talk about Boston socialite Harriet Hemenway, who was so outraged by the killing of birds in the name of fashion that she organized a boycott of the feather trade, helping to lay the foundation of the modern wildlife conservation and environmental protest movements. Though rare books and archival materials must remain in the library, we can move them from one "museum" to another with our imaginations and think about how they might tell a different story if viewed in a different context.

Conclusion: Women's History Is Everywhere

If you are an archivist or special collections librarian and think you do not have the depth of resources to support programming related to women's history, we hope this essay will inspire you to think again. Though full of women's history, our library at LSU is among those that have never intensively marketed themselves as women's history archives. In trying to build bridges to students and professors working in women's and gender studies, we have discovered that the lack of multiple, spot-on collections related to their precise topics of research is not necessarily a hindrance and that even a small cluster of materials of a general nature can be effective for the purposes of outreach and instruction in this subject area. Helping users see that women's history is often "hiding in plain sight" in readily available sources like university archives materials—student handbooks, photographs, institutional records, and so on—will hopefully lead users to a better understanding of the research process. So, too, can activities and projects that draw attention to the fact that women's history sometimes has to be sought out in an alternative way; for example, viewing sources through the lens of material culture, rather than traditional textual reading and analysis, can often yield interesting results. Our approach is one that most archival repositories, large or small, could replicate. It can also be adapted to other research areas, for in a sense, women's history is not alone: subjects like environmental history and the history of food can be equally elusive to catalog searchers, even though these subjects are almost always as much as a part of the archive as they are a part of everyday life.

For the past two decades, special collections librarians and archivists have been increasingly aligning themselves with their parent institutions' teaching and learning objectives. More than ever, we are now thinking like educators rather than service providers and gatekeepers. By supporting outreach and instruction activities based on primary sources from our collections, we are making our role as educators better known, advancing larger, institutional goals, and hopefully spreading the magic of archives and special collections in the process.

REFERENCES

American Library Association. 2013. "Information Literacy Guidelines and Competencies for Undergraduate History Students." https://urldefense.proofpoint.com/v2/url?u=http-3A__www.ala.org_rusa_resources_guidelines_infoliteracy&d=DQIFaQ&c=euGZstcaTDllvimEN8b7jXrwqOf-v5A_CdpgnVfiiMM&r=FuC2bgPKWy3lyLSFzYGLuQ&m=PWCP_LR5MxyIAsDDNXUJ31DJL0rUL_yPddiVX_J4tDA&s=3hfvcejxyyQZiT83Oq13Nh0T7oe24pvQ_gM1CwLEwH4&e=.

Price, Leah. 2015. "Book Sleuthing: What 19th-Century Books Can Tell Us About the Rise of the Reading Public." https://urldefense.proofpoint.com/v2/url?u=https-3A__www.edx.org_course_book-2Dbook-2Dsleuthing-2Dwhat-2D19th-2Dcentury-2Dharvardx-2Dhum1-2D5x-23-21&d=DQIFaQ&c=euGZstcaTDllvimEN8b7jXrwqOf-v5A_CdpgnVfiiMM&r=FuC2bgPKWy3lyLSFzYGLuQ&m=PWCP_LR5MxyIAsDDNXUJ31DJL0rUL_yPddiVX_J4tDA&s=2-4S2XxdCq9eabx_DoyTScgRsjHCIoG0G_AUhDHPdiw&e=.

Ulrich, Laurel Thatcher. 2015. "Tangible Things: Discovering History Through Artworks, Artifacts, Scientific Specimens, and the Stuff Around You." https://urldefense.proofpoint.com/v2/url?u=https-3A__www.edx.org_course_tangible-2Dthings-2Ddiscovering-2Dhistory-2Dharvardx-2Dusw30x-2D0&d=DQIFaQ&c=euGZstcaTDllvimEN8b7jXrwqOf-v5A_CdpgnVfiiMM&r=FuC2bgPKWy3lyLSFzYG-LuQ&m=PWCP_LR5MxyIAsDDNXUJ31DJL0rUL_yPddiVX_J4tDA&s=V1XZfy6aFcKRYVZi6cu9TEjoDfUn3J9BxiFN-ZhRCRU&e=.

The Herstory of the Book
Resources for the Study of Women in Book History

MAGGIE GALLUP KOPP

At this time of dramatic technological shifts in the creation and dissemination of the written word, numerous students and scholars are eager "to study all aspects of the creation of books, whether as physical artifacts, examples of fine art, products of unique production methods, or unique cultural symbols" (Finkelstein and McCleery 2013, 8–9). In spite of (or perhaps because of) frequent debates over the obsolescence of the print in a world of e-readers and online publishing, the history of books—their technological, cultural, and commercial contexts—provides a rich vein of inquiry for students at all educational levels.

In the United States book history blossomed as a field of study in the late 1970s and early 1980s and is well-established at many academic institutions. Book history is interdisciplinary, encompassing fields such as literary studies, art history, journalism, and social history; as such students from across campus may be interested in studying some aspect of the book. Part of the appeal stems from the dual nature of books. On one hand, books are *physical objects* which provide examples of material culture and historical people, places, and moments. By engaging with a first edition of Jane Austen's *Pride and Prejudice* or a medieval Book of Hours owned by a European noblewoman, students can form tangible links to the books' creators and owners as well as to the culture in which the physical books were produced. In this sense, the book can be piece of art, a technology, or even a commercial product which can be studied for its artefactual value. On the other hand, books are also *texts* which illustrate the origin and spread of ideas over time. For example, a student of Emily Dickinson's poetry may compare facsimiles of her manuscripts, the first printed editions of her poetry, and modern editions to look at changes in how Dickinson's poems have been presented to readers since they were first made public. In this role, the book is a cultural symbol or a vehicle for a writer's ideas. Both the symbolic and artefactual aspects of books make them appealing subjects of study.

Book history, like many other related fields, may be approached through the lens of interdisciplinary women's studies. Women have long engaged with the written word both as creators and as consumers of books. Book history encompasses women's roles as artisans and tradespeople involved in the creation and dissemination of physical copies of books; for example, as scribes, bookbinders, typesetters, printers, illustrators, or as booksellers. The history of the book also sheds light on women's intellectual creation and

71

engagement with texts, as authors and readers of books. Thus book history can be used in the women's studies classroom as a lens for students to explore topics such as women's employment by looking at examples of women printers and bookbinders, or women's education and literacy by looking at texts created for and by women readers.

Using Primary Sources: The Physical and the Digital

Book history is heavily reliant on primary source material—physical books, both as subjects and objects of inquiry. Students of book history need examples of books from all periods to get a good sense of the physical features of books as well as the circumstances of their construction, dissemination, and reception. Binding structure, paper, and typefaces may provide clues about a book's creation as well as its subsequent custodial history, or provenance. Edition statements and publication information may illustrate a given text's popularity with the reading public; annotations and other ownership marks offer evidence of individual readers interacting with physical books and the texts within.

Unfortunately not every student will have access to these kinds of primary source materials, which are often housed in special collections libraries, and not every library will have ready access to materials created or owned by women. A women's studies professor in Pennsylvania examining depictions of women readers in medieval miniature paintings will not be able to fly to her class Paris one afternoon to view a unique manuscript book. A student writing a paper on American Colonial women's history may be hard pressed to find a nearby library that holds original examples of the output of colonial newspaper publishers like Ann Franklin (sister-in-law to Benjamin) or Anne Catherine Green, printer of an influential anti–British newspaper. Recognizing these limitations special collections libraries worldwide have recognized the need to digitize primary sources to assist researchers, and in response, are creating "extraordinary collections of visual and textual surrogates" (Conway 2015, 52). Special collections libraries and archives consider digital images of primary sources to be surrogates which facilitate access to their materials outside the reading room and minimize handling of unique, fragile objects.

While digitized primary sources do not provide the sorts of hands-on learning experiences one would expect by viewing the object *in situ*, digital surrogates can still be beneficial as learning objects both inside and outside the classroom. Viewing a fully digitized book can be superior to looking at a decontextualized illustration or reading a text in a printed anthology because the digital images approximate views of the book in its original state and provide visual cues to the material and cultural contexts of the book's production. The student of colonial women's history viewing a digitized newspaper from the period gets a much better idea of the context in which information was presented than she would by reading an article from Green's paper in a textbook. High-resolution digital images can also facilitate the study of details like illustrations, manuscript annotations, and bindings by allowing the user to zoom in and enlarge images. The women's studies class can in Pennsylvania can study that far-away medieval manuscript as an art object, analyzing minute details in the margin of a single page as a group. For women's studies students who wish to use books as primary sources, but do not have access to the right materials for their research (or the means to travel to repositories of that material), digital surrogates are invaluable. Fortunately there are numerous primary sources available online, either freely available or through subscription databases, which highlight women's involvement in the history of the book.

What follows is a list of online repositories of fully digitized book and manuscript material which exemplify women's involvement in the creation, dissemination, and consumption of books from the medieval period through the 20th century in the West. The resources selected are in English to facilitate research by students at all levels. Additionally, general search strategies for discovering examples of additional material, both in digital repositories and in local library catalogs, are provided.

Women in the Book Trades

Medieval Manuscripts

Thousands of medieval manuscripts have been digitized in their entirety by institutions in the United States and Europe, allowing students to view unique books made during the Middle Ages. However, surviving examples of book production by women scribes and binders are relatively rare, as they were the product of a few elite female religious communities across Europe. Because so many medieval libraries have been dispersed, it is difficult for scholars to quantify nuns' book production. A very few examples of manuscripts from British women's religious houses have been digitized; in addition, a small number of libraries have scanned images from manuscripts owned and produced by women's religious houses elsewhere in Europe. Some of the most famous medieval manuscripts produced by women have not been fully digitized, though they have been published in facsimile (for example, the Guta-Sintram Codex or the Gradual of Gisela von Kerssenbrock). Researchers at both online and physical repositories may find similar items by searching with keywords like "woman," "convent," "sister," "nun," "nunnery," and other terms denoting female roles.

DIGITAL RESOURCES
The Bodleian Library's Digital Collections contain several manuscripts owned by two elite nunneries in England, Barking Abbey and Syon Abbey (http://bodley30.bodley.ox.ac.uk:8180/luna/servlet), including texts in English.
The Beinecke Rare Book & Manuscript Library's Digital Collections site (http://brbl-dl.library.yale.edu) has also digitized several books used by medieval female religious communities in Europe, including two liturgical books with music (Beinecke MS 205 and MS 902).

The Hand Press Period (Late 15th through 18th Century Europe and the American Colonies)

After the new technology of printing spread from Gutenberg's workshop in Mainz, Germany to the rest of Europe, the historical record provides evidence of women's involvement in the print trade. Since printing, publishing, and bookselling were often family businesses in the hand-press period, it is not uncommon to find record of women printing and disseminating books on behalf of other family members (particularly as widows holding a business in trust for a son) or as proprietors in their own right. Searching library catalogues for the keyword "vidua" or its abbreviation "vid." (Latin for "widow") often turns up examples of books printed or published by women maintaining businesses after the death of their husbands, as the word shows up on imprint statements of books from this period. Variants of the word "widow" (e.g. "widdowe") may turn up examples of books from English women printers and booksellers.

Women can also be traced in the records of book trade guilds like the Stationer's Company of London. While women were not officially admitted to the Company until the 1660s, they appear in the Company records as business owners or as trustees for family members, as stockholders, and as beneficiaries of the Company's charity for impoverished tradespeople. The full records of the Stationer's Company are available on microfilm (published by Chadwyck-Healy 1986) at some major research libraries; the company also published a transcript of its registers in the late 19th century. Additionally, women in the book trade can also be traced in free, online databases which index personal names of known printers, publishers, and distributors from the 15th through early 19th centuries.

DIGITAL RESOURCES

Images of early British hand-press items can be discovered through Early English Books Online (EEBO, http://eebo.chadwyck.com/home), a subscription database available through ProQuest. It covers books printed in England from the 15th through 17th centuries.

The largest online collection of digitized books from the 18th century is Eighteenth Century Collections Online (ECCO, http://gdc.gale.com/products/eighteenth-century-collections-online/), a subscription database from Gale which provides access to print titles produced in the United Kingdom and America. Gale also offers the 17th and 18th Century Burney Collection database, which includes examples of British women newspaper publishers.

A Transcript of the Registers of the Company of Stationers of London, 1554–1640, edited by Edward Arber (London, 1875–77) has been digitized and is available online at two different sites: Vol. 1 at Internet Archive (https://archive.org/details/transcriptofregi01statuoft) and Vol. 2–5 via Hathi Trust (http://catalog.hathitrust.org/Record/001168984).

Book trade indices include The British Book Trade Index (http://www.bbti.bham.ac.uk/); The Scottish Book Trade Index (http://www.nls.uk/catalogues/scottish-book-trade-index); and the London Book Trades Database (http://sas-space.sas.ac.uk/290/).

The 19th Century

By the middle of the 19th century, the print trades had become highly professionalized. As a result, women were likely to be employed in lower-skilled aspects of the trade like selling printed material, coloring prints, or sewing sheets during the binding process. In England, the Society for the Promotion of the Employment of Women, a charity founded in 1859 to open up new opportunities for skilled work for women, established a printing press to train and employ women as typesetters. Under the direction of Emily Faithfull, The Victoria Press published numerous works including feminist periodical *The English Woman's Journal* and *The Victoria Magazine.*

The Arts and Crafts movement in late 19th century Great Britain inspired a number of middle and upper-class women to learn the trade of fine bookbinding from top craftsmen in the trade. Women binders were usually trained privately, as was Sarah Prideaux, one of the most famous English binders of the period, and her American counterpart, designer Sarah Wyman Whitman. The Guild of Women Binders was organized in London in 1898 as a business venture for women fine binders from various arts and crafts organizations in the UK. A history of the Guild, entitled *The Bindings of To-Morrow: A Record of the Work of the Guild of Women-Binders and of the Hampstead Bindery,* was published in 1902, but no copy is currently available in digital repositories.

DIGITAL RESOURCES

A complete run of *The English Woman's Journal* can be found at the Nineteenth-Century Serials Edition site, http://www.ncse.ac.uk. Examples of other work from The Victoria Press can be found online at Google Books, Internet Archive, and Hathi Trust.

Digital images of work by Sarah Prideaux, The Guild of Women Binders, and others can be found at the British Library's Database of Bookbindings (http://www.bl.uk/catalogues/bookbindings/Default.aspx) and The American Bookbinders Museum (http://www.bookbindersmuseum.org/the-bindings-of-to-morrow/).

The Boston Public Library has created a digital photo album of Sarah Wyman Whitman bindings at https://www.flickr.com/photos/boston_public_library/sets/72157604192955355/.

The 20th Century to the Present

Continuing the Arts and Crafts tradition, women have been involved in fine printing and bookbinding since the turn of the last century. Irish author William Butler Yeats' sisters founded their own fine press (Dun Emer Press, renamed Cuala Press) in the early 20th century, as did author Virginia Woolf and her husband Leonard (The Hogarth Press, today an imprint of Random House). As the 20th century progressed, many artists have used the form and function of the book as a medium, a genre known as artist's books. Artists' books and the work of modern women fine printers are generally under copyright, but a few examples have been recreated digitally with the cooperation of the artists.

DIGITAL RESOURCES

Digital Exhibits of Dun Emer/Cuala Press items can be found at the libraries of Boston University (http://www.bc.edu/libraries/about/exhibits/burns/cuala.html) and Villanova University (https://exhibits.library.villanova.edu/jack-butler-yeats/cuala-press/). A digital exhibit of Virginia Woolf's work at the Hogarth Press is available from Columbia University Libraries (https://exhibitions.cul.columbia.edu/exhibits/show/lit_hum/woolf). None present the books in full.

Book artist Johanna Drucker has posted her 2012 artists' book *Stochastic Poetics* as a PDF file, along with a gallery of her other work, at her website, http://www.johannadrucker.com/.

The Beinecke Rare Book Library has worked with book artists Suzanne Heyd (http://beinecke.library.yale.edu/collections/highlights/crawl-space) and Erica van Horn (http://beinecke.library.yale.edu/collections/highlights/erica-van-horn) to provide digital images of a their work.

Women as Authors

Women have been involved in the creation of texts since the Middle Ages, and as women's literacy increased over the centuries, so too did their output in both manuscript and print. Individual women authors are easily searched in digital repositories like Google Books, and there are many electronic text-only versions of women's writing (such as Cambridge University Press' Orlando, http://orlando.cambridge.org/ or the Indiana Women's Writing Project, http://webapp1.dlib.indiana.edu/vwwp/). It is often more difficult for the researcher to locate specific examples of original manuscripts by women authors or to find collections of digitized books comprised solely of women's writings, but scholarly projects are appearing online which make available original manuscripts of well-known women authors.

DIGITAL RESOURCES

Academic publishers offer a number of curated digital collections of women's manuscripts for purchase or subscription. Examples include Adam Matthew Digital's Defining Gender 1450–1910, Perdita Manuscripts 1500–1700, and Women in the National Archives, Kew (which focuses on women's suffrage in Britain); Alexander Street Press's products British and Irish Women's Letters and Diaries, North American Women's Letters and Diaries, North American Women's Drama, and LGBT Thought and Culture; Gale's British Literary Manuscripts Online; and ProQuest's Gerritsen Collection-Women's History Online and Queen Victoria's Journals.

The British Library has digitized copies of famous medieval English texts created by and for women, such as *The Book of Margery Kempe* (BL Add MS 61823, online at http://www.bl.uk/manuscripts/FullDisplay. aspx?ref=Add_MS_61823), the oft-studied autobiography of a middle-class English woman mystic of the early 15th century.

The British Library has also created an interactive version of 13-year-old Jane Austen's *History of England*, at their *Turning the Pages* website (http://www.bl.uk/turningthepages).

The manuscript of Anne Bradstreet's *Meditations Divine and Morall* is available at Harvard (http://pds.lib. harvard.edu/pds/view/20085634).

Manuscripts by Phillis Wheatley are available at the Massachusetts Historical Society (http://www.masshist. org/endofslavery/index.php?id=57).

The University of Colorado–Boulder's *Women Poets of the Romantic Period* (http://cudl.colorado.edu/luna/ servlet/UCBOULDERCB1~65~65) presents a number of fully digitized printed works from authors Anna Letitia Barbauld and Felicia Hemans as well as many lesser-known poets.

The Shelley-Godwin Archive (http://shelleygodwinarchive.org/), a multi-library project which is still under construction, has digitized Mary Shelley's *Frankenstein* manuscripts. The site will eventually include manuscript material from Shelley and her family members Mary Wollstonecraft, Percy Bysshe Shelley, and William Godwin.

The Emily Dickinson Archive reproduces the poet's manuscripts held at Harvard's Houghton Library (http:// www.edickinson.org/).

The Beinecke Library has digitized the manuscript of Hannah Rafts' *The Bondswoman's Narrative*, which is considered the first novel by an African-American woman (http://beinecke.library.yale.edu/collections/ highlights/hannah-crafts-bondwomans-narrative).

The Harry Ransom Center at the University of Texas has digitized a number of manuscripts by 19th and early 20th century British and American women authors (http://hrc.contentdm.oclc.org/#nav_top), including Christina Rossetti, the Brontë sisters, and Charlotte Perkins Gilman.

The Library of Congress has digitized the typescripts of unpublished plays by 20th century African-American novelist Zora Neale Hurston (https://www.loc.gov/collections/zora-neale-hurston-plays/about-this-collection/).

Besides the manuscripts of well-known published authors, many libraries worldwide have created digital collections of women's diaries, cookbooks, and other ephemeral manuscript books produced by women which were never published.

DIGITAL RESOURCES

The Recipe Books Collection at London's Wellcome Library (http://wellcomelibrary.org/collections/digital-collections/recipe-books/), which reproduces a handful of 17th century English manuscripts containing women's recipes for food and medicine.

Duke University Libraries' Women's Travel Diaries Collection (http://library.duke.edu/digitalcollections/ womenstraveldiaries/about/), which contains a number of travel diaries written by British and American Women of the 19th and 20th centuries.

Women as Book Owners and Readers

Women's interaction with books as collectors and owners can be difficult to trace through digital repositories. The medieval period is perhaps best covered through digital resources, since there are many digitized copies of medieval manuscripts commissioned by and for women (especially noblewomen) available today. Books from this period are popular with students and scholars from many disciplines, especially literature and art history, and studying text and illustration together can lead to insights about the women for whom these books were made. For women of later periods, scrapbooks and commonplace books which contain hand-copied extracts of texts can suggest readers' reading habits and interests.

Evidence of women's interaction with books as readers and collectors from the hand-press period to the present can also be found by investigating individual books' provenance: studying readers' annotations and ownership marks such as signatures and bookplates. Unfortunately for the researcher this information is not always noted in library catalogs or digital repositories and it can be difficult to find interesting examples for primary source research. Secondary sources on women book collectors and authors may point to individual titles known to have been owned by famous women throughout history. Individual libraries may also contain collections of books brought together by individual women collectors, or primary source documents such as reading lists put together by individuals or women's reading groups.

DIGITAL RESOURCES

The University of Aberdeen's *St Albans Psalter* website (https://www.abdn.ac.uk/stalbanspsalter/english/index.shtml) provides visitors with a wealth of information about the 12th century manuscript presented to Christina of Markyate, an Anglo-Saxon visionary. Both text and images were chosen to reflect her life and her religious practice.

The National Library of Scotland has digitized The Murthly Hours, (http://digital.nls.uk/murthlyhours/), a 13th century prayerbook made for a woman, with later texts added in French and Gaelic.

Once again, the British Library's *Digitised Manuscripts* offers a number of famous medieval and Renaissance examples of women's book ownership and reading practices, including *Ancrene Riwle* or *Ancrene Wisse* (BL Cotton MS Cleopatra C VI, online at http://www.bl.uk/manuscripts/FullDisplay.aspx?ref=Cotton_MS_Cleopatra_C_VI). The text is an early 13th century manual written for the use of female hermits, or anchoresses. The BL has also digitized a number of their well-known illuminated Books of Hours and other liturgical books made for female owners. Examples include books owned by anonymous women, such as the De Brailes Hours (BL Add MS 49999, online at http://www.bl.uk/manuscripts/FullDisplay.aspx?ref=Add_MS_49999), as well as books owned by royalty like Isabella of Castile (her Breviary, BL Add MS 18851, online at http://www.bl.uk/manuscripts/FullDisplay.aspx?ref=Add_MS_18851) and her daughter Joanna (her Book of Hours, BL Add MS 18852, online at http://www.bl.uk/manuscripts/FullDisplay.aspx?ref=Add_MS_18852). Another interesting example of female reading practices is Royal MS 7 D X, a collection of religious texts translated into three different languages by Queen Elizabeth I when she was just 12 years old (http://www.bl.uk/manuscripts/FullDisplay.aspx?ref=Royal_MS_7_D_X).

Reading: Harvard Views of Readers, Readership, and Reading History provides several examples of women's commonplace books from the 18th and 19th centuries (http://ocp.hul.harvard.edu/reading/commonplace.html) as well as the records of women's reading clubs from the 19th and 20th centuries (http://ocp.hul.harvard.edu/reading/bookclubs.html).

The Library of Congress has digitized seven scrapbooks assembled by Elizabeth Smith Miller and her daughter Anne Fitzhugh Miller in the course of their work for the National American Woman Suffrage Association (http://memory.loc.gov/ammem/collections/suffrage/millerscrapbooks/).

In the 19th and 20th centuries, magazines and newspapers marketed to female audiences provide evidence of women's reading practices as well as evidence of women as writers, editors, and publishers in the periodical press. Magazines and other journals from the 20th century are especially rich visually with advertisements, illustrations, and photographic content which provide evidence of material culture, fashion, and marketing to women over the centuries. Magazines and newsletters from feminist organizations are also popular objects of study, both for their intellectual content as well as their representations of the print culture of the various feminist movements.

DIGITAL RESOURCES

A number of publishers offer digital collections of women's magazines. Products include ProQuest's Women's Magazine Archive and Vogue Magazine Archive and Gale's 19th Century UK Periodicals: New Readerships: Women's, Children's, Humor and Leisure/Sport.

One of the first successful 19th century women's magazines, Sarah Josepha Hales' *Ladies' Magazine,* is online at Harvard University (http://ocp.hul.harvard.edu/dl/ww/002016758) along with a number of issues of other historic journal volumes related to women's history. Various volumes of other 19th century titles like *Godey's Lady's Book* and *The Englishwoman's Domestic Magazine* can be found in repositories like HathiTrust and The Internet Archive.

Early 20th century feminist journals *The Freewoman* and *The New Freewoman* are available at The Modernist Journals Project (http://www.modjourn.org/journals.html).

Digitized Second Wave Feminist periodical collections include The Chicago Women's Liberation Union

Newsletters (http://www.cwluherstory.org/CWLU-News/); *WomaNews*, a second wave feminist newspaper digitized by the University of Florida (http://ufdcweb1.uflib.ufl.edu/ufdc/?a=rwg&b=UF00076708); and Duke University's *Women's Liberation Movement Print Culture* collection (http://library.duke.edu/digitalcollections/wlmpc/).

Other Online Resources for Women and Book History

There are a number of online exhibits which feature partially digitized examples of women's involvement in the book trades from the medieval period through 20th century. While not providing complete surrogates to use for in-depth book history research, students may find them useful as introductions to key themes and participants in the history of women and the book.

Chez La Veuve: Women Printers in Great Britain 1475–1700 (http://www.library.illinois.edu/rbx/exhibitions/chez_exhibit/index.html), an online exhibit at the University of Illinois Library, introduces several English women printers with title page images of selected examples of their work.

Unseen Hands at Princeton University Library (http://libweb2.princeton.edu/rbsc2/ga/unseenhands/index.html) features American women colonial printers and booksellers as well as other female printers, illustrators, bookbinders, and designers from American and Europe in the 16th through 20th centuries.

Cornell University Library's *Women in the Literary Marketplace, 1800–1900* exhibit (http://rmc.library.cornell.edu/womenLit/intro.htm) uses digitized letters and images from books to discuss the cultural changes which allowed 19th century women to achieve professional careers as authors.

The Women's Library @ LSE (http://digital.library.lse.ac.uk/collections/thewomenslibrary) showcases a number of objects (both fully and partially digitized) from The Women's Library collections at the London School of Economics, with items from the 16th century through First, Second, and Third Wave Feminisms.

The Library of Congress has digitized print items from the National American Woman Suffrage Association Collection (http://memory.loc.gov/ammem/naw/nawshome.html), covering the period 1848–1921.

Girl Zines in the Sophia Smith Collection at Smith College (http://smithlibraries.org/digital/exhibits/show/girlzines) introduces this genre of third-wave feminist publication with images of zine covers.

REFERENCES

Conway, Paul. 2015. "Digital Transformations and the Archival Nature of Surrogates." *Archival Science* 15:51–69.

Finkelstein, David and Alistair McCleery. 2013. *An Introduction to Book History*, 2d ed. New York: Routledge.

Supporting Trans* Teens
in the Public Library

M'ISSA FLEMING

Introduction

Most Young Adult Librarians are concerned with creating as safe a space for teens in their libraries as possible. There are a variety of ways to make and maintain these spaces, and many kinds of literature available that discuss what safe means, who should specifically be made safe, and how best to do so. In this essay, I will discuss how best to support trans* and gender-questioning youth in the teen spaces of public libraries. I will use the term trans* to indicate all the variations of gender identity that exist outside of binary conceptions of male and female. This includes, but is not limited to, transsexual teens (teens that identify as the gender opposite to the one they were assigned at birth and intend to alter or have altered their bodies to match), transgender teens (those who identify as the gender opposite to the one they were assigned but may not wish to alter their physiology), and gender non-conforming teens (there are a range of gender expressions that are not exclusively masculine or feminine and a variety of words that convey this such as genderqueer, genderfluid, and androgynous). Adolescence is a time of exploration; there will inevitably be teens who question and explore gender identity whether or not they settle on expressions that are within the trans* continuum. When I use the term trans* it is my hope that these teens are still on our minds when we create safe spaces. I refer to other teens as cisgender, denoting that their gender identity matches with the sex they were assigned at birth. This essay is intended to outline the kinds of support we can offer, framed with the discrete components of physical space, social space, and programming. Primarily, this is an effort to illustrate how librarians might begin considering what we have to offer this population of teens.

I think it is valuable to briefly discuss why trans* teens need specific support. According to GLSEN's "From Teasing to Torment: School Climate Revisited, A Survey of U.S. Secondary School Students and Teachers" (2016), LGBTQ students are significantly more likely to experience bullying related to gender expression than their peers, and consistently report feeling less safe in school than their peers. The surveyed teachers are less likely to intervene when hearing negative remarks about transgender people than they are to address sexist or homophobic remarks. Mustanski, et al.'s "The Effects of Cumulative Victimization on Mental Health Among Lesbian, Gay, Bisexual, and Transgender

Adolescents and Young Adults" (2016), indicates that transgender teens with a steady or increasing rate of victimization (as was the case for many transgender participants) were much more likely to experience depression and PTSD than their cisgender peers. The National Transgender Discrimination Survey (2011) includes many disheartening statistics regarding mental health and physical safety of trans* people, notably that more than half of the trans* youth respondents who reported harassment had attempted suicide. While libraries are not the appropriate institutions to conduct intervention programs, many are well equipped to provide a basic safe space.

Martin and Murdock discuss what a safe space means for queer youth in their 2007 work *Serving Lesbian, Gay, Bisexual, Transgender, and Questioning Teens*. They discuss including books with queer content in all different kinds of book displays, becoming comfortable using direct language regarding queerness in front of teens, how best to deal with teens that use homophobic language—their suggestions span a wide range of considerations and concerns. It makes sense that they include transgender teens in this book because, as they indicate in the preface, transgender teens experience a large amount of the same challenges as LGBQ youth, regardless of how they identify their sexuality. However, transgender teens face some challenges differing from those of LGBQ teens, and the difference is worth exploring. We can't afford to overlook the specific needs of this population or to allow ignorance to prevent teen spaces from being as welcoming as possible.

I find it necessary to discuss my own context before launching into these ideas. I have been fortunate to work with teens at the New Orleans Public Library for four-plus years. There are 10 to 15 regular teens in the library every day; most of these are cisgender African American boys between the ages of 11 and 17 from low-income families. I am white, genderqueer, middle-aged, able-bodied, and raised middle class—a privileged background that requires consistent consideration of how I can use this for effective advocacy. Kind older teens and adults (and the books they handed me) changed the trajectory of my life during my mid-teens, so part of my enthusiasm for my job stems from a joy in supporting other folks through the challenges of becoming an adult.

I studied the construction of gender in college, and I use this background frequently when interacting with teens as they (kindly or unkindly) assess their own and each other's gender roles and presentations. While being genderqueer puts me in the trans* continuum, and gender studies are a helpful background, neither makes me an expert at what is best for trans* teenagers, in or out of a library. It does make me more aware that making trans* teens comfortable is necessary, and maybe more equipped than I would be otherwise to start to adjust the space and programming with that in mind. Regardless, the suggestions I propose are hopefully accessible to librarians of all genders, and are offered with full acknowledgment that I am still learning what the best forms of support may be. I also acknowledge that my privilege plays a part in what I consider possible. For example, typical library authority figures, be they administrators or managers, often respond positively to the way a well-educated middle-class white person conveys a request for certain policy shifts, etc. Some of these suggestions are based on the idea that you will be considered in the same way and given as much autonomy and access as I am, which may or may not be the case. Regardless, I hope that even considering these approaches will help to broaden our professional interest in the specific needs of these teens.

Inclusion in the Physical Space

Much has been made of the aesthetics of teen zones; most are decorated and arranged in a way that lets teens know the space is specifically designed for them to relax and be comfortable. There are a variety of posters up on the walls—the teens in our library are into manga, so many are manga and anime-related. We have the "READ" poster series posted, which depicts a wide variety of folks they might look up to with books they love, exhorting them to read. In the context of the manga and anime posters, we display as many characters who defy conventional gender roles such as Princess Mononoke, as we do mainstream representations like the characters in *Oh! My Goddess*. The same goes for the role models on the READ posters—we have Missy Elliot, and some female athletes, but more variation would be desirable. All these inclusions are fairly subtle, but a present part of the atmosphere. Less subtle is a poster from the Teaching Tolerance division of Southern Poverty Law, which defines all elements of sex and gender very simply and explicitly. It is face-height in a section in which the teens spend much time. As a result, they've probably all read it at some point and have some embedded context for the concept that sex, gender, and sexuality are discrete entities. The poster is free and can be printed directly off the Teaching Tolerance website. Finally, we are in the process of creating a sign indicating exactly what a "safe space" entails where freedom of gender expression is directly named.

Other components of the physical space include the kinds of information that are readily on hand. In the same display box as the information on homeless resources, the library's databases, STIs, and event bookmarks, we have information for local trans* resources. We are lucky enough to have a variety of trans* support and activism groups in our area, so we include information for these groups as another easy way to ensure trans* teens know they are welcome in the space and that we support their information needs. While some teens will feel confident enough to ask us for those contacts, or are internet savvy enough to find contacts themselves, others could easily spend long and unnecessary hours assuming they're much more alone than they really are. If your library isn't close to any of those kinds of groups, including national resources on a bookmark alongside the more general info-sheets could be very useful. Trans* teens shouldn't continue to be a neglected population, especially considering how frequently they are bullied and how likely they are to suffer psychological damage from it. Offering information about these kinds of resources requires very little time or effort on our parts, and offers significant returns.

Book displays are another component of what's visually available in any teen space, and my coworkers and I try to make the most of these at all times. As Martin and Murdock suggest, not limiting books with trans* characters to Pride Month is crucial. More expansive inclusion guarantees an accurate picture of reality is conveyed, where trans* people are part of every population that could be celebrated during any given month. If you're interested in this idea but don't have background or context to know what kinds of books have applicable content during Women's History Month, Black History Month, etc., there are a few simple routes to take. The Rainbow Booklist is a committee of ALA's GLBT-RT that chooses the best books for teens and kids with queer content published each year. Ten of the best books are chosen, but everything of note is included with brief descriptions, and it's divided by age of audience, fiction, and non-fiction. Goodreads has a seriously expansive list of YA with trans* characters; searching for biographies of famous

SEX? SEXUAL ORIENTATION? GENDER IDENTITY? GENDER EXPRESSION?

KNOW THE DIFFERENCE

TOLERANCE.ORG

SEXUAL ORIENTATION is our physical, emotional or romantic attraction to others.

GENDER IDENTITY is a deeply held sense of being male, female or another gender. Gender identity is not related to sexual orientation.

SEX is biological: internal and external reproductive organs and sex chromosomes.

GENDER EXPRESSION is the way individuals show their gender to the world. Gender expression is not related to sexual orientation.

SEX, SEXUAL ORIENTATION, GENDER IDENTITY AND GENDER EXPRESSION are distinct concepts, but they combine uniquely in each person to make us who we are. Understanding these terms—and how they do and do not intersect—can help us better appreciate and respect the diverse spectrum of our identities.

TEACHING TOLERANCE

trans* folks in a variety of roles and professions can be an excellent supplement. There are many more ways that the physical space in libraries can be made more inclusive, but these aspects are relatively easy to address and well worth the time and consideration they require.

Inclusion in Social Space

The atmosphere of the Teen Zone is shaped at least as much by the interpersonal environment as it is by the physical space. There are two specific approaches I use when trying to make the atmosphere of the Teen Zone welcoming to patrons of all genders. The first is not far from what Martin and Murdock recommend in their chapter entitled "Offering Effective Service and Providing Safe Spaces." Even when I'm not directly engaged with the teens, I am keeping an eye and an ear on the area. Any time I hear anyone policing anyone else's gender, even in play, I speak up. This is most often necessary in casual conversations between cisgender teen boys; comments like "don't be such a girl" or "she's such a dude" are often intended harmlessly. My response is uniformly one that addresses both the implication that one gender expression is better or worse than another, while simultaneously reminding them that no one gets to tell anyone else how they're supposed to express themselves in the Teen Zone. Sometimes it's egregious enough that I pull the teens aside and have a more serious talk. Other times it's such a passing comment that I can just say something vaguely humorous about how they don't get to be the gender police and that suffices. Regardless, the regular teens have learned enough about why that isn't part of a safe space that when they bring friends into the Teen Zone, if the friend says something in that vein, it's the regular patron that says "you can't say that here." Perhaps someday this will include a short explanation of why. For now, I'm just thrilled that they're willing to curb their peers and don't always need me to maintain the standards of a safe space. One of the most recent times I interfered with someone telling a joke whose humor rested in reinforcing binary gender norms, whatever I said wasn't that serious—I'd already had the longer conversation with both teens involved and so was able to simply refer to it. I ended with a general statement of it being inappropriate to police anyone's gender and I got a "hell, yeah!" from three teens I'd never met before who were using the computers across the way. It was an excellent reminder that maintaining that space audibly, no matter how many times I think a teen has heard it, can have an excellent effect on patrons' feeling of welcome in a place intended to be safe for everyone.

The other main component of the social space is the relationship-building I do with the teens themselves. I do my best to be approachable and always ask a lot of questions about how they are, what they're up to, etc. Teens are aware that I am interested in them, and willing to disrupt any bullying or gender regulation in the Teen Zone, which makes me an easy person to come to with questions or assertions of their identities, gendered or otherwise. This kind of comfort can be achieved even when you're not as actively gregarious or hands-on. For example, if you're able to audibly affirm someone else's variety

Opposite: **A poster that defines elements of sex and gender simply and explicitly (reprinted with permission of Teaching Tolerance, a project of the Southern Poverty Law Center, www. tolerance.org).**

of expression—be it a teen or a superstar—either would let teens, whose ears are listening for cues that they're welcome or accepted, know that they might find an ally in you.

In the cases when a teen has entrusted me with a declaration of their gender expression or state of questioning, there are several things I try to do. The first, and most obvious, is to listen. Regardless of how much or little context we have with teens' struggles, YA librarians have to practice having open ears for the issues that patrons are experiencing. Without listening carefully, I might assume that it's just the same as some other problem I have handled, and totally botch the interaction through that assumption. From this point, there are several guiding questions that may be helpful:

- So you're saying ___? (Repeat back their concerns, questions, and context to make sure you've understood correctly.)
- What pronoun do you prefer when we are speaking to one another?
- Are you changing your name?
- What pronoun and name are you comfortable having me use around your peers?
- Is it okay to take a call from your parent and use that name and pronoun?
- If I visit your school, what name and pronoun should I use?

Another important set of questions relate to what kind of support they want when interacting with their peers and library staff:

- Do you want to have individual conversations with my coworkers, do you want me to, or do you not care right now?
- What level of assistance, if any, do you want when you tell your peers your new pronoun and/or name?
- Do you want my help explaining what being transgender means, or do you want to take it on yourself and ask for help if you need to?
- Do you want me to correct your peers when they use an incorrect pronoun or do all the correcting yourself—or to have no correcting at all?

Regardless of my feelings regarding their peers' level of respect and willingness to understand people with different identities than their own, I try to actively respect the wishes of each teen involved and not overstep in my eagerness to be supportive.

A final component of this process is continuing to check in with teens I see on an ongoing basis. I run much less of a risk of accidentally implying that a teen should be entirely settled and have it all figured out when I remember to check in. These are some things I've asked:

- Is it still okay for me to use your old pronoun when I'm talking to your mom?
- How did it feel when I stepped in to help you explain to the ten year old at the program that just because you look like a girl doesn't mean you have to be one? Do you want me to do that any differently next time?
- Do you want me to keep correcting your boyfriend when he calls you "she"?

I try to make a consistent effort to stay up to date on how any of these teens are feeling on any of these issues. Ideally this maximizes their understanding that they have my support and that I'm not invested in them being any particular identity as much as I'm invested in their general well-being.

Programming

Our Teen Zone has a fairly regular cast of characters during the school year, and few occasions where we would have a program that attracts socially unconnected teens, or that would benefit from formal go-round-style introductions. During the summer reading programming, however, we get a fair number of new teens who have had no previous contact with the regulars. Some of these programs are discussion or conversation-oriented, where it becomes helpful to have each person introduce themselves. In my daily life of non-work meetings and social meet-ups, it has become conventional to include pronoun preference as a component of a brief introduction. This makes it easy for participants to accurately and politely refer to someone's point during the discussion without assuming the speaker's gender. It is understood in these contexts that a multitude of gender expressions exists and that asking someone's pronoun is both conscientious and respectful. This past summer I tried bringing this practice into teen programs, realizing that there were teens in attendance that were likely to be mis-gendered by their peers. I hoped that including pronouns into the introductions would prevent some of that, or at least set a precedent to refer to when correcting any mis-gendering. The more I consider the issue, though, the less appropriate I believe it is to reserve the practice of including pronoun preference in introductions for occasions when I think a trans* teen might be present. It seems likely that not only would saving it for these occasions create a trend of singling out teens whose gender presentation is unusual, but it also assumes that I will always be able to tell when someone is in the trans* continuum—an unwise assumption at best.

Currently in my social world, I save the question of pronoun preference to environments where that is already a shared context. Bringing it into our Teen Zone is bringing this practice far out of context, but the costs seem to significantly outweigh the benefits. Without the practice, the teens and I will find it extremely easy to make assumptions regarding each-others' genders in practice, which creates very little space for trans* teens to feel welcome or included. Rare is the teenager, even the ones who specifically come out to me as trans*, that feels entirely comfortable correcting strangers in a group of their peers regarding their pronoun preference. Including the practice provides trans* teens with two crucial things. First, they know from the outset of the program that the librarian supports and encourages them to make their own assertion of identity. Second, they know that the librarian is likely to support their self-designation if another participant mis-genders them, regardless if it's intentional or accidental. Those benefits seem huge to me—with a single question added to introductions, I'm suddenly able to convey a specific welcome that was previously left to chance.

The main drawback that I can imagine is one of initial awkwardness. The first time I included it in the introductions, a handful of teens immediately asked "what's a pronoun?" in tones of serious suspicion that I was including something tedious and possibly related to the grammar section in English class. If I was less comfortable with this group of teens, that might have felt seriously challenging. Knowing most of them fairly well meant that whether or not they thought it was a weird and unnecessary inclusion, they would do it anyway—they wanted pizza and most already had at least one really serious conversation with me about gender and/or sexuality and inclusion or prejudice under their belts. I understand that this is not going to be the case in every teen space. However, if you're serious about making the teen area inviting to everyone, this is probably the most pivotal inclusion you could make to express to trans* teens that you welcome them and support their presence. If this feels too weird to start cold, that's totally fine. Much as Martin and Murdock suggest shutting yourself in a room and saying the words "lesbian," "gay," "queer," etc., until you're sure you can say them without wincing in front of teenagers, you can approach pronouns gradually. Practice asking the question by yourself, then ask a few of your social groups or other adult meeting spaces if pronoun preference could be included in the introductions as practice for you. Not only will this be a good training ground, but you will have suddenly opened those spaces to further inclusion and made your peers in these environments understand that you're invested in inclusion. From there you will hopefully feel more comfortable starting to include pronouns in group introductions with teens, and start to find the explanations of why more comfortable as well.

Conclusion and Further Directions

There are many other ways to be an excellent ally that don't fall easily into this breakdown. An example is inviting trans* folks to lead programs (not necessarily on the topic of gender); another is advocating for your library's card applications to allow gender to be an optional, fill in the blank box. A critical further consideration is the presence of gender-neutral bathrooms in the library itself, a crucial component to trans* patrons feeling welcome in the space. This is not an exhaustive list of best practices—do what works for you at the pace you're able.

My ambition is to maintain a space for teens in my library that is as welcoming as humanly possible to as many kinds of humans as possible. Given that trans* teens continue to be marginalized, made invisible, and subsequently endangered by themselves and others, it follows that making every effort to make teen areas specifically welcoming to this population is a part of my job. I'm interested in how other librarians are making their own spaces more welcoming to this population. I'm also interested in what trans* teens have to say about their interactions in public libraries—if they feel like we have their back enough without these measures or if these practices do in fact make them feel more safe and welcome. There's a lot to learn still, and I am glad to have the opportunity to share the start of what I'm learning here.

References

Grant, Jaime M., Lisa A. Mottet, Justin Tanis, Jack Harrison, Jody L. Herman, and Mara Keisling. "Injustice at Every Turn: A Report of the National Transgender Discrimination Survey." Washington: National Center for Transgender Equality and National Gay and Lesbian Task Force, 2011.
Greytak, E.A., J.G. Kosciw, C. Villenas and N.M. Giga. "From Teasing to Torment: School Climate Revisited: A Survey of U.S. Secondary School Students and Teachers." New York: GLSEN, 2016.
Martin, Hillias J., and James R. Murdock. *Serving Lesbian, Gay, Bisexual, Transgender, and Questioning Teens: A How-to-do-it Manual for Librarians.* New York: Neal-Schuman, 2007.
Mustanski, Brian, Rebecca Andrews, and Jae A. Pucket. "The Effects of Cumulative Victimization on Mental Health Among Lesbian, Gay, Bisexual, and Transgender Adolescents and Young Adults." *American Journal of Public Health* 106, no. 3 (March 2016): 527–533.

"Sex in the Library"

*Promoting an Undergraduate Gender Studies
Research Program in an Academic Library*

LYNN D. LAMPERT, ELLEN E. JAROSZ
and COLEEN MEYERS-MARTIN

Beginning in 2012, the Obviate Library at California State University Northridge partnered with faculty in the Gender and Women's Studies Department, Queer Studies Program, and the campus Pride Center to successfully develop an undergraduate research competition and outreach programming through its Bullough Endowment. These efforts led to annual outreach programming, where library personnel collaborate with discipline faculty and the Pride Center to develop a week of programming showcasing undergraduate research projects that make significant use of primary source materials from the Library's Vern and Bonnie Bullough Collection on Sex and Gender. The Oviatt's "Sex in the Library" programming is a dynamic example of how an academic library can best promote awareness and effective usage of its special collections materials in the area of gender studies while simultaneously providing programming that allows lesbian, gay, bisexual, transgender, intersex and queer (LGBTIQ) subjects and voices to be heard on campus. For the purposes of this essay, LGBTIQ is being broadly applied as an inclusive abbreviation encompassing a large spectrum of identities. This includes all who do not strictly identify as heterosexual or cisgender. In addition to describing the "Sex in the Library" programming, this essay also reviews the literature pertaining to LGBTIQ library programming and presents best practices that can be employed for gender studies outreach in academic libraries.

Literature Review

While there was precedent on campus for the Obviate Library's "Sex in Library" programming, academic libraries have not always engaged in promoting their collections in the areas of gender studies and LGBTIQ research. In the past two decades, academic libraries have made strides in delivering programming that showcases how students and faculty can best use special collections materials in the area of gender studies and LGBTIQ research. These programming efforts have also simultaneously provided opportunities to allow LGBTIQ themes to be discussed through disciplinary and current social contexts at both the undergraduate and graduate studies levels. These recent developments reflect a marked change from past practices which Marvin J. Taylor characterized as "closeted" and discriminatory in his 1993 article, "Queer Things from Old Closets: Libraries—Gay and Lesbian Studies—Queer Theory." As James Carmichael notes, citing the 1999 American Library Association's Annual Gay, Lesbian, Bisexual and Transgender taskforce program, "Daring to Save Our History: Gay and Lesbian Archives," the turn to the 21st century represents a more open and accepting focus on gay collections and archives as the "'boom' in gay archives and collections arrives at a felicitous moment when the availability of online technology … precipitated a new awareness of the accessibility of archives among professionals in the field" (2000, 93).

Today many libraries are doing more than just collecting, digitizing and promoting special collections that further LGBTIQ studies. As Peggy McEachreon (2016) shows, many libraries worldwide are now developing programming that both markets and supports collections and LGBTIQ human rights and social justice. McEachreon also identifies programming and special events held at libraries worldwide that have supported subjects such as the censorship of literature, HIV/AIDS, LGBTIQ pride and highlighted previously obscured and sometimes deliberately silenced collections.

In tandem with these above efforts in the library and information science literature, it is important to also note the pivotal role that archivists, subject specialists and outreach librarians continue to play in promoting gender studies and LGBTIQ research. Many academic libraries now staff specialists in the areas of gender studies and queer studies. The growth of these library positions has paralleled the growth of academic departments and disciplinary programs. Recent research on the unique work of gender studies librarianship specialists working within archives and libraries can be found in Greenblatt's comprehensive volume *Serving LGBTIQ Library and Archives Users: Essays on Outreach, Service, Collections and Access* (2011).

Tracing the development of these library roles and programs, Greenblatt's work discusses the interdisciplinary nature of gender studies librarianship and describes the difficulties that still exist for both librarians building collections and researchers working to retrieve information to support both LGBTIQ and gender studies research. Some of these struggles emerge in terms of funding considerations and collection gaps from past missed acquisitions. Greenblatt reminds readers of the power that gender studies librarians, whether they are embedded within women's studies, queer studies or gender studies departments, bring to both building and promoting LGBTIQ collections and programming.

While articles focused on collection building, instruction and reference services that support gender studies research abound, there are fewer studies that focus on the value that collaborative library outreach programming can bring to these research areas as well as climate improvement for LGBTIQ students and studies alike. As John C. Hawley's *Expanding the Circle: Creating an Inclusive Environment in Higher Education for LGBTQ Students and Studies* (2015) notes, collaboration with student-centered units and campus organizations dedicated to supporting the LGBTIQ population on campus is critical to developing successful undergraduate programming that creates a campus climate receptive to discussing gender studies issues and research through public programming.

California State University Northridge and the Obviate Library

California State University Northridge (CSUN) is one of the 23 campuses that make up the California State University system. CSUN is a diverse university community of 38,310 students and more than 4,000 faculty and staff, sited on a 356-acre campus in the heart of Los Angeles' San Fernando Valley. CSUN's Obviate Library has a collection containing 2.1 million volumes, of which over 1.5 million are books, and over 250,000 bound periodical volumes. The archives and manuscript collection exceeds 14,000 linear feet of materials, with nearly 45,000 items housed in Special Collections. As a teaching institution, the Obviate Library provides approximately 24,000 students with library instruction sessions annually. During these sessions librarians guide students on how to find and evaluate credible and scholarly information for university level research papers. The Obviate Library has a dedicated outreach program that serves many non–CSUN and CSUN communities through tours, instruction and special programming.

The History of the Bullough Collection and Endowment

The Bullough Collection and Endowment document social attitudes and studies of sex and gender from ancient times to the present and support ongoing collection development associated with CSUN curricula and research. CSUN faculty member Vern Bullough was an historian and noted scholar of sex and gender. His professional interest in human sexuality focused on its sociology and the history of its study, and he worked extensively around human sexuality themes throughout his career at CSUN, publishing dozens of books on the subject over four decades.

Having amassed a robust personal research library of books and other resources documenting sex and gender over the course of his career, Bullough and his wife, Bonnie, donated the foundation of what would become the Vern and Bonnie Bullough Collection on Sex and Gender to the Obviate Library in 1973, the vast majority of which is housed in the Special Collections and Archives unit within the Obviate Library. The Bulloughs continued making donations through the 1990s, and also worked with librarians and staff in the Obviate Library to acquire rare and archival materials on gender and sexuality from other individuals and groups to develop the collection. In 1996 Bullough established the Endowment for Human Sexuality at the Obviate in honor of Bonnie's passing earlier that year. In addition to supporting continued growth and development of the collection, the endowment also initially supported programming at the Center for Sex and Gender Research on campus.

As the collection has grown over the intervening years, it has become an increasingly unique and complex record of social attitudes towards sex and gender roles, and the broader study of sex and gender around the world over several centuries. In addition to a diversity of topical content, it also includes a diverse set of formats. The oldest volume in the collection is a 1584 edition of the collected works of Italian physician Girolamo Fracastoro, which contains his cure for syphilis, and the poem he wrote giving the disease its modern name.

In addition to books and periodicals on a host of topics, including medicine, marriage, fashion, midwifery, childrearing, gender roles, nudism, fetishism, pornography, and others, the collection includes an extensive quantity of archival collections. Archival holdings are particularly strong in the areas of cross-dressing, the homosexual community in Los Angeles, prostitution, the transgendered community, children and gender, gender and psychology, and legal obscenity.

While the collection itself has steadily grown more extensive and robust over the years, Bullough's desire to support programming on campus at CSUN's Center for Sex and Gender Research became unworkable when the center closed. For some years the endowment was used exclusively to support and build collections on sex and gender topics in library, especially in Special Collections and Archives. Despite this growth and the great richness of the collections, use by undergraduate students in particular was quite limited during this period, due in part to the myriad challenges they face when working with rare, unique, and archival materials in a research context for the first time.

Reaching Out to the Campus Community:
The Bullough Endowment Committee

In 2012, after the Obviate Library's Collection Development Coordinator conducted a review of all library endowments at the behest of library administration, she realized the Bullough endowment could be used to support programming in addition to library collections. While the original endowment agreement referred to a center that no longer existed, she reached out to the new Queer Studies Program (QS), the Gender and Women's Studies Department (GWS), and CSUN's Pride Center in the Student Union to ascertain whether there was interest across campus in organizing programming in the spirit of Bullough's original wishes. Shortly thereafter the Dean of the Library convened the Bullough Endowment Committee.

In addition to members from QS, GWS, and the Pride Center, the committee also has several members from the library, including the subject specialists for QS and GWS, and the Head of Special Collections and Archives, among others. While the committee readily agreed that collection support should continue to be a priority, it also considered a number of annual, bi-annual, and other programming options when it met each month. It ultimately settled on organizing an annual student symposium highlighting the research of undergraduates enrolled in the capstone courses in QS and GWS. The endowment would provide $500 research awards for the two most outstanding projects.

"Sex in Library"

In spring 2014, the Bullough Endowment Committee launched the first student symposium focused on sex and gender, titled "Sex in Library: Scholarship, Exploration, and Intersectionality in the Archives." Each year the subtitle of the event changes, while the main title, "Sex in Library," remains consistent. The symposium itself is a multi-day event, featuring student presentations from QS and GWS on different days of the week. While subsequent symposia have been organized in a much shorter period of time, planning for the first year's program took nearly a year.

Additionally, a major component of the GWS department's senior capstone course has been a student-organized conference at the end of the semester for many years. The QS program, in contrast, was created much more recently, and had no such established practice. The committee endeavored to be as accommodating as possible of GWS's traditions throughout the planning process while incorporating its student conference as GWS's contribution to the "Sex in Library" event.

In the fall semester of 2013 committee members from QS and GWS reached out to the faculty members in their departments who would be teaching the undergraduate capstone courses the following spring semester. Their goal was both to gauge interest in the possibility of incorporating primary, archival research into the final research projects each student completed in their courses, and willingness to modify their syllabi and other course content to accommodate that kind of a project. Both capstone instructors liked the idea, and were also curious to learn more about the contents of the collection themselves. They visited the Special Collections and Archives reading room together to view a pre-selected set of collection materials in order to have some idea of what their students might be working with that spring.

After modifying their draft syllabi to reflect the change, both instructors scheduled one-shot library instruction sessions for their classes in Special Collections and Archives in addition to the sessions they had already planned with the appropriate subject specialists. These 90-minute Special Collections sessions focused in part on highlighting the contents of the Bullough Collection, but also on introducing undergraduate students to some of the basic, core concepts needed to successfully conduct primary research with archival and other rare materials in a special collections environment. Students were then asked to draw connections between these newly introduced skills, the content presented in the session with the GWS or QS subject specialist, and the information literacy skills they had already acquired in their 100- and 200-level courses. Finally, they were given time to browse some collection materials identified by the librarian in consultation with their instructors on topics the students were interested in pursuing.

While the content of the two library sessions is nearly identical, there are some differences in course structure and in the assignments. Following the session many students schedule research consultations with the librarian in Special Collections and Archives, their subject specialist, or both. In the QS course some of these meetings are required, while in the GWS course they are all optional. Also notably, students in the QS capstone course are required to incorporate at least one item from the Bullough Collection in their research projects, while students in GWS are instead offered the option of doing so.

Those students who wish to be eligible for the $500 awards must have used at least one item from the Bullough Collection in their research, and must turn their award applications in a week before the "Sex in Library" student symposium begins. Bullough Committee members attend the presentations of each student applicant in addition to reading their applications and a brief statement describing their experiences working with the Bullough Collection. The Bullough Committee evaluates student projects according to several criteria shared with the applicants in advance. These include the originality of their research, incorporation of archival and other materials found in the Bullough Collection, and their use of supporting literature. Committee members also evaluate how successfully students present their theoretical framework, findings, and Bullough Collection content during the "Sex in Library" event.

"Sex in Library's" structure has varied each year as the committee strives to improve the event and increase its profile on campus. The most recent program included a keynote address to a packed house by noted feminist scholar Sandra Harding, while previous events have featured local community activists like Andy Sacher, director of The Lavender

Effect organization, and trans activist Miss Major. Announcement of the student awards has also changed from year to year. They were initially handed out at a closing reception hosted by the Dean of the Library at the conclusion of the event, but this past year were instead announced at the Rainbow Graduation Celebration, a special event for LGBTIQ graduates, their families and friends, and other allies, in an effort to increase the profile of the event.

Best Outreach Practices for Gender Studies Programming

Developing a multi-faceted outreach and promotional strategy to support gender studies programming in its initial phases, as well as during its expansion period, will be essential for success. Through careful planning, gender studies outreach and communication efforts can be tailored to your institution in order to reach your targeted communities and to provide the most meaningful impact. Best practices for outreach and promotion of gender studies programming at an academic institution will include the following planning steps and implementation.

Identify and gather library and campus stakeholders who support the development of the programming and who are willing to participate in communicating the project to the campus and community. Who are the individuals, departments and organizations or groups that are invested and involved in gender studies programming on your campus? LGBTIQ Centers, queer studies programs, gender and women studies departments and student organizations, clubs and groups can all be considered. Invite them to become members of your team in developing and carrying out an outreach and promotional plan. Find out what resources they have to support this process. You may discover these colleagues have talent for designing promotional materials, possess an interest or experience in utilizing social media or creating webpages. They also may be able to put you in contact with other interested parties who can support the process.

Define your message by identifying the most useful information to promote about your programming and events. As with many disciplines, gender studies programming has its own unique history. One effective form of communication within promotion is the use of narratives pertaining to that history. Creating a personal connection with your targeted audience through messaging that includes gender studies narratives will make your communications more meaningful and impactful. People want to see and hear stories of how gender studies programming can enrich their lives (Lamb, 2016). The goal of your messaging will be two-fold: (1) to inform people about the rewards of gender studies programming, collaborating departments and groups on campus and, (2) to invite people to attend and participate in specific events. Informing people will involve utilizing promotional materials and vehicles that communicate the vision of the gender studies programming and providing information about the events such as who will be speaking and what activities will be taking place. Benefits received from participating in the events should be highlighted. A call to action that asks people to RSVP or to sign up should be included in communications and promotion materials.

Defining your audience will be as important as defining your message. This will enable you to target the communities you wish to reach most. What groups of people do you want to share your message with and provide an opportunity to participate? LGBTIQ Centers, Queer Studies Programs, Gender and Women Studies Departments and student organizations such as the student union, again, can be considered. Brainstorm with your team in order to target specific instructors, classes, and other campus departments to support you in building and communicating your message to as many communities as possible.

The methods you choose to deliver your message to these targeted communities should include a wide variety of communication popular formats and mediums. For example, an online promotion will reach people virtually through Facebook, Instagram, Snapchat, Twitter, YouTube, the library website and other social networking sites. Videos and blogs go a long way in telling a story and communicating a message. If your outreach and promotional team is able to garner giveaway items from local vendors, these items can be used for promotion before and during an event.

More traditional promotional strategies include the distribution of banners, lawn signs, posters, A-frame posters, brochures, bookmarks and fliers. These materials can be distributed throughout the dorms and campus grounds. Outreach promotional booths located in popular areas on campus can reach passersby with information and campus newspaper ads can communicate the programming effectively. These materials help brand your programming events and generate enthusiasm and awareness.

The community at large can be informed through press releases sent to local press outlets that are willing to publicize and welcome campus and community members to the events. Additional approaches to outreach include announcements in classrooms; tours of your LGBTIQ Center; email messaging; as well as word-of-mouth promotion. Having the support of library staff and classroom faculty within the communication process will help forward your message exponentially.

Coordinating the day-to-day staffing needs of implementing an effective outreach campaign will require consideration. It is likely you will meet regularly with the stakeholders who volunteered to serve on your outreach and promotional team. However, there will be a need for additional support staff who will carry out some of the details of the programming as well. Are there enough staff members within your department to carry out your message within the delivery systems you have selected? The use of student assistants and support staff from other participating departments may be sources of assistance. Identifying the staffing needs required to fulfill your outreach plan and programming will support a smooth process.

It will be important to evaluate the success of both the programming and outreach efforts. Assessing your events and promotion may involve several methods of inquiry including but not limited to in-person surveys at the end of events; email or library website questionnaires; feedback from social media sites; in-person communications; focus groups following events; headcounts taken at events; or by utilizing a combination of these methods. Within your assessment strategies and tools you will aim to identify whether the programming met your goals, and the manner in which it met those goals. Determining how participants learned about the programming, and if they were informed about the event through more than one source, will also be information to identify and gather through the assessment.

Developing an effective outreach and promotional strategy to support your gender studies programming will require a multi-faceted approach and careful planning. Gathering stakeholders; developing messaging; identifying desired audiences; and selecting communication vehicles that will best reach your targeted audiences will be essential to the success of your communications. Assessment of your outreach also will be necessary in order to develop and build meaningful programming. Effective gender studies outreach and promotion has the ability to create meaningful connections with campus communities. Through the use of varied communication tools and strategies, the gender studies programming message has the capacity to broaden its reach, provide relevant support, and enrich the lives of its stakeholders as well as campus and community members.

Conclusion

As deJong and Koevoets admonish, "Teaching gender studies should not stop at teaching students how to navigate library spaces, or how to locate and analyze archival materials, but also inspire them to produce situated perspectives out of their findings" (2013,159). It is imperative to remind all librarians engaged in gender studies outreach & LGBTIQ programming that "As the new generation of feminist activists, scholars, and professionals, students of gender studies face the multiple challenges of reflecting critically on the stories scientists and scholars have been telling, on the status of the objects they are telling stories about, and on how they may tell such stories differently. These are all political activities that take place within material conditions as well as narrative traditions, and libraries and archives … [AND] play a seminal role in the political practices of knowledge production" (deJong and Koevoets, 2013,159).

The Obviate Library's "Sex in Library" programming embodies that pursuit, by fostering the growth of research skills in students while also encouraging students and participants to disseminate their findings with their peers and the community. In addition, the collaborative programming forged between the university library, GWS and QS departments, and campus Pride Center reflects a solidified and dynamic effort to empower student researchers to share their voices beyond their classrooms, and in many instances participate in a program that supports and cultivates political activism for social justice. This is critical work that is meaningful to students, faculty, the campus community and the library.

REFERENCES

de Jong, Sara, and Sanne Koevoets. 2013. *Teaching Gender with Libraries and Archives: The Power of Information.* Central European University Press.

Carmichael, James V., Jr. 2001. "'They Sure Got To Prove It on Me': Millennial Thoughts on Gay Archives, Gay Biography, and Gay Library History." *Libraries & Culture.* 35 (1): 88–102.

Greenblatt, Ellen. 2011. *Serving LGBTIQ Library and Archives Users: Essays on Outreach, Service, Collections and Access.* Jefferson, NC: McFarland.

Lamb, Annette. 2016. "Message Design, Branding & the Library's Story." *Marketing 4 Libraries.* http://eduscapes.com/marketing/7.htm.

McEachreon, Peggy. 2016. "Libraries 'Coming Out' in Support of LGBTQIA+ Human Rights and Social Justice." In *Perspectives on Libraries as Institutions of Human Rights and Social Justice*, 183–208. Emerald.

Taylor, M. J. 1993. Queer Things from Old Closets: Libraries—Gay and Lesbian Studies—Queer Theory. *Rare Books and Manuscripts Librarianship* 8 (1): 19.

Third Wave Library Activism

The Dynamic Possibilities of a Women's and Gender
Studies and University Library Partnership

CARRIE E. MORAN *and* LEANDRA PRESTON-SIDLER

"To make riot grrrl move into the future in a new way with a bunch of new names and a bunch of new energy, younger people have to learn about it and apply it to their own lives and own modern conversation. And they are."

—Kathleen Hanna

Introduction

Riot grrrl and the academy may seem like an uneasy partnership. The University of Central Florida Women's and Gender Studies program's emphasis on third wave feminism paired with a third wave feminist librarian liaison is bringing theory into practice in unexpected ways. This essay details the burgeoning partnership between a Women's and Gender Studies Program (WGST) and the campus library at a large, public university. The relationship began with a push from WGST to acquire streaming videos and specialized content for online classes. Both self-identified "third wave feminists," the librarian and WGST liaison quickly recognized the possibilities of the partnership. In addition to expanding streaming video content, the library and WGST collaborated to host a successful film screening and interdisciplinary discussion panel. Future plans include themed Open Mic nights (in collaboration with the WGST mentoring program and community partners) and a Third Wave Feminist Conference. This collaboration has involved the library's Reference, Teaching & Engagement, Acquisitions & Collections, Circulation, and Special Collections departments, as well as the WGST Director and faculty. This essay will highlight the reciprocal relationship between the women's and gender studies program and the library, and discuss how libraries and gender-based programs can work together to enrich academic institutions and communities.

The University of Central Florida is the second largest public university in the United States, with a student body of approximately 63,000. UCF offers 93 bachelor degree programs, 84 master degree programs, and 31 doctoral degree programs in twelve colleges (University of Central Florida, 2016). As a research I university with a heavy commuter population, online programs have been an integral part of the university's expansion. The Women's And Gender Studies Program is one of many at UCF where a degree can be attained entirely online.

The UCF Libraries system is composed of a main library, two branch libraries, and seven regional campus libraries. In 2013, UCF moved to a subject librarian service model where the academic departments on campus were assigned to individual librarians. These librarians perform proactive outreach, collection development, academic support for students in those disciplines, and research support for faculty in those disciplines. The majority of subject librarians are part of the Research & Information Services Department, however, librarians from the Teaching & Engagement Department, branch locations, and regional campus locations also serve as subject librarians.

The Women's and Gender Studies Program is part of the College of Arts & Humanities. The program has evolved from Women's Studies to "Women's and Gender" Studies to expand offerings and attract a broader student body, including possibilities for transgender, masculinity, and queer studies. The WGST program at UCF is known for its emphasis on Girls Studies, which includes a Girls Studies track consisting of several courses focused on girlhood studies (Girls Studies, Girls and Leadership, Virtual Girls, and Girls and the Body), as well as an award-winning mentoring program geared toward girls who tend to garner less attention in school settings, as they are neither deemed "gifted" or "at-risk," common terms used to categorize girls in academic and behavioral contexts. Faculty members in the program include Girls Studies experts and activists who also maintain blogs related to girls and Girls Studies' scholarship.

The UCF Young Women Leaders Program (YWLP) consists of "big sisters," undergraduate students who are paired with "littles" for one-on-one and group meetings every other week on middle school grounds to engage in activities related to bullying, self-esteem, leadership, body image, as well as other concepts related to personal and professional success. A Women's and Gender Studies faculty member serves as the coordinator and is active throughout the process each semester. She also secures grants and anything else needed to sustain the program. YWLP is an important component of the WGST Program and serves as a powerful impetus to drive activities bringing students and the community together. The UCF library has hosted displays featuring girl-based texts and houses a collection of YWLP creations in their Special Collections department, as well as a collection of student-created zines from a third wave feminisms course.

Common Ground

Women's and Gender Studies and the library at UCF have always collaborated, though most frequently in the process of identifying and acquiring content for students. However, subject librarian assignments recently shifted due to retirements and reassignments, enhancing the dynamic of librarian-academic area relationships. Subject areas are assigned to make use of the strengths of each librarian by focusing on academic backgrounds, research interests, and personal interests. The original librarian assigned to the Women's & Gender Studies Program was responsible for a related discipline, interdisciplinary studies. When she changed departments within the library, she took on several more subjects, and a decision was made to transfer WGST to one of the newest subject librarians who was taking over psychology and social work. This decision was based on the librarian's personal interest in feminism and professional interests in LGBTQ+ Studies.

Another strategy implemented by the UCF library program related to the selection of subject librarian duties includes pairing librarians with undergraduate or graduate degrees in given subjects with their assigned subject areas (ex. business, English, psychology). There are also librarians who have professional experience in specialized libraries that relate to their assigned subjects, such as the science librarian having previously worked as the librarian for a molecular research institute. Finally, UCF has librarians who have switched careers and use that prior career knowledge in their subject librarian duties, such as the nursing librarian. Such critical and thoughtful assignment strategies encourage not only informed but passionate collaborations between academic areas and the university library.

Communication

Though the library understood the reasoning and need for assignment modifications, the first challenge of the subject librarian model was to communicate this change to affected academic departments and faculty, and to accurately represent the benefits of having a particular librarian assigned to their specific department. Each subject librarian creates a newsletter at the beginning of the semester to distribute physically or virtually. There are no standards for this communication, but librarians typically include news about collection items, promote services like instruction or research consultations, and promote library events of interest.

Newsletters are also an ideal forum for introducing a librarian who has been assigned to a new department. In this case, the new WGST librarian felt it was important to connect with WGST faculty by sharing a common interest: third wave feminism. The WGST librarian included this description in her standard biography: "In my life I've identified as riot grrrl, and am a proud third-wave feminist." This line resonated with WGST faculty because it demonstrated that their new librarian was well versed in their subject and personally connected to the discipline.

The initial newsletter, delivered for the spring 2016 semester, also had information on a new collection purchased to support Women's and Gender Studies students, promoted the re-vamped WGST Research Guide, and included a statement about the library for WGST faculty to include on their syllabus. Providing a syllabus statement provides a dual purpose: it informs faculty about library services and makes it easier for faculty to communicate the importance of the library to their students. Further, if faculty already had statements about the library on their syllabus, they were likely in need of an update considering how rapidly library services evolve at a dynamic research university.

The primary form of communication between the WGST librarian and faculty has been email. The small size of the WGST department (currently two full-time lecturers and a program chair) makes it easier to converse about events and collection development using this communication channel. As mentioned previously, the WGST librarian also works with two of the larger departments on campus, psychology and social work. Email is a less effective tool for reaching larger departments, for which attending departmental faculty meetings has proved a better strategy.

Face-to-face meetings with the WGST librarian and faculty have been more sporadic depending on which projects or initiatives are being pursued. Once a bond was formed, the WGST librarian connected with some of the WGST faculty on Facebook. Social media has helped foster personal connections, opening up conversation about research interests, opportunities, and conferences of note.

Streaming Video

The UCF WGST librarian wears many hats in the library, and her official title is user engagement librarian. Part of her role in the UCF Libraries is to promote and market online services, and streaming video has been central to that effort. The UCF Libraries owns many Alexander Street Press collections, and a few titles through Films Media Group's Films on Demand platform. The library also licenses titles on an as-needed basis from Swank DigitalCampus, and has a demand driven acquisition program through Kanopy.

These four services work in tandem to cover the streaming video needs of academic faculty, however, titles can be purchased with streaming rights in special cases. The Alexander Street Press collections that relate to the academic goals of the WGST department include Ethnographic Video, LGBT Studies in Video, and New World Cinema in Video. The Swank DigitalCampus platform provides access to feature films from a variety of studios, and must be used for classes with an online component. Kanopy is the UCF Libraries' newest streaming video platform.

The Kanopy service runs on a demand driven acquisition model, where a certain threshold of time viewing a film must be met in order to trigger a purchase. The collection is large and updated regularly with over 16,000 titles as of July 2016. The videos also include public performance rights, a boon for event planning. Kanopy is essential to the WGST department, as it includes films from the Media Education Foundation that are used in several WGST courses.

Women's and Gender Studies at UCF offers 90 percent of its courses online, so streaming videos are a key resource for WGST courses. The transition from VHS to DVD to streaming has been a gradual one and, while streaming offerings have substantially improved the past few years, it has been a challenge with fiscal constraints and high prices. The WGST librarian has worked closely with faculty to identify titles by priority and locate grants and funds to meet student needs. We hope to continue working together to make all required films available streaming for UCF's online student population, particularly as streaming videos can be accessed by all students, whether online or traditional.

As streaming video garners more interest across departments, demand for related presentations and training has increased. The WGST librarian and one of the WGST faculty had the opportunity to present on streaming video with another librarian and Social Work faculty at an annual campus faculty development conference. This conference occurs in the week after the close of the fall and spring semesters, and is well attended by academic faculty. This presentation was a way for the library to showcase our services and our partnerships with various academic departments. It also allowed academic faculty to share their work and class activities with their colleagues, and was a positive experience for each of the presenters.

Events

Wonder Women

In an increasingly digital environment, the academic library has emerged as a valuable physical resource. Academic libraries offer computers, study areas, exhibit walls, classrooms, and event spaces. Academic departments often lack access to these resources, and librarians can market the physical library space to their academic faculty. The WGST librarian is part of the Teaching & Engagement department that is responsible for library outreach, and event planning has become an integral part of this role.

Many library events and promotions are linked to campus, community, and national events. The Teaching & Engagement department keeps a calendar of relevant events, such as Women's History Month in March. The WGST librarian saw an opportunity to host an event with this theme that could make use of and promote library resources such as streaming video, Special Collections & University Archives, and our physical space. To pursue this opportunity, the WGST librarian reached out to the WGST faculty via email.

The WGST librarian offered a choice of three films selected from the Kanopy platform that included public performance rights, with the idea to use a large library classroom to screen the film. The idea grew into a film screening and panel discussion, with refreshments provided by the WGST department. The film collectively selected was *Wonder Women! The Untold Story of American Superheroines*. This hour-long documentary tracks the evolution of the Wonder Woman character while highlighting key developments in feminism and women's rights.

Panel selection developed organically, with a focus on using experts from within the university. Panelists included Leandra Preston-Sidler, WGST associate lecturer; Michael Furlong, assistant librarian; and Jay Boyar, film department instructor and film critic. Dr. Preston-Sidler spoke to the feminist themes from the film, Mr. Furlong is a comic and graphic novel expert, and Mr. Boyar discussed film and superheroes. In addition to the film and panel, the original *Ms. Magazine* with Wonder Woman on the cover was on display from UCF's Special Collections. The UCF Libraries' Art Specialist created several photo booth props for attendees to take Wonder Woman-themed photos.

The event was marketed and promoted through various channels. Flyers were posted throughout the library. The event was posted on the Facebook and Twitter pages of the UCF Libraries and WGST Program, as well as the UCF Libraries' and university website. The library's digital signs displayed an ad for the event in the few weeks prior. It was also included on the campus-wide events calendar and weekly events email. A blurb about the event was included in the weekly newsletter distributed to all faculty via the Faculty Center for Teaching and Learning. This particular action led to several faculty offering extra credit or research participation credit for attendance at the event.

On the day of the event, the WGST librarian reserved the event space for one hour prior to set up. Refreshments and the display items were set up in the back of the room and, as attendees arrived, they mingled in that area. The photo booth props were utilized more by the WGST and library attendees; however, several others made use of them. Approximately 50 people attended the event, making it one of the larger events in the history of the UCF Libraries. A significant number of attendees were in a class that offered participation credit for attendance. The professor of that course provided anonymous surveys for those attendees to fill out after the experience.

The survey proved an unexpected highlight, as the WGST librarian was able to review them after the event. The class included many students with no interest in any of the film topics, so it was interesting to read their perspectives. The film was screened first by streaming it from Kanopy on a computer connected to an overhead projector. The computer went to sleep after the first twenty minutes, and the film experienced a few buffering issues. In planning future events, computer settings will be modified to prevent the former issue, and the film will be pre-loaded to avoid connection lags.

There was a short break between the film and panel to allow attendees to get refreshments or use the restroom. The panel had a list of questions provided by the filmmakers but, ultimately, discussion grew organically based on audience feedback. Major themes from the film were addressed and, in an especially poignant moment, panelists and attendees shared personal she-roes. Several students remarked on this powerful moment in their survey responses.

Several people left before the panel, but most stayed for the discussion. Event planning on a large campus is always challenging, but this event was ultimately successful. For future events, the WGST librarian would like to make use of the other subject librarians and their contacts to encourage more faculty/class participation. A large poster was placed in the library entrance the day of the event, but could have been posted for an entire week to potentially draw more attendees. This event had a few community attendees, and future events could be better advertised in community forums. The success of this event inspired plans for future event collaborations.

Open Heart Open Mic

The next collaboration grew out of a discussion between the WGST librarian and WGST Program Director. The WGST librarian writes and performs poetry in the community, and suggested that it would be fun to hold an open mic event in the library. An open mic event had previously been held in the fall 2015 semester in collaboration with Student Accessibility Services and was relatively successful. The WGST librarian hoped for a more consistent open mic event series, but sought an on campus partner for the event.

An email exchange between the WGST librarian and WGST faculty prompted a face-to-face meeting to solidify open mic event plans. During the email exchange, organizers decided that each event would tie into a specific theme and themes and dates were chosen for each month. The first event focus is Hispanic Heritage, then LGBTQ+ History, followed by an emphasis on Indigenous Peoples. Each month features one faculty and one student performer, in order to ensure at least two readings on the theme. The goal is to inspire audience members to speak, and also draw attendees who wish to see the featured performers. In the initial meeting, we selected faculty speakers for the first two events and discussed future themes. Each month, a different coordinator will plan the details of that specific month, including the speakers, promotion, and refreshments. Attendees are encouraged to bring food for a potluck-style refreshment area. The name decided upon during this initial planning meeting was Open Heart Open Mic.

The UCF Libraries' Art Specialist designed a custom logo for the event to be used for promotion on UCF Libraries' and campus wide calendars, as well as calendars distributed by various on campus organizations such as the Office of Diversity and Inclusion, the Latino Faculty & Staff Association, the Multicultural Student Center, and the Pride

Faculty & Staff Association. There are plans for the event to be included on various social media platforms, in the weekly faculty email, emails distributed to staff, and to specific departments with students who are likely to participate.

Remaining collaborative details for our open mic events have been, and will likely continue to be, worked out through email. As expected, flexibility for events is often necessary, and the dates of the first two events were moved to accommodate schedules. A large library classroom was reserved for each event. The events were scheduled on different nights, with varied start times to maximize attendance and participation. There is hope for this series to continue into future semesters, and attendance numbers will help decide future possibilities and events. Marketing and promotion for our events is enhanced by the collaborative nature of our work and promotions span across campus, particularly through social network and online avenues.

Third Wave Conference

The final planned collaboration between the WGST librarian and department is a Third Wave Conference. One of the WGST faculty who teaches a third wave feminisms course was inspired by a Facebook post about Kathleen Hanna, a favorite artist and riot grrrl of both women. The goals of this event are to hold a daylong event in the library that will include a zine making workshop, conference paper presentations, poster presentations, and a keynote speaker. Of course, Bikini Kill, Le Tigre, and Julie Ruin will be playing all day. The city of Boston named April 9, 2015, as "Riot Grrrl Day" in honor of Hanna's performance in the city (Kreps). A daylong event is ambitious, but previous collaborations point to the potential for great success.

Conclusion

The spirit of riot grrrl DIY culture permeates the collaboration between the WGST Program and WGST librarian at UCF, as both value the power of art and education as social justice, and respect the continuing necessity for feminism both within and beyond the academy. There is a tacit agreement to keep pushing boundaries, and asking for what is needed to bring Women's and Gender Studies issues to as many UCF students, faculty, staff, and community members as possible. The WGST Program has been a key driver of pursuing streaming video collections within the UCF Libraries, and this drive has benefitted myriad academic programs. As more successful events are held in the UCF Libraries, there has been more support within the library for events of all types. This collaboration is still growing, and the possibilities are endless.

REFERENCES

Davis, Allison P. "Girls Like Us: A Q&A With Kathleen Hanna." *The Cut*, 2013. Accessed August 12, 2016.
Kreps, Daniel. "Kathleen Hanna Honored With 'Riot Grrrl Day' in Boston." *Rolling Stone.* Accessed September 1, 2016.
Moran, Carrie. "STARS" Site. Accessed September 04, 2016.
"UCF Facts—University of Central Florida–Orlando, FL." University of Central Florida. Accessed September 4, 2016.

Beyond Women's History Month

Strengthening Collection Development
and Programming at Public and School Libraries
through Women's Studies Resources

JOY WORLAND

As community educational and cultural resources and disseminators of information, school and public libraries are in a unique position to ensure that library collections include high quality books promoting gender equality, and programming that highlights the existence and importance of these materials. We live in an era when we still haven't had a female president, college administrators and students at high school and colleges are discussing sexual consent and how to handle misconduct in a way that is fair to all parties, and even in a liberal pocket of the country, more than one library patron has raised the cry, "We need more books by men!," despite the disproportionate number of male authors represented in the library collection. Celebrities argue about claiming or disowning the word feminism and what it means, and mainstream media offers conflicting messages on what female empowerment looks like. Much as librarians help patrons sift through the glut of information on the internet to find accuracy and quality, discerning collection development and programming librarians can present vetted resources and experiences for patrons seeking a nuanced and balanced approach to gender issues.

Collection Development Resources

Collection development librarians need not have a personal interest in feminism to make collection decisions that reflect gender equality and inclusiveness and high quality. There are several organizations, book lists, websites and social media resources that provide current, vetted and reviewed material from which to choose. The "We Need Diverse Books" campaign includes books by and for women and girls of diverse backgrounds. Publications like *Booklist* and other large review sources typically highlight Women's History Month. Additionally, certain publishers can be counted on to offer a more significant offering of books with feminist authors and contents than often is true of some more mainstream publishers.

"We Need Diverse Books"

The "We Need Diverse Books"[1] project advocates for more inclusiveness in book publishing, with the goal of offering children empowering experiences through engagement with books in which they see characters from diverse backgrounds, sometimes mirroring the reader's own racial, gender, or sexual identity. WNDB defines diversity as "all diverse experiences, including (but not limited to) LGBTQIA, people of color, gender diversity, people with disabilities, and ethnic, cultural, and religious minorities."[2] As such, although feminism in not their specific focus, many of the books they promote embody feminism, particularly intersectional feminism, which embraces the connections amongst different forms of discrimination and marginalization, such as racism, sexism, and classism.

Publishers

A good representation of publishers with a feminist focus can be developed by browsing lists of recommended feminist lists such as the Amelia Bloomer Project lists[3] and seeing what publishers are frequently cited. For comprehensive information on publications, publishers, new books, see the University of Wisconsin–Madison Office of the Gender and Women's Studies Librarian website.[4]

As a start, here are some publishers to look to for quality and quantity in feminist publications, including fiction and non-fiction works, ranging from children's books to academic works:

Second Story Press.[5] Founded in 1988, Second Story Press is "dedicated to publishing feminist-inspired books for adults and young readers."

Seal Press[6] is a member of the Perseus Book Group. Based in Berkeley, CA, Seal was "founded in 1976 to provide a forum for women writers and feminist issues," and represents "the diverse voices and interests of women—their lives, literature, and concerns."[7]

The Feminist Press.[8] More academic than other publishers mentioned here yet still accessible, Feminist Press is based at the City University of New York. In the 1970s Feminist Press was instrumental in publishing and promoting classic but neglected feminist icons such as Charlotte Perkins Gilman. They continue to champion diverse feminist authors from all over the world.

Green Dragon Press.[9] Based in Canada, this is a good resource for American librarians searching English language material from beyond U.S. borders. In addition to books, Green Dragon Press has other media such as posters and curriculum support materials that can be incorporated into programming at school and public libraries as well as classrooms.

Orca Books.[10] Also based in Canada, independent publisher Orca Books publishes books from board books through adult books, with a good representation of female protagonists and authors, historical figures, and accessible fiction with progressive themes.

Lee & Low Books.[11] Early pioneers in promoting multi-cultural books for children and youth, in addition to their racially and ethnically diverse catalog, Lee & Low publishes books that challenge gender stereotypes.

Other Resources

Amelia Bloomer Project.[12] A project of the Feminist Task Force of the Social Responsibilities Round Table of the American Library Association, the charge of the Amelia Bloomer Project is to create an annual list of recently published recommended feminist books, fiction and non-fiction, for all ages up to 18. ABP lists are practical and often inspiring tools for librarians, teachers, parents, and readers to find books vetted by a committee of nine. The list is annotated and does not have a set number of books so varies in length year to year, but always has a Top Ten List. The list is broken down into three age groups and divided into fiction/non-fiction for each group, making it easy to navigate and use as a resource to recommend books to specific readers. Often the lists reflect the political and cultural tone of the specific year, with a theme emerging either because of current events or the year's publishing trends. The list can always be relied on to represent a broad understanding of feminism, as the committees are made up of members from different backgrounds and generations, as well as different types of libraries. The project maintains the Wordpress blog referenced above as well as a public group on Facebook. Nominations are posted on these sites throughout the year so it is easy to have a pulse on what the committee is reading even before the annotated list appears in January of each year.

A Mighty Girl.[13] Self-described as "the world's largest collection of books, toys and movies for smart, confident, and courageous girls,"[14] this project promotes media highlighting current and historic personalities and narratives exemplifying empowered girls and women. A Mighty Girl is active on social media, so busy librarians can easily follow them without having to go to the website regularly for information, although that is also a good resource.

Bitch Media.[15] Bitch Media is "a nonprofit, independent, feminist media organization dedicated to providing and encouraging an engaged, thoughtful feminist response to mainstream media and popular culture."[16] They publish a magazine, a weekly digest of online articles, podcasts, and more. There are always book and movie reviews from a feminist perspective as well as more broad coverage of feminist issues that might also inform collection development decisions. Bitch Media has a sensibility that appeals to a demographic that is hard to coax into libraries, young adults who are out of school and working but are not parents. Staying in touch with what Bitch is covering provides clues to librarians for materials and themes with appeal to these potential patrons.

Ms. Magazine.[17] The iconic magazine started in 1972 and is now published by the Feminist Majority Foundation. Print and online versions of the magazine exist, as well as a blog and social media presence. *Ms.* book reviews cover many genres, sometimes include Young Adult books as well as adult books, and are a reliable source for recently published books with feminist credibility.

Women in Libraries.[18] Women in Libraries is published online by the American Library Association Social Responsibilities Round Table Feminist Task Force. It includes book reviews of adult books, fiction and non-fiction, with feminist topics. This is a good source for academic women's studies material, but the scope of its reviews is not limited to those.

Our Shared Shelf.[19] Actress and activist Emma Watson has started a virtual feminist book club via Goodreads. Anyone can join (close to 100,000 people worldwide already have as of this writing), and the format is to discuss one book per month. Following what books the club is reading as well as scanning the many comments for suggestions for other books will give a collection development librarian a good sense of what their patrons who identify as feminist will be looking for at the library. This could be an excellent tie-in for programming as well. Watson is a household name and face and brings intelligent, young, celebrity cache to feminism in a way that is appealing to teens. Having a library book club reading and discussing the books as they are featured in Our Shared Shelf would be one way to incorporate this into local programming. Watson also has Our Shared Shelf events that could be attended virtually from the local library or shown later as part of a program. The first of these is a sold out interview in London between Watson and Gloria Steinem, whose 2015 book *My Life on the Road* was the inaugural book for Our Shared Shelf. The video of the interview will be uploaded to Our Shared Shelf.

There are several social media sites and websites focused on feminist books and feminism in libraries. Two examples are Feminist Librarian,[20] and Feminist Library on Wheels.[21] These often have discussions of books as well as links and references to other resources relevant to feminist media. They are also often quite funny, irreverent, and opinionated, good to share with teens.

Programming and Conference Ideas

Many libraries provide programming and displays for Women's History Month in March. Ways to liven that up and make it more engaging to young people, boys as well as girls, self-identified feminists and others, is to partner with organizations and people outside of the library. Examples of this are to bring in local women who do diverse types of jobs: an entrepreneur, an astronaut, a dogsledder, an athlete, an artist, various kinds of scientists. There are many book tie-ins for various jobs, and using the resources above, librarians can find newly published books to present that are likely to be unfamiliar to patrons.

Collaboration is key here, as local individuals as well as organizations may be available to provide unique perspectives and narratives form their own experience. A local example here in Vermont is Vermont Works for Women,[22] an organization that "helps women and girls recognize their potential and explore, pursue, and excel in work that leads to economic independence."[23] Program collaborations as well as collection selections that support the work of organizations like this strengthen the library collection as well as community connections.

Many libraries have permanent or pop-up Maker Spaces and technology programs. These are great opportunities to bring in women mentors with unique skills in specific areas to inspire and teach less experienced people of different ages and genders. There are several national and in many areas local organizations dedicated to encouraging and mentoring girls in coding and other STEM areas. "Girls Who Code" is a "national non-profit organization working to close the gender gap in the technology and engineering sectors."[24] The organization offers a structure for local Girls Who Code clubs and volunteering. These could be spearheaded or at least on location at school or public libraries. Similarly, Girl Develop It[25] is a national organization with local chapters in more than 50 cities, and the opportunity to start more. Their focus is also expanding technology education and experiences to girls. If starting or hosting regular meetings of groups like this is beyond the staffing, space, or even interest of libraries, one-day workshops are a possibility, or information sessions so patrons know what resources are available in their communities. As always with library programming, related print and digital resources available at the library can be highlighted during the programs.

"Sisters in Crime" is an organization with worldwide membership whose mission is to "promote the ongoing advancement, recognition and professional development of women crime writers."[26] This is not only a resource for women mystery writers, but their writers are also available at very reasonable fees to do library visits. This is a good entry point for readers of mysteries to enjoy an author visit and also get perspective on women writers in the publishing world. Discussion points with Sisters in Crime authors could range from the female characters of their books to their experiences as women authors and even to the feminization of mystery as a genre.

A good resource for ideas, Inter Library Loan, and potential program collaboration is the department of Gender and Women's Studies at a local university or college if there is one. Some institutions have special libraries dedicated to this department, and most will likely have a larger, more comprehensive collection of feminist materials than a public library. Some universities also have outreach librarians, so tapping into their work as a way to reach out to high school students or adults for special events related to gender issues could be an asset to both organizations and the community.

There are opportunities to plan and/or attend programs with feminist content at American Library Association conferences as well as state library associations. The Feminist Task Force of ALA has meetings at the Annual conference and is often looking for people to take on or update projects. They sometimes offer Feminist Night at the Movies, which is a chance not just for movie watching, but also for post-film discussion. These movie nights could easily be replicated at a public library and at the very least can be referenced for ideas about what movies to purchase for collections. The Amelia Bloomer Project often presents authors featured on their recommended book list, sometimes in conjunction with the Rainbow Book List Committee,[27] which is charged with creating an annual book list of recommended GLBTQ fiction and nonfiction titles for young readers from birth through age 18.

A key component to remember when hosting authors, whether at conferences or locally is to be specific about what you as the host want the focus of the content and tone to be. Sometimes authors write what to a reader with a feminist perspective reads as an empowering narrative of groundbreaking, stereotype-breaking anthem, without necessarily intending for it to be read in that way. It's OK to ask them to hit on feminist talking points, particularly if you want to emphasize certain topics because of your anticipated audience, because it's Women's History Month, or you want to inspire attendees to think of a book in a new way. This can kick off some pretty amazing and unexpected conversations!

Conclusion

Feminism conjures up complex reactions: inspiring, empowering and positive for some, but unfortunately sometimes negative for others. For a concept that so embraces inclusion, it can too often be off-putting to men and boys or women who choose not to self-identify with the "label," even when sometimes their lives exemplify some aspects of feminism. Part of the inclusive mission of libraries can be applied to this by making collections and programming informative yet entertaining, accessible and interesting. Building a comprehensive feminist collection means honoring historical movements such as the suffrage movement, the important work of Second Wave Feminists, intersectional feminism, eco-feminism, and more: in other words, the complexities of 21st century feminism.

Rather than display and promote scholarly textbooks about women's history, show teens and adults alike the wonderfully engaging *Notorious RBG: the Life and Times of Ruth Bader Ginsburg*, the 2015 book by Irin Carmon and Shana Knizhnik based on their Tumblr project that helped make Ginsburg an internet star and a household name to a new generation while also highlighting her enormous legal and cultural influence.

Content created by young women is being shared through traditional publishing avenues as well as online, often starting online first and then being picked up by mainstream publishers. Supporting this effort through collection development will carve a connection to library patrons, especially but not only young women. So make sure Tavi Gevinson's *Rookie Yearbooks* are in your collection, or Petra Collins' collection of photography by young female artists, *Babe*. Programming tie-ins abound with these celebrations of creativity manifested through the written word, art, editing, and creating and sharing of content.

The specific materials, the Tavi Gevinsons of the current time, or the internet stardom of icons like Ruth Bader Ginsburg will shift with time, but libraries will remain in a unique position to create and curate inclusive, diverse collections, and to offer programs that promote social awareness. Dedicating one month a year to women's history is a meagre start, an unsatisfactory nod toward inclusion. Instead try treating feminist content as an integral part of collection development and programming as an opportunity to demarginalize feminism. Focusing on feminism and promoting its ideals and representations in books, movies, digital content and other library materials to all patrons, regardless of age or gender, is a powerful method for libraries to remain current and broaden their impact on society.

NOTES

1. https://urldefense.proofpoint.com/v2/url?u=http-3A__weneeddiversebooks.org&d=DQIFaQ&c=euGZstcaTDllvimEN8b7jXrwqOf-v5A_CdpgnVfiiMM&r=FuC2bgPKWy3lyLSFzYGLuQ&m=6FhfammyCv-5uOV716B7Y8lHlIurRlGoTBv602IrP4g&s=CmzK_QTpJckfCPqfbM3ioMzjwcBNjJ2V9l0rL3Y4y7M&e=

2. https://urldefense.proofpoint.com/v2/url?u=http-3A__weneedddiversebooks.com&d=DQIFaQ&c=euGZstcaTDllvimEN8b7jXrwqOf-v5A_CdpgnVfiiMM&r=FuC2bgPKWy3lyLSFzYGLuQ&m=6FhfammyCv-5uOV716B7Y8lHlIurRlGoTBv602IrP4g&s=RU0XXO2YV6ez5xj6qMesr3e7uHUeoicgg7yTLgGYJXk&e=

3. https://urldefense.proofpoint.com/v2/url?u=http-3A__ameliabloomerproject.wordpress.com&d=DQIFaQ&c=euGZstcaTDllvimEN8b7jXrwqOf-v5A_CdpgnVfiiMM&r=FuC2bgPKWy3lyLSFzYGLuQ&m=6FhfammyCv-5uOV716B7Y8lHlIurRlGoTBv602IrP4g&s=Osy2TP2uYSBOsYxSqQYMEiXntebOTXoaDJxOi-bCFa_c&e=

4. https://urldefense.proofpoint.com/v2/url?u=http-3A__www.library.wisc.edu_gwslibrarian_&d=DQIFaQ&c=euGZstcaTDllvimEN8b7jXrwqOf-v5A_CdpgnVfiiMM&r=FuC2bgPKWy3lyLSFzYGLuQ&m=6FhfammyCv-5uOV716B7Y8lHlIurRlGoTBv602IrP4g&s=JkLtXZB2RMaldKlPaJ_kL_TnTxbPyBfD-KbmK1wsxeY&e=

5. https://urldefense.proofpoint.com/v2/url?u=http-3A__secondstorypress.ca&d=DQIFaQ&c=euGZstcaTDllvimEN8b7jXrwqOf-v5A_CdpgnVfiiMM&r=FuC2bgPKWy3lyLSFzYGLuQ&m=6FhfammyCv-5uOV716B7Y8lHlIurRlGoTBv602IrP4g&s=XpesDY3H5Dy685098MEhhEjBeWVcOs2YObmVJZErjGk&e=

6. https://urldefense.proofpoint.com/v2/url?u=http-3A__sealpress.com&d=DQIFaQ&c=euGZstcaTDllvimEN8b7jXrwqOf-v5A_CdpgnVfiiMM&r=FuC2bgPKWy3lyLSFzYGLuQ&m=6FhfammyCv-5uOV716B7Y8lHlIurRlGoTBv602IrP4g&s=-urBXuoUNrda_IwPoYadQDc9xq5e8UFQlVQYP83XshE&e=

7. https://urldefense.proofpoint.com/v2/url?u=http-3A__sealpress.com&d=DQIFaQ&c=euGZstcaTDllvimEN8b7jXrwqOf-v5A_CdpgnVfiiMM&r=FuC2bgPKWy3lyLSFzYGLuQ&m=6FhfammyCv-5uOV716B7Y8lHlIurRlGoTBv602IrP4g&s=-urBXuoUNrda_IwPoYadQDc9xq5e8UFQlVQYP83XshE&e=

8. https://urldefense.proofpoint.com/v2/url?u=http-3A__feministpress.org&d=DQIFaQ&c=euGZstcaTDllvimEN8b7jXrwqOf-v5A_CdpgnVfiiMM&r=FuC2bgPKWy3lyLSFzYGLuQ&m=6FhfammyCv-5uOV716B7Y8lHlIurRlGoTBv602IrP4g&s=FFcsaoB3xeChzyLSjAtGgk8reMHrtd00Ogc_ahyw0lw&e=

9. https://urldefense.proofpoint.com/v2/url?u=http-3A__greendragonpress.com&d=DQIFaQ&c=euGZstcaTDllvimEN8b7jXrwqOf-v5A_CdpgnVfiiMM&r=FuC2bgPKWy3lyLSFzYGLuQ&m=6FhfammyCv-5uOV716B7Y81HlIurRlGoTBv602IrP4g&s=k3d9ik_i8MWz2czDvJ-xys6OeghA0tziiUs6T01YzqE&e=

10. https://urldefense.proofpoint.com/v2/url?u=http-3A__orcabook.com&d=DQIFaQ&c=euGZstcaTDllvimEN8b7jXrwqOf-v5A_CdpgnVfiiMM&r=FuC2bgPKWy3lyLSFzYGLuQ&m=6FhfammyCv-5uOV716B7Y81HlIurRlGoTBv602IrP4g&s=jT-nJKDSellz2RRsrX2kFV8sIMK_rlwsXCH1Nppt2YY&e=

11. https://urldefense.proofpoint.com/v2/url?u=http-3A__www.leeandlow.com&d=DQIFaQ&c=euGZstcaTDllvimEN8b7jXrwqOf-v5A_CdpgnVfiiMM&r=FuC2bgPKWy3lyLSFzYGLuQ&m=6FhfammyCv-5uOV716B7Y81HlIurRlGoTBv602IrP4g&s=VluvNAClkU0GhDaxrFarSsNCl5_OTJ_qii92ulo442c&e=

12. https://urldefense.proofpoint.com/v2/url?u=https-3A__ameliabloomer.wordpress.com&d=DQIFaQ&c=euGZstcaTDllvimEN8b7jXrwqOf-v5A_CdpgnVfiiMM&r=FuC2bgPKWy3lyLSFzYGLuQ&m=6FhfammyCv-5uOV716B7Y81HlIurRlGoTBv602IrP4g&s=aKAwbF6xUgrZirrHvTZ6TMsiCOLuiD3q4CxJ0fTOBI4&e=

13. https://urldefense.proofpoint.com/v2/url?u=http-3A__www.amightygirl.com&d=DQIFaQ&c=euGZstcaTDllvimEN8b7jXrwqOf-v5A_CdpgnVfiiMM&r=FuC2bgPKWy3lyLSFzYGLuQ&m=6FhfammyCv-5uOV716B7Y81HlIurRlGoTBv602IrP4g&s=BxyXvBGJPbnfh2NvYRtgqJwBC2ftCbN4CiHSw_ZisHw&e=

14. https://urldefense.proofpoint.com/v2/url?u=http-3A__www.amightygirl.com&d=DQIFaQ&c=euGZstcaTDllvimEN8b7jXrwqOf-v5A_CdpgnVfiiMM&r=FuC2bgPKWy3lyLSFzYGLuQ&m=6FhfammyCv-5uOV716B7Y81HlIurRlGoTBv602IrP4g&s=BxyXvBGJPbnfh2NvYRtgqJwBC2ftCbN4CiHSw_ZisHw&e=

15. https://urldefense.proofpoint.com/v2/url?u=https-3A__bitchmedia.org&d=DQIFaQ&c=euGZstcaTDllvimEN8b7jXrwqOf-v5A_CdpgnVfiiMM&r=FuC2bgPKWy3lyLSFzYGLuQ&m=6FhfammyCv-5uOV716B7Y81HlIurRlGoTBv602IrP4g&s=uBAM7FMrI69vG8bKGdKRiVbDdQ3_TphYc3hxD2VO5FI&e=

16. https://urldefense.proofpoint.com/v2/url?u=http-3A__bitchmedia.org&d=DQIFaQ&c=euGZstcaTDllvimEN8b7jXrwqOf-v5A_CdpgnVfiiMM&r=FuC2bgPKWy3lyLSFzYGLuQ&m=6FhfammyCv-5uOV716B7Y81HlIurRlGoTBv602IrP4g&s=N51DU72Guqv7uWZ8cpa6Pef1O3hCmqnWkbb7M5MHOVM&e=

17. https://urldefense.proofpoint.com/v2/url?u=http-3A__www.msmagazine.com&d=DQIFaQ&c=euGZstcaTDllvimEN8b7jXrwqOf-v5A_CdpgnVfiiMM&r=FuC2bgPKWy3lyLSFzYGLuQ&m=6FhfammyCv-5uOV716B7Y81HlIurRlGoTBv602IrP4g&s=WZ9weBmuRQqGEKiW3Fzn8qF8HDI5fnoTsEiy4nfMZzI&e=

18. https://urldefense.proofpoint.com/v2/url?u=https-3A__ftinfo.wikispaces.com_Women-2Bin-2BLibraries&d=DQIFaQ&c=euGZstcaTDllvimEN8b7jXrwqOf-v5A_CdpgnVfiiMM&r=FuC2bgPKWy3lyLSFzYGLuQ&m=6FhfammyCv-5uOV716B7Y81HlIurRlGoTBv602IrP4g&s=Q6hcKCuYvcz3YU4SLZIJvlUMOtQVttfGQb7wvfF3jUM&e=

19. https://urldefense.proofpoint.com/v2/url?u=https-3A__www.goodreads.com_group_show_179584-2Dour-2Dshared-2Dshelf&d=DQIFaQ&c=euGZstcaTDllvimEN8b7jXrwqOf-v5A_CdpgnVfiiMM&r=FuC2bgPKWy3lyLSFzYGLuQ&m=6FhfammyCv-5uOV716B7Y81HlIurRlGoTBv602IrP4g&s=pTjRzlx_UXdbdVGPq8CfejZYpL6PQ5EoPOt_qhtzUJQ&e=

20. https://urldefense.proofpoint.com/v2/url?u=https-3A__www.facebook.com_librariansunite_&d=DQIFaQ&c=euGZstcaTDllvimEN8b7jXrwqOf-v5A_CdpgnVfiiMM&r=FuC2bgPKWy3lyLSFzYGLuQ&m=6FhfammyCv-5uOV716B7Y81HlIurRlGoTBv602IrP4g&s=Z5qOhP2BIGjLmUTNLD4t8KBy__aop8—tuQQ7EW-3FE&e=

21. https://urldefense.proofpoint.com/v2/url?u=http-3A__feministlibraryonwheels.com_&d=DQIFaQ&c=euGZstcaTDllvimEN8b7jXrwqOf-v5A_CdpgnVfiiMM&r=FuC2bgPKWy3lyLSFzYGLuQ&m=6FhfammyCv-5uOV716B7Y81HlIurRlGoTBv602IrP4g&s=6Pk7LOc8xnwcWVBK0W2lF9R7mIeLWTd_4Ipj1NKSGnA&e=

22. https://urldefense.proofpoint.com/v2/url?u=http-3A__vtworksforwomen.org&d=DQIFaQ&c=euGZstcaTDllvimEN8b7jXrwqOf-v5A_CdpgnVfiiMM&r=FuC2bgPKWy3lyLSFzYGLuQ&m=6FhfammyCv-5uOV716B7Y81HlIurRlGoTBv602IrP4g&s=Tde1qKGA9SjJijN5iUQSr7HLXMqKgiJDahrW2mfZguY&e=

23. https://urldefense.proofpoint.com/v2/url?u=http-3A__vtworksforwomen.org&d=DQIFaQ&c=euGZstcaTDllvimEN8b7jXrwqOf-v5A_CdpgnVfiiMM&r=FuC2bgPKWy3lyLSFzYGLuQ&m=6FhfammyCv-5uOV716B7Y81HlIurRlGoTBv602IrP4g&s=Tde1qKGA9SjJijN5iUQSr7HLXMqKgiJDahrW2mfZguY&e=

24. https://urldefense.proofpoint.com/v2/url?u=http-3A__girlswhocode.com&d=DQIFaQ&c=euGZstcaTDllvimEN8b7jXrwqOf-v5A_CdpgnVfiiMM&r=FuC2bgPKWy3lyLSFzYGLuQ&m=6FhfammyCv-5uOV716B7Y81HlIurRlGoTBv602IrP4g&s=SHqC-nY00SHE72QiK9BI9sCwAwA1TojJyU7tKiHSyG4&e=

25. https://urldefense.proofpoint.com/v2/url?u=https-3A__www.girldevelopit.com_&d=DQIFaQ&c=euGZstcaTDllvimEN8b7jXrwqOf-v5A_CdpgnVfiiMM&r=FuC2bgPKWy3lyLSFzYGLuQ&m=6FhfammyCv-5uOV716B7Y81HlIurRlGoTBv602IrP4g&s=PR1iGPk2lR1hxnEhTsyoI0jePI6CrPrL0J2yCXpct-4&e=

26. https://urldefense.proofpoint.com/v2/url?u=http-3A__www.sistersincrime.org&d=DQIFaQ&c=euGZstcaTDllvimEN8b7jXrwqOf-v5A_CdpgnVfiiMM&r=FuC2bgPKWy3lyLSFzYGLuQ&m=6FhfammyCv-5uOV716B7Y81HlIurRlGoTBv602IrP4g&s=08BYupVcieWUi7iEnHI_azxELE-cRi8T6viuzjHBkn0&e=

27. https://urldefense.proofpoint.com/v2/url?u=http-3A__glbtrt.ala.org_rainbowbooks_archives_1207&d=DQIFaQ&c=euGZstcaTDllvimEN8b7jXrwqOf-v5A_CdpgnVfiiMM&r=FuC2bgPKWy3lyLSFzYGLuQ&m=6FhfammyCv-5uOV716B7Y81HlIurRlGoTBv602IrP4g&s=e1tmuwgviSz6WXFptzv3YvU3gPVlC4ls9MBGfw6hAoc&e=

REFERENCES

Amelia Bloomer Project. Blog. February 3, 2016, https://urldefense.proofpoint.com/v2/url?u=http-3A__ameliabloomer.wordpress.com&d=DQIFaQ&c=euGZstcaTDllvimEN8b7jXrwqOf-v5A_CdpgnVfii MM&r=FuC2bgPKWy3lyLSFzYGLuQ&m=6FhfammyCv-5uOV716B7Y81HlIurRlGoTBv602IrP4g&s= WGJYJ9nW1Mgb6Q3x6YX5kFtQBr0prBmm-nYsodnQR6M&e=.

American Library Association. https://urldefense.proofpoint.com/v2/url?u=http-3A__www.ala.org_&d= DQIFaQ&c=euGZstcaTDllvimEN8b7jXrwqOf-v5A_CdpgnVfiiMM&r=FuC2bgPKWy3lyLSFzYG LuQ&m=6FhfammyCv-5uOV716B7Y81HlIurRlGoTBv602IrP4g&s=ONxIG1yuZBnMAv9fcHo75tEPnge A3mFbD130mZfRiJk&e=.

Bitch Media. https://urldefense.proofpoint.com/v2/url?u=https-3A__bitchmedia.org_&d=DQIFaQ&c= euGZstcaTDllvimEN8b7jXrwqOf-v5A_CdpgnVfiiMM&r=FuC2bgPKWy3lyLSFzYGLuQ&m= 6FhfammyCv-5uOV716B7Y81HlIurRlGoTBv602IrP4g&s=OYl8irubCrT-hmsCL0W7pX80xmg2Bu10x DxY_15wiME&e=.

Booklist 111, no. 14 (2015).

Carmon, Irin, and Shana Knizhnik. *The Notorious RBG: the Life and Times of Ruth Bader Ginsburg.* New York: HarperCollins: 2015.

Collins, Petra, ed. *Babe.* New York: Prestel, 2015.

Feminist Librarian's Facebook page. https://urldefense.proofpoint.com/v2/url?u=https-3A__www.facebook. com_librariansunite_&d=DQIFaQ&c=euGZstcaTDllvimEN8b7jXrwqOf-v5A_CdpgnVfiiMM&r= FuC2bgPKWy3lyLSFzYGLuQ&m=6FhfammyCv-5uOV716B7Y81HlIurRlGoTBv602IrP4g&s=Z5qOhP2 BIGjLmUTNLD4t8KBy__aop8—tuQQ7EW-3FE&e=.

Feminist Library on Wheels. https://urldefense.proofpoint.com/v2/url?u=http-3A__feministlibraryonwheels. com_&d=DQIFaQ&c=euGZstcaTDllvimEN8b7jXrwqOf-v5A_CdpgnVfiiMM&r=FuC2bgPKWy3lyLSF zYGLuQ&m=6FhfammyCv-5uOV716B7Y81HlIurRlGoTBv602IrP4g&s=6Pk7LOc8xnwcWVBK0W2lF 9R7mIeLWTd_4Ipj1NKSGnA&e=.

The Feminist Press. https://urldefense.proofpoint.com/v2/url?u=http-3A__www.feministpress.org_&d= DQIFaQ&c=euGZstcaTDllvimEN8b7jXrwqOf-v5A_CdpgnVfiiMM&r=FuC2bgPKWy3lyLSFzYGLuQ& m=6FhfammyCv-5uOV716B7Y81HlIurRlGoTBv602IrP4g&s=dBljBA7bhTxBNNOlsdtUIiGsZPyPMUCz VFlVdt946mc&e=.

Gevinson, Tavi. *Rookie Yearbook Four.* New York: Razorbill, 2015.

Girl Develop It. https://urldefense.proofpoint.com/v2/url?u=https-3A__www.girldevelopit.com&d=DQIFa Q&c=euGZstcaTDllvimEN8b7jXrwqOf-v5A_CdpgnVfiiMM&r=FuC2bgPKWy3lyLSFzYGLuQ&m= 6FhfammyCv-5uOV716B7Y81HlIurRlGoTBv602IrP4g&s=KB9ECN3VuWZ5ibbsOiMN41PveOXvMihH KZIAsBJG6Rg&e=.

Girls Who Code. https://urldefense.proofpoint.com/v2/url?u=http-3A__girlswhocode.com&d=DQIFaQ&c= euGZstcaTDllvimEN8b7jXrwqOf-v5A_CdpgnVfiiMM&r=FuC2bgPKWy3lyLSFzYGLuQ&m=6Fh fammyCv-5uOV716B7Y81HlIurRlGoTBv602IrP4g&s=SHqC-nY00SHE72QiK9BI9sCwAwA1TojJyU7tKi HSyG4&e=.

Green Dragon Press. https://urldefense.proofpoint.com/v2/url?u=http-3A__greendragonpress.com&d= DQIFaQ&c=euGZstcaTDllvimEN8b7jXrwqOf-v5A_CdpgnVfiiMM&r=FuC2bgPKWy3lyLSFzYGLuQ& m=6FhfammyCv-5uOV716B7Y81HlIurRlGoTBv602IrP4g&s=k3d9ik_i8MWz2czDvJ-xys6OeghA0tzii Us6T01YzqE&e=.

Lee & Low Books. https://urldefense.proofpoint.com/v2/url?u=https-3A__www.leeandlow.com&d=DQIF aQ&c=euGZstcaTDllvimEN8b7jXrwqOf-v5A_CdpgnVfiiMM&r=FuC2bgPKWy3lyLSFzYGLuQ&m= 6FhfammyCv-5uOV716B7Y81HlIurRlGoTBv602IrP4g&s=sCzKvGgabnx93bRl06R6IW1Yldx75wcJZmzu 5QaBY74&e=.

A Mighty Girl. https://urldefense.proofpoint.com/v2/url?u=http-3A__www.amightygirl.com_&d=DQIFaQ &c=euGZstcaTDllvimEN8b7jXrwqOf-v5A_CdpgnVfiiMM&r=FuC2bgPKWy3lyLSFzYGLuQ&m= 6FhfammyCv-5uOV716B7Y81HlIurRlGoTBv602IrP4g&s=Bqeg06kXlIEuuH718TU-BOeHG8kWUov2t 5h34RgeVd4&e=.

Ms. Magazine Online. https://urldefense.proofpoint.com/v2/url?u=http-3A__www.msmagazine.com&d= DQIFaQ&c=euGZstcaTDllvimEN8b7jXrwqOf-v5A_CdpgnVfiiMM&r=FuC2bgPKWy3lyLSFzYGLuQ& m=6FhfammyCv-5uOV716B7Y81HlIurRlGoTBv602IrP4g&s=WZ9weBmuRQqGEKiW3Fzn8qF8HDI5 fnoTsEiy4nfMZzI&e=.

Orca Books. https://urldefense.proofpoint.com/v2/url?u=http-3A__www.orcabooks.com&d=DQIFaQ&c= euGZstcaTDllvimEN8b7jXrwqOf-v5A_CdpgnVfiiMM&r=FuC2bgPKWy3lyLSFzYGLuQ&m= 6FhfammyCv-5uOV716B7Y81HlIurRlGoTBv602IrP4g&s=eyBxBuFHdhU6kw3tFYs6tKhpa_hiW2r7M XwPV_4H9MI&e=.

Our Shared Shelf. https://urldefense.proofpoint.com/v2/url?u=https-3A__www.goodreads.com_group_show_ 179584-2Dour-2Dshared-2Dshelf&d=DQIFaQ&c=euGZstcaTDllvimEN8b7jXrwqOf-v5A_CdpgnVfii MM&r=FuC2bgPKWy3lyLSFzYGLuQ&m=6FhfammyCv-5uOV716B7Y81HlIurRlGoTBv602IrP4g&s= pTjRzlx_UXdbdVGPq8CfejZYpL6PQ5EoPOt_qhtzUJQ&e=.

Rainbow Book List List. https://urldefense.proofpoint.com/v2/url?u=http-3A__glbtrt.ala.org_rainbowbooks_&d=DQIFaQ&c=euGZstcaTDllvimEN8b7jXrwqOf-v5A_CdpgnVfiiMM&r=FuC2bgPKWy3lyLSFzYGLuQ&m=6FhfammyCv-5uOV716B7Y81HlIurRlGoTBv602IrP4g&s=Mp8I0GpSJpZHz0J_1R3HsBdSJXA04h5f5bfo0bSlu0w&e=.

Seal Press. https://urldefense.proofpoint.com/v2/url?u=http-3A__sealpress.com_&d=DQIFaQ&c=euGZstcaTDllvimEN8b7jXrwqOf-v5A_CdpgnVfiiMM&r=FuC2bgPKWy3lyLSFzYGLuQ&m=6FhfammyCv-5uOV716B7Y81HlIurRlGoTBv602IrP4g&s=jM0BuPqrv9zDKoNobaBPmrSy39STcUBBslNf-Nl3uk4&e=.

Second Story Press. https://urldefense.proofpoint.com/v2/url?u=http-3A__secondstorypress.ca_&d=DQIFaQ&c=euGZstcaTDllvimEN8b7jXrwqOf-v5A_CdpgnVfiiMM&r=FuC2bgPKWy3lyLSFzYGLuQ&m=6FhfammyCv-5uOV716B7Y81HlIurRlGoTBv602IrP4g&s=kfzlfwPE6UAHcz7P1pnNFvGHzasUw4IyIuD7UwgSHo8&e=.

Sisters in Crime. https://urldefense.proofpoint.com/v2/url?u=http-3A__www.sistersincrime.org_&d=DQIFaQ&c=euGZstcaTDllvimEN8b7jXrwqOf-v5A_CdpgnVfiiMM&r=FuC2bgPKWy3lyLSFzYGLuQ&m=6FhfammyCv-5uOV716B7Y81HlIurRlGoTBv602IrP4g&s=ZUSBRu-3G9fKBsJ10KDaqcCKTl7jQo2SC13Nah49G0k&e=.

Steinem, Gloria. *My Life on the Road*. New York: Random House, 2015.

University of Wisconsin–Madison Office of the Gender and Women's Studies Librarian. https://urldefense.proofpoint.com/v2/url?u=https-3A__www.library.wisc.edu_gwslibrarian_&d=DQIFaQ&c=euGZstcaTDllvimEN8b7jXrwqOf-v5A_CdpgnVfiiMM&r=FuC2bgPKWy3lyLSFzYGLuQ&m=6FhfammyCv-5uOV716B7Y81HlIurRlGoTBv602IrP4g&s=Mr4CxsR4eQkswsUFkzx4kskRR6TKsmFNWBfiaZCihBo&e=.

Vermont Works for Women. https://urldefense.proofpoint.com/v2/url?u=http-3A__vtworksforwomen.org_&d=DQIFaQ&c=euGZstcaTDllvimEN8b7jXrwqOf-v5A_CdpgnVfiiMM&r=FuC2bgPKWy3lyLSFzYGLuQ&m=6FhfammyCv-5uOV716B7Y81HlIurRlGoTBv602IrP4g&s=Iqx_HtyxCbzrXheRBIOD6r5mDCJjthA1-3zYzFa9IpQ&e=.

We Need Diverse Books. https://urldefense.proofpoint.com/v2/url?u=http-3A__weneeddiversebooks.org_&d=DQIFaQ&c=euGZstcaTDllvimEN8b7jXrwqOf-v5A_CdpgnVfiiMM&r=FuC2bgPKWy3lyLSFzYGLuQ&m=6FhfammyCv-5uOV716B7Y81HlIurRlGoTBv602IrP4g&s=bxTJ-b211SOqhm4JddZg4jKayBsQ_GXaters2YX-YV0&e=.

Women in Libraries. https://urldefense.proofpoint.com/v2/url?u=https-3A__ftfinfo.wikispaces.com_Women-2Bin-2BLibraries&d=DQIFaQ&c=euGZstcaTDllvimEN8b7jXrwqOf-v5A_CdpgnVfiiMM&r=FuC2bgPKWy3lyLSFzYGLuQ&m=6FhfammyCv-5uOV716B7Y81HlIurRlGoTBv602IrP4g&s=Q6hcKCuYvcz3YU4SLZIJvlUMOtQVttfGQb7wvfF3jUM&e=.

Partnering Across Campus to Engage the LGBTQ+ Community

ANTHONY WRIGHT DE HERNANDEZ
and SAMANTHA R. WINN

This essay will provide guidance on improving outreach and collection development to LGBTQ+ constituents based on the experiences of two University Libraries faculty at Virginia Tech. Virginia Tech is a Research 1 university and public land-grant institution located on the eastern edge of the Appalachian region. The University Libraries comprise four public-serving branches: Newman Library, the main facility located in the center of campus; the Veterinary Medicine Library; the Art + Architecture Library; and the Northern Virginia Resource Center located in the National Capital Region. Across these facilities, Virginia Tech University Libraries serve a broad range of faculty, staff, student, and alumni constituents.

All University Libraries employees are expected to contribute to the University's inclusion and diversity goals in accordance with the Virginia Tech Principles of Community. The University Libraries have traditionally relied upon individual employee interest to develop ad hoc programming for LGBTQ+ focused events. This strategy resulted in several short-term collaborations across campus, but rarely translated into enduring and mutually beneficial partnerships. Key barriers to sustainability included personnel turnover and limited coordination across library departments. Since 2014, the University Libraries Diversity Council has served as a springboard for programming and outreach to cultural and identity-based communities. Diversity Council members maintain regular contact with LGBTQ+ leaders in the campus community, support library departments developing temporary programming and short-term projects, and promote events happening in the Libraries.

Hiring personnel with explicit responsibility for inclusion and diversity initiatives has further bolstered the long-term viability of outreach initiatives with LGBTQ+ communities. In October 2014, Special Collections hired a dedicated archivist to develop and manage collections related to the history of traditionally marginalized groups. A resident librarian was hired in August 2015 as part of the Diversity Alliance for Academic Librarianship. Like the collections archivist position, the resident librarian was hired with clear expectations to support inclusion and diversity initiatives across the Univdersity Libraries.

Foundations of Outreach

Assessing the institution's historic relationship with the LGBTQ+ community is an important first step. As Huddleston (2015, 28) notes, "archivists [and librarians] should examine their own institutional history, and be aware of instances that may raise concerns for LGBTQ people." It is deeply important to understand historic events on campus and in the community that have hindered trust. Conversely, previous collaborations that engendered trust can serve as springboards for future initiatives. As representatives of the institution, employees working with the LGBTQ+ community will always be accompanied by the legacy of past interactions and the broader context of campus history.

Strategies for assessing institutional history with the LGBTQ+ community Review the archives University archives can provide a wealth of information, including official correspondence and policy documents in administrative files, records of student and alumni groups, ephemera from campus events, and local newspaper coverage.

Discuss historic relations with community stakeholders Librarians should go directly to the source to learn how the community views the institution. The quickest way to find the answer is to simply ask. Librarians should be prepared for pushback or tense conversations, especially if the relationship has historically been marked by low trust. Demonstrating sincere interest, transparency, and willingness to accept critical feedback will provide a foundation for future good relations.

Conduct a Campus Climate Survey

The LGBTQ+ community is not always as visible as other traditionally marginalized communities. Gathering information from publicly active members of the community will only tell part of the story. Conducting a voluntary and anonymous survey can help to include perspectives from individuals who are not open about their status as members of the community.

Records in the Virginia Tech university archives provided a wealth of information about the institution's relationship with the LGBTQ+ community. However, the official recorded depicted a narrowly optimistic recollection weighted in favor of the administration. It was important to consider additional sources. Speaking informally with members of the faculty and staff LGBT Caucus revealed a richer and more complicated history. Several interviewees highlighted past incidents that had alienated community members. To better understand the needs of individuals who did not feel comfortable publicly identifying themselves as LGBTQ+ on campus, outreach faculty reviewed a campus climate survey conducted by the LGBT Caucus in 2014 (LGBT Caucus, 2015).

Establishing Trust

Earning the trust of the LGBTQ+ community before initiatives begin is deeply important for future success. The amount of time and effort needed to establish trust— or in some cases, restore it—will depend on the institution's legacy of interactions with the community. At Virginia Tech, outreach faculty demonstrated a desire to build mutually beneficial relationships by seeking out community leaders and sharing resources without expectations or demands. They attended open community events and meetings of LGBTQ+ organizations (with permission from the organizations); actively participated in campus inclusion and diversity workshops; and maintained regular contact with members of the LGBTQ+ community outside of formal event planning. In addition to restoring a foundation of trust in the institution, building relationships with faculty, student leaders, and active alumni allowed the outreach team to develop projects with community members who had not previously engaged with the University Libraries.

Prerequisites for employees working with the LGBTQ+ community: Knowledge of proper terminology People working with this community need to have an appropriate vocabulary to discuss the issues faced by the community. Knowing the correct terms to use is the foundation for these conversations. As in any public-facing position, individuals will also benefit from cultural competency training and multicultural communication workshops.

Familiarity with LGBTQ+ history in their community: Conducting a basic assessment of institutional history with the community is a great way to start creating a relationship. New employees should be educated about the history before beginning outreach work. It is important to continue building upon the initial assessment as new relationships and initiatives develop.

Understanding diversity within the LGBTQ+ community: "[Trans and queer students of color] have different experiences when navigating their sexual orientation and gender identity than their white counterparts. White, cisgender men have long dominated public images of the LGBTQ+ community at the expense of queer and trans folks of color" (Consortium of Higher Education LGBT Resource Professionals 2016, 3). Employees should recognize the diversity of this community and consider how the work they are doing affects various subgroups within the community.

A firm understanding of the campus climate: Knowing how members of the LGBTQ+ community feel about the climate on campus is essential to doing this work. If the community does not feel welcomed or valued, the library may find it more challenging to reach and engage with its members.

Organizational Support

Institutions committed to outreach should be prepared to invest in these efforts with time and funding. Employees who are expected to bear the financial and temporal burden of training on their own are at risk of burning out.

Personal knowledge of LGBTQ+ identities may provide a useful foundation for engagement, but administrators should not assume that LGBTQ+ employees are automatically equipped to reach the community on behalf of the institution. Regardless of individual identities, outreach employees should take time to learn about the local context and history. Attending continuing education workshops and cultural competency training hosted by campus and regional LGBTQ+ organizations can help outreach employees learn more about the community they hope to serve. Supporting employee participation in community-based workshops and educational events also allows institutions to demonstrate a desire to serve the community.

Faculty engaged in outreach for the University Libraries took advantage of several opportunities for continuing education and certification. The Virginia Tech Intercultural Engagement Center offers targeted education workshops on topics relating to the

LGBTQ+ community through its SafeZone program. Virginia Tech's University Organizational and Professional Development office provides additional training through its Diversity Development program, including workshops on the history of LGBTQ+ civil rights. In addition to edifying participating faculty, these programs provided regular opportunities to connect with campus stakeholders.

Models of Outreach

There are many ways to conduct outreach. Regardless of which model an institution chooses, it is important to remember that the library needn't do all of the work itself. Instead, the library can better engage with and serve the community by reaching out to other groups on campus already working with the LGBTQ+ community.

Examples of institutional outreach partners

- Office of Inclusion/Diversity
- Student Affairs and other student-facing service groups
- Residential Life
- LGBTQ+ student, alumni, and faculty/staff groups
- Cultural and identity-based campus centers
- Alumni Relations
- Academic Departments

Liaison Approach

Benefits:

- Liaison structure is well understood at academic institutions
- Support structure for liaisons may already exist within the library
- Community groups can build a relationship with the liaison

Drawbacks:

- Prone to a lone soldier pitfall
- May need to rebuild relationships if liaison leaves
- Not as straightforward as a traditional subject liaison role

Designating a specific liaison to work with and support the LGBTQ+ community is an easy model to adopt. It fits within existing structures at many institutions and can help to give the library a face for the LGBTQ+ community. One of the first inclusion and diversity efforts undertaken by Virginia Tech's resident librarian was to establish himself as the Diversity outreach librarian. Modeling an existing subject liaison program, the Diversity outreach librarian works directly with Virginia Tech's Intercultural Engagement Center (IEC). In this role, the resident functions as a subject liaison to various LGBTQ+ groups on campus.

Within his first year as liaison, the resident worked on various projects to help establish the library as a partner for projects benefiting the LGBTQ+ community. He partnered with the University Libraries Diversity Council, the IEC's LGBTQ community advocate, the SafeZone program, the LGBT Caucus, the LGBTQ+ Center, and HokiePRIDE on initiatives designed to support the LGBTQ+ community.

Examples of Partnering as Liaison

IEC LGBTQ Community Advocate, LGBT Caucus, Ex Lapide Society (LGBTQ+ alumni network), University Libraries Diversity Council: One of the resident's first projects was to promote an event showcasing a new LGBTQ+ oral history collection within the University Archives. By targeting advertising to relevant communities and existing advocates, word of the project reached those most impacted by it. This type of outreach attracted the attention of both the *Collegiate Times*, the campus newspaper, and *The Interloper*, Virginia Tech's LGBTQ magazine, resulting in favorable stories about the Libraries' support for the LGBTQ+ community.

SafeZone, University Libraries Diversity Council: To engage further with the campus LGBTQ+ community, the resident completed SafeZone training and became a SafeZone facilitator. The SafeZone program invites all members of the campus community to learn basic information about LGBTQ+ identities with the goal of creating a supportive environment. The 101 session is often the first introduction non–LGBTQ+ individuals receive to concepts in sexuality studies and varied personal identities. As a facilitator for the program, the resident led SafeZone 101 sessions in the main library and arranged for the library to host additional sessions. He also worked with the University Libraries Diversity Council to include two sessions as part of the University Libraries' professional development day. As a result, 50 new library employees became SafeZone certified.

LGBT Caucus, LGBTQ+ Center: The resident partnered with the LGBT Caucus to support a petition for the creation of an LGBTQ+ Center. The petition was successful and the new center opened in fall 2016. The new center coordinates both HokiePRIDE, the student LGBTQ+ organization, and the LGBT Caucus. Taking initiative to establish a strong partnership with the University Libraries from the outset, the resident hosted a meeting with the center's newly hired director and the chair of the University Libraries Diversity Council to offer library support for any center initiatives.

HokiePRIDE: Most liaisons focus on supporting faculty and academic departments, but liaison work for the LGBTQ+ community includes providing direct support to student groups. In this capacity, the resident reached out to the president of HokiePRIDE to suggest library spaces for the group to meet and encourage the group to include its historic records in the university archives. The resident also recommended tools and methods to help the group manage its own library of resources.

Collection Development Approach

Benefits:

- LGBTQ+ users can find resources across a broad spectrum of disciplines and topics
- Diverse research collections support a more inclusive environment on campus
- More research on LGBTQ+ issues can be conducted

Drawbacks:

- Harder to reach community stakeholders
- Requires more monetary investment
- Requires significant buy-in from various members of the library faculty

Library collections, both circulating and archival, provide another method for reaching the LGBTQ+ community. In contrast to the traditional model of collection development for academic programs, Vince Graziano notes that collecting for the LGBTQ+ "requires a collaborative collection development strategy" among several subject specialists

(Graziano 2016, 124). This approach allows libraries to incorporate relevant resources across many disciplines.

Implementing a collection development strategy to the LGBTQ+ community requires planning and assessment. The first step is to review the existing resources. As Graziano (2016) noted in his article, it can be surprising how much a collection already has in this area. Partnering with faculty and staff who conduct research in this area is key to identifying collection priorities. In addition to academic faculty specializing in LGBTQ+ or sexuality studies, employees in student services or resident life who work closely with the community are often an excellent resource. LGBTQ+ members of the campus community may also provide feedback and input about what resources are appropriate and useful.

Virginia Tech does not have a program for LGBTQ+ or sexuality studies, although the Women's and Gender Studies minor includes related courses. Nonetheless, the circulating collection includes many resources relevant to LGBTQ+ topics. As Diversity Outreach Liaison, the resident works with stakeholders in the Intercultural Engagement Center and the Women's and Gender Studies minor to determine whether the current library collections meet their research needs.

Special collections and university archives present another opportunity for community facing collection development. To effectively document the history of LGBTQ+ groups both on campus and in the surrounding area, libraries must demonstrate transparency and commit to building trust with the LGBTQ+ community. Wakimoto, Hansen, and Bruce (2013) note that community focused archives rely upon donations from the community and reflect the community they serve. They also observe that administering a community archives may require adjustments to traditional archives access policies. As a group that has been historically marginalized from campus histories, priority should be placed on giving the community an active voice in its own documentation and empowering campus groups to identify records for future acquisition. As Robinson (2014) noted, campus archivists may need to work closely with the LGBTQ+ community to help them see the value of ephemeral and sometimes highly personal records. Privacy concerns are particularly acute, as Huddleston (2015) demonstrates in her case study of an archival outreach program for LGBTQ+ communities in Utah.

The LGBTQ+ label represents a vast spectrum of intersecting identities, including race, class, gender identity, ability, age, religious affiliation, national origin, and veteran status. Collection development should respond to the needs of the local community and reflect an intersectional approach. Exhibits, collections, and events should reflect the broad experience of the LGBTQ+ community. In contrast, the community is not well-represented when an institution presents the perspectives and experiences of affluent, cisgender, and white gay men or lesbians. In addition to limiting the research utility of library collections, this practice of exclusion will alienate members of the community that the library hopes to reach.

Special Projects Approach

Benefits:

- Involve library employee time for a defined period
- Often highly visible
- May come with designated funds

Drawbacks:

- Can be seen as opportunistic
- Require significant marketing to reach stakeholders
- Temporary benefits

Conducting outreach through special projects gets the library noticed. Special projects can include targeted events, seminars, oral history campaigns, grant initiatives, and other one-time endeavors. Special projects afford the library an opportunity to target its outreach for specific times of the year or to coincide with specific events. Since special projects have a defined end date, it can be easier to secure partner support. Working within a special projects model requires a leader who can spot an opportunity and lead a project through conceptual planning and implementation phases. Once a project has concluded, it is important to have another in progress or ready to begin.

In the fall of 2014, members of the Ex Lapide Society, the LGBTQ+ alumni association, initiated a conversation with campus units about documenting their history at Virginia Tech. In response, Special Collections faculty leveraged existing relationships with faculty in the History Department to develop an oral history campaign to document the experiences of LGBTQ+ individuals in the 20th century American South. The first interviews were collected during the second annual Ex Lapide Fall Reunion in October 2015, which overlapped with Gay in Appalachia, a community-wide arts series hosted annually.

Special Collections partnered with local stakeholders throughout the project's planning and implementation phases. Being responsive to community requests and engaging regularly with the community cultivated significant trust for the Libraries. The finished project was showcased with a month long exhibit in Special Collections and a two-day pop-up event, "Sharing Our Voices: A Celebration of the Virginia Tech LGBTQ Oral History Project," which featured archival materials, ephemera, recorded interviews, historic films, and an interactive web exhibit.

The project led to an ongoing collecting drive to increase representation of LGBTQ+ history in the university archives and local history collections. This effort relies on partnerships developed with the LGBTQ+ community through work on the oral history project.

Promotion Based Approach

Benefits:

- Raises awareness of the library as a service point
- Increases use of existing LGBTQ+ resources
- Demonstrates that the library is proud of having LGBTQ+ resources

Drawbacks:

- Can be resource intensive
- May be seen as niche by general audience

Targeted promotion will help connect the community with collections and bring in potential partners. Libraries should also consider spaces and classrooms as a resource.
Examples of promotion strategies

- Hold special events to highlight new additions in special collections or archives
- Highlight seasonal displays and new acquisitions
- Work with academic departments to develop projects
- Work with LGBTQ+ campus organizations to advertise collections
- Create LibGuides to direct users to LGBTQ+ resources
- Actively promote library spaces for LGBTQ+ programs
- Invite student groups and community groups to hold their meetings in the library
- Designate or identify inclusive bathrooms

Common Pitfalls

The Lone Soldier: As noted by Jody Gray (2010, 77) at the University of Minnesota, "One person alone cannot work with all of the diversity populations." Administrators should not to assume one person can do all the work of reaching a community. To truly engage with the LGBTQ+ community, the library should demonstrate inclusive practices beyond diversifying library employees and collections. An institution committed to partnering with the community will incorporate LGBTQ+ perspectives and topics throughout its operations and programming.

Things to avoid: Hiring an LGBTQ+ employee and expecting them to assume all outreach responsibility A member of the community may have a unique interest and insight into supporting the community but it is unfair to place the entire burden on one person and this actually serves to further marginalize the employee.

Assuming that an LGBTQ+ employee will automatically be accepted by the community They will still need to build relationships on behalf of the library. If there has been tension between the community and the library in the past, they won't be able to establish a productive relationship without demonstrated support from the rest of the library.

Putting on a Show: Events and programming should reflect the institution's commitment to maintaining mutually beneficial relationships with local stakeholders. Advertising the library as a space for LGBTQ+ groups to hold events and meetings or install displays can demonstrate strong support. In contrast, programming that narrowly serves library interests may be seen by the community as opportunistic.

Things to avoid: Only doing events in June and October. LGBTQ+ history month and National Coming Out Day are great opportunities to engage the community, but efforts may seem disingenuous if they are limited to these windows. Information about LGBTQ+ issues and perspectives can be incorporated into other cultural heritage and identity celebrations. Similarly, LGBTQ+ focused events should reflect a broad spectrum of intersectional identities represented in the community.

Only participating in library-led events Library events are a great way to incorporate LGBTQ+ topics into information literacy and outreach campaigns. Libraries should not neglect opportunities to engage with the community at their own events and across campus. Partnering with LGBTQ+ groups to host something at the library is a great way to demonstrate meaningful support.

Rewriting History: Assessing the institution's historic relationship with LGBTQ+ community is the first step in a long process of reconciliation. Accordingly, the institution should be prepared to critically examine its historic role in harming and marginalizing LGBTQ+ individuals. Memorializing positive anniversaries, historic gains, and campus pioneers should not overshadow the full narrative. Actively soliciting input from LGBTQ+ faculty, staff, students, alumni, and community leaders will help outreach staff find a balance between honoring the community's complex history and celebrating progress.

Things to avoid: Dictating the process of engagement with the community Interacting with traditionally marginalized communities on their own terms is a powerful expression of an institution's commitment to reconciliation. This is particularly true for documenting relations between the community and the institution. Institutional records will depict a narrow segment of the story; the LGBTQ+ community may offer unique interpretations, insights, and perspectives. Outreach staff should work with community stakeholders to highlight these stories.

Inflexible documentation practices: As Huddleston (2015) and other scholars have demonstrated, official records have long been used to expose and harm members of the LGBTQ+ community. In addition to communicating transparently throughout the process, library and archives staff should carefully consider privacy concerns when documenting historic struggles. Special precautions should be taken to avoid outing individuals, exposing private medical information without permission, and describing materials using inappropriate terminology.

Looking Forward

Library faculty at Virginia Tech established a strong foundation for outreach between 2014 and 2016, paving the way for more ambitious initiatives going forward. Top priorities include establishing enduring relationships with the LGBTQ+ community and developing a sustainable program that does not rely on specific individuals. The following strategies are planning to strengthen the University Libraries' LGBTQ+ outreach:

- Increase collaboration between library departments for event and exhibit planning
- Provide more training for library employees, especially public facing staff and faculty in liaison roles
- Increase library employee participation in community and campus-based LGBTQ+ events.
- Build capacity to support campus and community collections that the library does not directly manage, including resource libraries in campus centers, faculty teaching collections, and community archives.

BIBLIOGRAPHY

Consortium of Higher Education LGBT Resource Professionals. 2016. "Recommendations for Supporting Trans and Queer Students of Color." New York: Consortium of Higher Education LGBT Resource Professionals, Inc. https://urldefense.proofpoint.com/v2/url?u=https-3A__lgbtcampus.memberclicks.net_assets_tqsoc-2520support-25202016.pdf&d=DQIFaQ&c=euGZstcaTDllvimEN8b7jXrwqOf-v5A_CdpgnVfiiMM&r=FuC2bgPKWy3lyLSFzYGLuQ&m=o7Q2juceWHuBefD-sqEayhORg33dqZY4hrK03tVQiAs&s=h-mYVs6QjIcYDvY7iCgPu1UimAtRpPkaK9wgC4qC6kA&e=.

Gray, Jody. 2010. "A Different Approach to Diversity Outreach: Partnerships and Collaboration at the University of Minnesota." *College & Research Libraries News* 71 (2): 76–78. https://urldefense.proofpoint.com/v2/

url?u=http-3A__crln.acrl.org_content_71_2_76.full&d=DQIFaQ&c=euGZstcaTDllvimEN8b7jXrwqOf-v5A_CdpgnVfiiMM&r=FuC2bgPKWy3lyLSFzYGLuQ&m=o7Q2juceWHuBefD-sqEayhORg33dqZY4hr K03tVQiAs&s=4z7yFLpetEYJv6sqJuMjaYxXXG4vp4gjP7LwSYhp4vY&e=.

Graziano, Vince. 2016. "LGBTQ Collection Assessment: Library Ownership of Resources Cited by Masters Students." *College & Research Libraries* 77 (1): 114–127. doi:10.5860/crl.77.1.114.

Huddleston, Julia. 2015. "A Vibrant and Vocal Community: Establishing an Archival Outreach Plan for the LGBTQ Community in Utah and Similar States." *Provenance, Journal of the Society of Georgia Archivists* 33 (1): 24–35. https://urldefense.proofpoint.com/v2/url?u=http-3A__digitalcommons.kennesaw.edu_provenance_vol33_iss1_7&d=DQIFaQ&c=euGZstcaTDllvimEN8b7jXrwqOf-v5A_CdpgnVfiiMM&r=FuC2bgPKWy3lyLSFzYGLuQ&m=o7Q2juceWHuBefD-sqEayhORg33dqZY4hrK03tVQiAs&s=XOjKV UBsg4GzCcXKuQ6umhkBp44PK_h4BmFobyduIng&e=.

LGBT Caucus at Virginia Tech. 2015. "LGBTQ Climate Survey Report." Blacksburg, VA: LGBT Caucus at Virginia Tech. https://urldefense.proofpoint.com/v2/url?u=http-3A__www.inclusive.vt.edu_content_dam_inclusive-5Fvt-5Fedu_resources_publications_reports_lgbtq-2Dclimate-2Dsurvey.pdf&d=DQIFaQ&c=euGZstcaTDllvimEN8b7jXrwqOf-v5A_CdpgnVfiiMM&r=FuC2bgPKWy3lyLSFzYGLuQ&m=o7Q2juce WHuBefD-sqEayhORg33dqZY4hrK03tVQiAs&s=Hs0-kB18e1Ri4ull1pZTmVNBmvVY38_Pa6PagrHS7 pE&e=.

Robinson, Jr., Franklin A. 2014. "Queering the Archive." *QED: A Journal in GLBTQ Worldmaking* 1 (2): 195–199. https://urldefense.proofpoint.com/v2/url?u=https-3A__muse.jhu.edu_article_547802&d=DQIFaQ &c=euGZstcaTDllvimEN8b7jXrwqOf-v5A_CdpgnVfiiMM&r=FuC2bgPKWy3lyLSFzYGLuQ&m=o7Q2 juceWHuBefD-sqEayhORg33dqZY4hrK03tVQiAs&s=zeXZC-wX1OB3DSISGYKnj_yRG1sFZ3I8k4NR fE1NDIE&e=.

Wakimoto, Diana K., Debra L. Hansen, and Christine Bruce. 2013. "The Case of LLACE: Challenges, Triumphs, and Lessons of a Community Archives." *The American Archivist* 76 (2): 438–457. doi: 10.17723/aarc.76.2. kqv813v23vl24741.

Evolution of the Curriculum
Using Archives to Inform Collection Development for Women's Studies

LAUREL BLISS *and* ANNA W. CULBERTSON

What factors inform current topics in the Women's Studies curriculum? Have topics adequately evolved to address current social issues or are they more informed by a core holdover of topics from the discipline's nascence? Areas of academia that explore sociological topics are generally understood to evolve alongside the social issues themselves. Is the Women's Studies curriculum consistent with this notion or have significant moments and events been obscured by generalization? These questions are best answered by looking both within and outside of the curriculum—by surveying what we've accomplished both academically and socially—and what correlations can be made of the current status of each. While this query begins with a survey of change as evidenced by presiding mainstream social perceptions, it is not complete without taking into consideration the granular moments that bring about each transformation. Likewise, a survey of course offerings applicable to women's history, both prior to and since the establishment of the Women's Studies major, allows an analysis of correspondences in the curriculum.

The library at San Diego State University, one of the first two universities in the country to offer a Women's Studies major, provides exceptional resources for tracing the curriculum and developing a narrative timeline. Not only does the library preserve a complete run of course catalogs and class schedules spanning SDSU's history, but we also hold the records of the Women's Studies program, as well as numerous other women's organizations on campus and around the region. Moreover, the library's support of the Women's Studies program through the provision of a subject librarian and a dedicated collection development budget lends a wealth of added data to this analysis. These factors presented an interesting opportunity for a collaborative research project between the two authors of this essay—one a subject librarian for Women's Studies and the other a special collections librarian. Ideally, the results will allow us to direct (or redirect) collection development, liaison and outreach efforts accordingly. Even more ideally, this data will also determine which former issues may remain at rest or might merit resurrection.

Background of Women's Studies at SDSU

The first question we asked was this: what was the state of the curriculum when this major was introduced? Women's studies as a discipline represents a particularly notable fissure in the foundation of the academic establishment. Prior to the appearance of Women's Studies degrees, the absence of women as topics in education at all, beyond practical applications of one's womanhood such as home economics and physical education, is striking. Of particular note is the absence of women from literature and philosophy course descriptions. In fact, based solely upon course catalogs, it is almost as if women did not exist—at least not outside the household or grocery store. It is also worth mentioning that courses were already offered by 1970 in Afro-American (now Africana) studies, Asian studies, and Latin-American studies, the latter since 1942. This suggests that whatever the discipline, it was the actions of men, regardless of their race or ethnicity, that largely defined topics in mainstream academia.

This data raised additional questions: when did home economics courses first appear, and what was the state of the curriculum at that point? Until 1921, SDSU was a state normal school, meaning it trained teachers. A glimpse of the graduates listed at the end of each catalog from 1899 and 1909 reveals that on average, less than 10 percent were male. The first appearance of home economics was an announcement in the 1907–1908 catalog for courses to be offered the following year in "Domestic Science." The heading in the subsequent catalog was changed to "Household Arts" and included only cooking and sewing. Over the decades, Household Arts would become Home Economics, and the program would expand to include all aspects of family management, including nutrition, health care, wardrobe selection, home buying, repairs, "successful marriages" and financial planning. The course descriptions alone offer fascinating insight into gender relations throughout the 20th century. For example, in the 1950s, only one introductory Home Economics course, General Home Arts, is listed as being open to both men and women. A course dealing exclusively with domestic violence first appears in the catalog for 1980–81. The Home Economics courses described above continue to be offered well into the 1990s, and by 2000, becomes a "Family Life Education" certificate in the Child & Family Development program.

The first listings in a Women's Studies program appear in the 1971/72 general catalog. Ten courses were offered, with one associate professor listed. Subjects ranged from women in comparative cultures, women in history, women in literature, human sexuality, and a course on field experience. Over the next few years, more courses and faculty members were added. Additional subjects like women in the arts, women and law, and psychological aspects of women broadened the depth of coverage. A minor in Women's Studies was first offered in 1976/77, with a major added in 1983/84.

Current Courses in the Women's Studies Program

If we move ahead in time and consider the curriculum in the present day, we can see at a glance that the two foundational courses for the Women's Studies major are WMNST 101 Women: Self, Identity and Society and WMNST 102 Women: Images and Ideas. Both courses are frequently taught by graduate teaching assistants and lecturers, although tenured/tenure-track faculty teach sections as well. These courses were introduced in the 2002/03 cycle, taking the place of Women and the Social Sciences and Women in the Humanities.

The 2015/2016 general catalog description of WMNST 101 is "Interdisciplinary introduction to Women's Studies thought and scholarship in the social sciences, to include such areas as gender-based language, personality development and self-concept, social evolution, family structures, and economic life." It is also classified as a General Education Foundations course, which help students cultivate skills in reading, writing, research, communication, computation, information literacy, and use of technology. Instructors choose specific areas to cover, such as examining social justice organizations or creating a gender-focused profile of a country.

The 2015/2016 description for WMNST 102 is "Major cultural representations of women in ancient through contemporary societies from perspectives in the humanities, including philosophy, religion, art, literature, and history." By analyzing and critiquing different forms of media, they explore the social constructions of categories such as gender, race, class, sexuality and ability in women's lives. Instructors often assign a final project that requires the critical analysis of scholarly resources as well as an oral presentation.

Beyond the foundational courses, the bulk of Women's Studies courses fall in the 300s levels, intended for undergraduates, and the 500s, acceptable for advanced degrees. Enrollment in 300 level courses usually requires completion of a general education course at the foundations (basic) level, while enrollment in 500 level courses requires 3 upper division units in Women's Studies. This codification of requirements and levels parallels courses in other disciplines, and fits into the standard structure for an undergraduate major.

Content in the 300 and 500 level courses has been strongly interdisciplinary and constant for many years. Topics such as Women in American History (first appearance in the general catalog was in 1973/74); Women and Violence (2000/01); and Feminist Thought (1984/85) are hugely popular. Newer courses like Gender, Science, and Technology (2007/08) also bring in large enrollment numbers. As the program has grown in size, more 300 and 500 level courses have been available for majors to choose from, addressing issues of law, politics, health care, and the arts.

Special courses such as independent study, internships, research projects, writing workshops, and thesis preparation are offered every semester. WMNST 596 Topics in Women's Studies examines an issue such as feminist organizations and activism, and can be repeated with new content. It is also being used as a writing workshop, to explore styles, norms, and argument in academic writing. This flexibility permits faculty to teach in an area of interest to them, with the possibility of turning it into a regular course. The Women's Studies program also gives extra credit to students who attend Women's Studies-related events and guest lectures on campus.

Trends in the Curriculum

A close analysis of the Women's Studies course listings in the annual general catalog allows us to construct a narrative timeline from 1971 to the present. We can see the courses that have endured, those that have dropped away, and the new areas of study that have developed and gained popularity. Our evaluation also reveals several patterns in the curriculum that we can use to inform our outreach and collection development.

One trend that has slowly emerged is that of globalization. The program began with a rather traditional approach of primarily looking at women in Western cultures, offering courses such as Women in Comparative Cultures (1971/72) and the aforementioned Women in American History. Gradually the offerings became more international in scope, with the creation of Women in Cross-Cultural Perspective (1983/84). Women of Latin America (1999/2000), which became Latinas in the Americas (2004/05), marked the first instance of a course that examined the roles of women in a non–European setting. Given SDSU's location on the border with Mexico, choosing a Latin-American focus made a great deal of sense. Women in Asian Societies (2000/01) followed shortly thereafter. Ten years later, the creation of Women in Muslim Societies (2010/11) reflects the growing interest in the socio-political status of women in Muslim societies around the world.

A second trend is LGBT issues, which have long been a part of the Women's Studies curriculum. Courses like Human Sexuality (1971/72) and Women's Sexuality (1979/80) covered "current research and theories on the psychological, social, and psychophysiological aspects of women's sexuality; examination of the relationships among social expectations, sexual customs and traditions, and sexual behavior, responses, identity." More overtly LGBT-friendly courses like Women-Identified Woman (1982/83) and Lesbian Lives and Culture (1995/96) have allowed students to explore stereotypes, current conditions, and social movements. Simply using the word "lesbian" in a course title can be seen as a major milestone.

Anita Harker Armstrong and Jamie Huber point out that "new areas of scholarship were predicted by many to pose significant changes to WGS [women and gender studies] as we know it—specifically in the area of transgender studies" (Armstrong and Huber 2015, 222). One change has been where those topics are covered. For instance, two current courses in the LGBT program, Lesbian and Gay Identities and Lesbian and Gay History and Culture, were formerly listed under general studies, rather than Women's Studies, even though one was actually taught by a Women's Studies professor. The LGBT program itself is explicitly not affiliated with any department.

A third significant curricular trend is internships. Giving students the opportunity to be socially active through engagement in field experience has remained an essential part of the curriculum, although the terminology and context has certainly changed. The 1971/72 course description for Women's Studies 198 Field Experience says "Exploration and analysis of sex discrimination in public and private agencies in the San Diego area as they relate to women through supervised experience and observation, understanding principles and utilizing skills in organizing and effecting change." The existence of sex discrimination is assumed, and the focus is on effecting change in these organizations. In 1976/77, the description was shortened to "Observation and analysis of public and private agencies in the San Diego area which deal primarily with women," which seems like a much more passive and watered down experience for students.

The course description for today's equivalent, WMNST 598 Women's Studies Internship, says "Application of women's studies theories and scholarship to community service and activism. Internship includes 120 hours of work in local public and private agencies serving women and girls." Based on this brief write-up, the priority seems to be the numbers of hours worked, rather than producing social change. This shift in the role of internships has happened throughout the field. For example, Judith Taylor and Kim de Laat argue that "the focus on praxis that has prevailed in women's studies since it began has been gradually infringed upon by a larger culture and etiquette of internships in which students' initial interests in practicing their politics, making a difference, or becoming part of a community of people interested in producing social change are morphed into job training and introduction to the real world" (Taylor and de Laat 2013, 104). It is hard to say at this point if the emphasis on job training will be something that continues.

Faculty Teaching Women's Studies

Any discussion of the curriculum should also address the faculty teaching those courses. In the early years of the program, the number of faculty members who offered courses was quite modest, at two or three, and most were at the assistant professor level or were lecturers. Each year shows different names listed, which seems to indicate that professors rotated in and out of the program. Beginning in the early 1980s, the numbers began to slowly grow as full and associate professors started to offer courses. On average, five full professors and two associates taught in the program throughout the rest of the 1980s and the 1990s. The early 2000s saw the resumption of assistant professors in the program, with two or three, bringing the total number of tenured/tenure-track faculty to around 10, where it remains today.

Looking at the faculty included in the general catalog, we can see some of the names appearing year after year. We can track the progress of careers, as names move from the assistant category to associate to full, and even to program chair. Having this degree of consistency in the teaching faculty, particularly in the last 20 years, speaks to the enduring strengths of the program. It is worth noting that several of the current tenured/tenure-track faculty in Women's Studies also teach in other programs, such as Asian Studies and French/Francophone Studies. Additionally, over 50 faculty based in other departments offer occasional courses on gender issues in their discipline. This allows the Women's Studies program to offer a much broader range of courses than might otherwise be possible, and supports the interdisciplinary nature of the discipline.

Collecting Materials in Women's Studies

Developing a collection in support of research in Women's Studies has not been a unified process. The subject specialist has a mandate and funding to add books to the main circulating collection, while the Special Collections librarian focuses on adding primary, non-circulating material to Special Collections. Historically the contact between the two areas has been minimal, instead of one informing the other.

Funding for Women's Studies monographs in recent years has reflected the state of the library's budget, as well as the university, California State University system, and the economy in general. That is to say it has fluctuated greatly and never been more than modest at best. Occasional influxes of one-time money from the campus have permitted purchases of items like back files of journals or items of an interdisciplinary nature. At one point we had an approval plan in this area, but budget limitations meant cancelling that in favor of firm orders.

We have records for the past five years of book purchases for the main collection in the area of Women's Studies. Approximately 310 books were ordered during this period, with a mix of firm orders, titles requested by faculty members, and a few replacement copies. We do have additional titles in the reference collection and e-books that are part of large packages that are paid for on separate accounts, and therefore not included. Journal subscriptions, which are for the most part in large packages, are also not included. Furthermore, many books are purchased in related areas, such as history, law, and health. Those titles are of great value to Women's Studies researchers, but are paid for by fund allocations in those subject areas. Lastly, we occasionally receive book donations from Women's Studies faculty and alumni to support the collection.

Taking this five-year block of book purchases as a snapshot, we can see certain patterns of collecting that reflect both academic publishing and teaching in this area. We regularly purchase materials in areas like globalization, feminist movements, key female figures in history, body image and popular culture, sex trafficking, women in the Muslim world, and LGBT issues. These patterns correspond closely to key trends in the SDSU Women's Studies curriculum identified earlier, and directly support new courses being taught.

One very encouraging development affecting the library's collection as a whole has been the creation of a Lesbian, Gay, Bisexual and Transgender (LGBT) Studies program at SDSU, which began in January 2012. At a time when many programs are being merged together, not always comfortably, establishing a stand-alone program seems particularly noteworthy. As Breanne Fahs states, "the road to renaming, reclassifying, and regrouping women's studies and its allies is fraught with messiness, intellectual and ideological struggle, personal passions, and hard-earned political strategizing" (Fahs 2013, 497). LGBT Studies had previously been part of Women's Studies, and materials to support LGBT research had been purchased using Women's Studies funds. In 2014 the library established a separate LGBT monograph fund to support this program.

On a related note, we have cataloged the print and media collection of SDSU's Pride Center, so all of their materials are now included in the library's online catalog and can be borrowed with a university ID. We are working with SDSU's Women's Resource Center to do the same for their book collection. These campus collaborations have allowed us to improve access to a wide range of materials for Women's Studies researchers.

Finally, the Library's Special Collections & University Archives department is home to a wealth of primary sources and other unique materials that support historical and contemporary topics in Women's Studies. In the Rare Books Collection, there are many historical titles relating to international feminism, minority women, women artists, women and religion, sexual identity, female health, and body image, and individual titles dating back to the 16th century. There is a strong emphasis on sources in second-wave feminism, particularly owing to donations by SDSU professor emeritus and renowned lesbian scholar Bonnie Zimmerman. A substantial

The Second Revolution, April 12, 1971, the newsletter of the Women's Studies Program, San Diego State College (courtesy Special Collections & University Archives, San Diego State University Library & Information Access).

collection of ephemera includes postcards promoting suffrage and trade cards depicting women and femininity, domesticity and the American home, amongst many other topics. The collection also includes women's magazines dating back to the 1830s, etiquette and conduct books dating back to the 1670s and 19th century readers and textbooks related to the proper education and elocution of young girls.

Special Collections also houses nearly 40 archival collections of organizations and personal papers that support various aspects of Women's Studies. The archives of San Diego chapters of organizations such as National Organization for Women (NOW), YWCA and Older Women's League are just a few highlights. The papers of noted women's rights activists Tish Sommers, Bonnie Zimmerman, and Kathleen B. Jones are just a few collections of personal papers that enhance holdings. The Zines and Minicomics Collection, also described in a finding aid due to its extensive holdings and difficult cataloging formats, focuses heavily on the riot grrrl movement and third-wave feminism. The special collections librarian has focused most recent collection development efforts in the department on further developing sources in third-wave feminism and LGBT studies.

Conclusion

Creating a narrative timeline of the Women's Studies curriculum has provided a useful tool for outreach and collection development. It has also sparked ideas for future exploration. One area that seems interesting is using course syllabi to inform purchasing decisions. We now have an SDSU syllabi database, where teaching faculty can upload their syllabi so that everyone might have access, not just the students taking the class. This gives librarians information such as the course reading list and topics being covered in far greater detail than the short course descriptions currently available in the general catalog. While not everyone is uploading their syllabi and there is limited historic data available, it does offer promise.

A second strategy would be to examine lists of books and articles being requested through interlibrary loan. We have access to data that includes the program affiliation, which would allow us to see at a glance what Women's Studies majors and faculty members are requesting. Another approach is to look at requests wholesale and pull out items related to women's studies. This kind of analysis could reveal gaps in our collecting habits, as well as indicate areas of potential growth.

We also need to explore ways of sharing information more effectively amongst ourselves about how we're developing the collection, with the goal of integrating our purchasing decisions. For instance, the acquisition of a new archival collection should inform the purchasing of related secondary material for the main circulating collection. Likewise, Special Collections can more effectively build, redirect or refine relevant strengths in concert with the library's circulating holdings as well as current curricular needs by collaborating with the subject librarian for women's and LGBT studies. Staying generally communicative with each other about new course offerings and faculty research interests is the most obvious way to establish this balance. Collaborating on research guides is one way to foster this environment; co-teaching library instruction sessions is another. This synergy should be cultivated wherever and whenever possible to improve both individual and collaborative efforts.

References

Armstrong, Anita Harker, and Jamie Huber. 2015. "Where Are We Headed? What's in Our Way? How Can We Get There? Thoughts from Directors of Women's and Gender Studies Programs." *Affilia-journal of Women and Social Work* 30, no. 2: 216–231.

Fahs, Breanne. 2013. "Diving (Back) into the Wreck: Finding, Transforming, and Reimagining Women's Studies and Sexuality Studies in the Academy." *Feminist Studies* 39, no. 2: 496–501.

Taylor, Judith, and Kim de Laat. 2013. "Feminist Internships and the Depression of Political Imagination: Implications for Women's Studies." *Feminist Formations* 25, no. 1: 84.

Beyond Collections

Libraries, Ally Work and the Preservation of Women's, Gender and Sexuality Studies Programs

KARL ERICSON, MEGAN NOVELL
and ROSEMARY WEATHERSTON

Introduction

In common usage the word "ally" refers to individuals or groups that share interests and cooperate in support of those interests. In the disciplines of Women's, Gender, and Sexuality studies (WGSS), however, "ally" has a more specific definition and is better understood as a verb than a noun. To "ally" one's self is to use one's privilege within existing social structures and ideologies in support of individuals and groups marginalized by those structures and ideologies. The underlying goal of ally work is dismantling the oppressive systems, practices, and beliefs that create privilege and marginalization in the first place.

In this essay, we use the active definition of ally as a framework for newly imagining the relationships between academic libraries and WGSS programs and departments. We describe the numerous challenges facing many such programs and departments that create their urgent need for alliances, and identify the characteristics of academic libraries that prime them to take up that charge. Using a collaborative project between our own university's library and Women's and Gender Studies program as a case study, we highlight both the potential benefits and risks of libraries serving as allies in the preservation of WGSS programs and departments. The mutual benefits, we assert, far outweigh the risks and have positive implications for other types of libraries, academic programs, and community groups.

Challenges

In current U.S. financial, educational, and political climates, WGSS programs and departments have need of alliances. Despite some improvement in higher education's financial outlook (Moody 2016), continued increases in operating costs, stiff competition for student enrollment, and inadequate state spending on education still challenge many colleges and universities. These financial challenges are coupled with a more general spread of business- and consumer-based models of higher education, which emphasize financial returns on investment for both institutions and students. Under these conditions, disciplines such as WGSS—which have less uniform pathways to employment and emphasize less tangible "products" such as civic engagement and social activism—can become targets for funding cuts or outright elimination. In 2013, for example, North Carolina Governor Patrick McCrory asserted that state funds should not be used to help students to earn degrees in Women's and Gender Studies: "If you want to take gender studies that's fine, go to a private school and take it. But I don't want to subsidize that if that's not going to get someone a job" (quoted in Kiley 2013).

Other disciplines such as Ethnic Studies, African American Studies, philosophy, or the fine arts can also be vulnerable to the dismissal of their "use-value," especially if their number of majors is low. However, WGSS programs and departments face the added burden of sexually stigmatized subjects of study. Against the endemic sexism and homophobia of contemporary U.S. society, the disciplines' focus on issues of reproductive justice, gender identity, feminism, and sexualities are at best, devalued. At worst, they generate direct and virulent attacks.

These attacks can be against individual scholars, such as feminist media critic Anita Sarkeesian, who has received thousands of rape and death threats because of her work on misogyny in video games and other forms of popular culture (Valenti 2015). A renowned gender and religious studies scholar at our own institution, the late Dr. Jane Schaberg, experienced years of vitriolic attack—including having her car set on fire—because of her work in feminist biblical interpretation. Attacks also occur on the programmatic level. In 2014, for example, the University of Southern Carolina–Upstate attempted to close its Center for Women's and Gender Studies and reallocate those funds to the teaching of the Constitution, Declaration of Independence, and Federalist Papers. Supporters of the Center for Women's and Gender Studies linked these actions to the controversy over the Center's hosting of a symposium on LGBTQ issues and arts earlier in the year (Cooley 2014).

Even WGSS scholars and programs not under financial or political threat experience strains on their resources that many other faculty and disciplines do not. Among these are higher institutional service demands (NWSA 2001). WGSS faculty serve as subject experts at all levels of their institutions. They are routinely asked to sit on committees addressing complex issues such as Title IX compliance, sexual harassment and sexual assault prevention, family leave and transgender equality policy development, and diversity-based curriculum assessment. Individuals with personal interests or who are experiencing crises in areas of gender or sexuality, too, will seek out WGSS faculty for guidance and assistance. This can include other faculty and employees but is especially the case with students who self-identify as gender or sexual minorities or who have experienced gender- or sexual-based discrimination and violence. Some students seek academic mentorship and collaboration; others are in need of psychological, legal, and/or medical care. Such pedagogical and "affective labor" is vital and highly demanding but largely unrecognized within university reward structures (Sloniowski 2016).

The interdisciplinary nature of Women's, Gender, and Sexuality Studies also comes with resource demands most traditional disciplines do not experience (NWSA 2013). At some colleges and universities Women's, Gender, and/or Sexuality Studies are housed in full departments with tenure-track faculty lines, undergraduate majors, and M.A. and/or Ph.D. students. At other institutions, however, they occupy more structurally ambiguous positions such as programs or centers that offer certificates or minors, but no majors. Other programs are part of larger academic units that house a number of diversity-based fields. WGSS faculty, too, can occupy structurally demanding or ambiguous positions. This can range from joint positions, in which faculty split their duties between WGSS programs and other departments, all the way down to "volunteer" models of WGSS affiliation, in which faculty's work in WGSS is considered part of their service obligations and is completely uncompensated. Thus, many WGSS faculty have responsibilities in more than one academic unit and many WGSS programs experience a higher rate of faculty turnover than do traditional academic departments.

In light of these conditions, when we speak of "the preservation of Women's, Gender, and Sexuality Studies programs" we are referring both to supporting their continued existence and helping them maintain institutional continuity. Fortunately, we assert, the institutional privilege of academic libraries puts them in excellent positions to serve as allies for both these goals.

Privilege

"Privilege" refers to "structured and social opportunities, particularly those that are systematically granted on the basis of a social category of identity rather than merit or individual will" (Launis and Hassel 2015, 77). Privilege and "oppression"—"prejudice and discrimination directed towards a group and perpetuated by the ideologies and practices of multiple social institutions"—go hand in hand (73).

It's important to note that the systemic nature of both privilege and oppression means individual people, groups, or institutions do not choose their privileged or oppressed statuses. It's also important to recognize that privilege and oppression are not monolithic; rather, they are context-specific. White women for, example, may experience racial privilege at the same time they experience gender oppression. Libraries may be simultaneously venerated as "storehouses of knowledge" and marginalized as "service institutions."

While academic libraries struggle with their own budget challenges and the need to adjust to the rapidly changing landscapes of U.S. higher education, they still maintain significant material and ideological privileges. Valuable material resources available to most academic libraries include:

- Physical buildings, often in central locations, with meeting, display, and archival spaces
- A wide range of information technologies
- Permanent, full-time, and high quality staff
- Funds to purchase new resources and conduct programming

Perhaps even more valuable, however, are the non-material privileges garnered by academic libraries. One of these is institutional goodwill. The majority of members of college and university communities see libraries as providing useful resources and services. They also view libraries as occupying a place in-between disciplines, departments, and administrative units. This likeability and in-between status translates into libraries and their staff having access to and being met receptively by most entities on their campuses.

Libraries are also granted significant authority in the central enterprise of academia: the production and circulation of knowledge. Thus, when libraries recognize and highlight subjects, they confer legitimacy on those subjects. A concrete example of this ability to legitimize can be seen in the recent controversy over the Library of Congress's move to replace the search term "illegal aliens" with "noncitizens" and "unauthorized immigration" (Peterson).

By recognizing and creating awareness of their privileges within academic systems, libraries become better positioned to utilize their strengths in outreach, advocacy, and consultation. It becomes possible for them to actively engage with departments and programs as institutional allies.

Ally Work and Academic Libraries

Scholarship in and discussions of librarianship increasingly draw on the language of advocacy and activism in envisioning the future of libraries, and the critical librarianship movement explicitly concerns itself with enacting the principles of social justice in libraries. However, nearly all discussions of libraries as agents of social justice or social change focus on the efforts of individuals in libraries. Few have addressed the possibility of the institution of the library itself to ally with marginalized groups.

It is clear, however, that there is a precedent for alliances between academic libraries and Women's, Gender, and Sexuality Studies programs even if the relationships have so far not been articulated in these terms. Libraries at the University of Buffalo, Brooklyn College, Purdue University, and the University of Massachusetts Boston all have archival collections devoted to the history of the Women's Studies programs at their institutions, and libraries at both Portland State University and the University of Arizona have partnered with Women's Studies programs to organize special exhibitions in celebration of those programs' milestone anniversaries.

Ally work is not without its risks, however. Like individuals who use their privilege in support of oppressed groups, libraries that ally with social justice programs, especially programs that focus on minority experiences, risk their privileged status. A historic expectation that libraries remain neutral repositories of knowledge makes their advocacy risky, and libraries that openly depart from this construct open themselves to criticism from individuals and groups both on and off their campuses.

Still, in their discussion of the creation of a Black Lives Matter research guide at the University of Arizona Library, Nicole Pagowsky and Niamh Wallace argue that, for libraries to engage in effective alliances, cooperative action is essential: "[T]he campus should work as a community, in partnership, sharing the labor of support for diversity and social justice, and not leaving the burden of effort solely to the few units on campus with these explicit charges" (2015). As libraries adjust to their changing roles in higher education, an alliance model can acknowledge the many resources and unique status that the library can offer to other university groups, programs, and organizations and provide a framework to guide partnerships across campus.

What, then, does a library interested in allying with campus groups such as WGSS programs and departments need to do? Our thinking on this topic is indebted to Mia McKenzie's essay "No More 'Allies'" and Jamie Utt's article "So You Call Yourself an Ally: 10 Things All 'Allies' Need to Know."

First, listen and self-educate. Libraries interested in ally work must learn the histories, intentions, and concerns of the programs or groups with whom they work, since each program will have a unique set of circumstances informing their needs. Moreover, those circumstances and needs can change. Libraries should expect the learning process to be ongoing and that alliances will be fluid and contingent. In arenas of political activism some people who engage in ally work describe themselves as "currently operating in solidarity with" rather than as "an ally of" when speaking of their work with marginalized individuals and groups. As writer and activist Mia McKenzie asserts, this emphasis on action underscores that ally is "not an identity. It's a practice" (2014, 140). Such framing is useful on the institutional level as well. Libraries that wish to act as allies should not, however, rely on members of the marginalized groups and programs to educate them. Rather, they need to adopt a model of interaction that depends on their expending the majority of the effort. This can include initiating the conversations that can lead to productive relationships.

Second, once an alliance is established, libraries need to be consistent in their support. Stability is one of the greatest privileges libraries enjoy. Libraries can provide services and resources that aid programmatic continuity, through, for instance, hosting annual events or scheduling regular archival deposits. Codifying regular engagement with a library liaison can help to develop an alliance into an enduring relationship, especially as liaisons increasingly "see or imagine the impact of their work in the context of solving larger institutional problems" (Jaguszewski and Williams 2013).

Third, libraries committed to doing ally work should engage other units at their universities who have privileged statuses. For example, when the Clark Memorial Library at Shawnee State University partnered with the university's Women's Center to host a reading and discussion of a book about surviving sexual assault, the event included a dinner with the author to which the university's Director of Public Safety, Director of Human Resources, Athletic Director, Dean of Students, and Provost, among others, were invited. In uniting different campus leaders and members of the university community at this event, the library "demonstrated its influence on knowledge construction on campus" (Mathuews 2016).

The Black Lives Matter research guide at the University of Arizona shows how libraries can lead alliances on their campuses and also how such efforts can lead to deeper collaborations across the university. After the publication of their guide, the library partnered with the university's department of Africana Studies and faculty from the Gender and Women's Studies program to organize and sponsor a conference on racial justice. A shared motivation to effect social change and work for social justice can motivate other alliances between libraries and WGSS programs.

The WGS 25th Anniversary Project

Such motivation is at the heart of a developing alliance between the University of Detroit Mercy's Libraries and Instructional Design Studio and Women's and Gender Studies program. UDM is a private, Catholic institution in the Jesuit and Mercy traditions with approximately 4,920 students and 225 full-time faculty members. The academic libraries at UDM, which employ thirty librarians, administrators, and staff, are comprised of the McNichols and Dental campus libraries and the Instructional Design Studio, which supports online learning and digital special collections. The Library has a history of using its material resources to support other university units. For example, the library:

- Makes its public spaces available at no charge for campus and community events and displays
- Houses the Carney Latin American Solidarity Archive
- Helps organize the university's annual Celebration of Scholarly Achievement.

On a larger scale, the McNichols campus library recently moved personnel and collections from a floor of its building to provide space for a new TRiO program and permit the expansion of other student support agencies such as Disability Support Services and the Student Success Center.

UDM's Women's and Gender Studies Program is a small program, offering an academic minor but no major. The program is coordinated by rotating, part-time faculty directors but lacks any full-time or jointly appointed faculty. The vast majority of curricular development, events, educational programming, and community outreach efforts depend on the volunteer efforts of faculty from other departments. The program has periodically come under both internal and external attack for programming viewed as "anti–Catholic," such as productions of the play *The Vagina Monologues*. This is a charge that has been levied at the Library as well. In 2010, both WGS and the Library came under attack from external conservative Catholic groups for having links to Planned Parenthood and the National Organization of Women in their online research guides.

More positive examples of common interests between the Library and WGS include shared commitments to the social justice, outreach, and service aspects of our institutional mission, as well as long-standing relationships between WGS and Library faculty and staff. The ad hoc committee overseeing the WGS 25th Anniversary Project consists of the three co-authors of this article and Associate Librarian Kristine McLonis. Karl is an assistant librarian at the McNichols library and serves as the liaison to the WGS program. Kris has served for many years on the WGS Steering Committee. Megan is a staff member of the library and a part-time instructor in the WGS program. Rosemary directs the WGS program and has frequently collaborated with library staff and administration on community-based programming.

The Anniversary Project extends beyond shared interests and individual relationships and efforts, however. The aims of the project are twofold:

- To develop a series of programs, events, and displays at the McNichols Campus library to celebrate the 25th anniversary of WGS.
- To develop a WGS program archive. The archive will include both physical and digital collections of program artifacts as well as video oral histories of the founders of the WGS program.

We see two aspects of this collaboration illustrating the library's engagement as an institutional ally. First is its use of its material and ideological privilege in support of the needs of the WGS program. McNichols library public spaces will be made available for Anniversary events and displays. The WGS founders' oral history component is being integrated into an existing library project. Library staff will conduct the grant-writing needed to fund these efforts and will employ the team of interviewers and videographers, along with the technical support of the IDS to create space on the library's servers and to transfer data from WGS field recordings. The increased visibility afforded the WGS program and its subjects of study in the Library's public spaces and material and digital archives draws on the legitimizing authority of academic libraries. The WGS program's history and central areas of scholarship and teaching gain in stature when highlighted in these ways. Of primary importance, library faculty and staff are coordinating these efforts—proactively engaging with WGS faculty, educating themselves about the program's history and circumstances, and researching other ways the Library can support both the short and long term needs of WGS.

This points to the second way we see the WGS Anniversary Project extending beyond shared interests and individual efforts: its integration into Library structures and policies. The Dean of Libraries, Jennifer Dean, as well as the associate dean for Public Services, George Libbey, have supported the initiative, expressing their approval of and offering their assistance at every stage of the project's development. At an administrative level, library liaison policies and responsibilities are being reviewed with an eye towards codifying a more proactive role for liaisons as "advocate and … consultant, both with an emphasis on campus engagement" (Rockenbach et al. 2015). An advocate works to reveal possibilities in a collaborative process. An ally acts on those possibilities. By establishing an institutionalized approach to advocating for UDM's Women's and Gender Studies program, the Library is making a long term commitment to working towards its preservation.

Conclusion

While "the work librarians do is often conceived of as being about librarians, about the library," librarians and others are increasingly focused on the need to attend to "the larger institutional ecosystem in which the library operates" (Rockenbach et al. 2015). As librarians reimagine their roles, libraries as institutions can re-envision the ways they engage with and work to support their communities.

Although our discussion has focused on alliances between academic libraries and WGSS departments and programs, the relevance of this model for collaborations with other university groups, programs, and organizations is clear. Other academic disciplines grounded in social activism and civic engagement face many of the same challenges as do Women's, Gender, and Sexuality Studies and also have need of institutional allies. Outside of academia, this model may have even more relevance. When public libraries in both Ferguson, MO, and Baltimore, MD, stayed open during the protests against police brutality that rocked their communities, they were, in every sense, operating in solidarity with their communities. Libraries of all kinds occupy unique spaces, both physically and ideologically, and can use their privilege to move beyond collections and into the collective actions that are at the heart of ally work and, ultimately, of social justice.

REFERENCES

Cooley, Lauren. 2014. "University Cuts Women's and Gender Studies, Will Teach Constitution Instead." Campus Reform, May 19. https://urldefense.proofpoint.com/v2/url?u=http-3A__www.campusreform.org_-3FID-3D5628&d=DQIFaQ&c=euGZstcaTDllvimEN8b7jXrwqOf-v5A_CdpgnVfiiMM&r=FuC2bgPKWy3ly LSFzYGLuQ&m=ITNkhCLbCCrImEKEQruy_RRKtNaSk5U4dD06XD9cSCo&s=BPIzsXThnOdpm8Un fwtTISHiw_7PTUxPJVQ9kp0O734&e=.

Gonzalez, Julieta. 2000. "UA Women's Studies Honored by Library Exhibition for Its 25th Anniversary." UANews, February 22. https://urldefense.proofpoint.com/v2/url?u=https-3A__uanews.arizona.edu_ story_ua-2Dwomen-2Ds-2D&d=DQIFaQ&c=euGZstcaTDllvimEN8b7jXrwqOf-v5A_CdpgnVfiiMM&

r=FuC2bgPKWy3lyLSFzYGLuQ&m=ITNkhCLbCCrImEKEQruy_RRKtNaSk5U4dD06XD9cSCo&s=L_
6h4rvSNpNVkLjdIHDgLVjWLNllPhtFy1JNooPSRxQ&e=studies-honored-by-library-exhibition-for-its-
25th-anniversary.

Holden, Jessica. 2015. "In the Archives: Women's Studies Program Records." Open Archives News, November
5. https://urldefense.proofpoint.com/v2/url?u=http-3A__blogs.umb.edu_archives_2015_11_05_in-2Dthe-
2D&d=DQIFaQ&c=euGZstcaTDllvimEN8b7jXrwqOf-v5A_CdpgnVfiiMM&r=FuC2bgPKWy3lyLSFzY
GLuQ&m=ITNkhCLbCCrImEKEQruy_RRKtNaSk5U4dD06XD9cSCo&s=a9b1E4GzTxX6Oh1eJKUQc
2mXhewxsHWS2F3AXn7-78o&e=archives-womens-studies-program-records/.

Jaguszewski, Janice, and Karen Williams. 2013. "New Roles for New Times: Transforming Liaison Roles in
Research Libraries." Association of Research Libraries.

Kiley, Kevin. 2013. "North Carolina Governor Joins Chorus of Republicans Critical of Liberal Arts." Inside Higher
Ed, January 30. https://urldefense.proofpoint.com/v2/url?u=https-3A__www.insidehighered.com_
news_&d=DQIFaQ&c=euGZstcaTDllvimEN8b7jXrwqOf-v5A_CdpgnVfiiMM&r=FuC2bgPKWy3l
yLSFzYGLuQ&m=ITNkhCLbCCrImEKEQruy_RRKtNaSk5U4dD06XD9cSCo&s=aAdt20K1YqNKvYo
8u4i7BO9bYdOkQ1Wqkl7U0WPgjZU&e=2013/01/30/north-carolina-governor-joins-chorus-republi
cans-critical-liberal-arts.

Mathuews, Katy. 2016. "Moving Beyond Diversity: A Call to Action for Academic Libraries." Progressive Librarian 44.

McKenzie, Mia. 2014. "No More 'Allies.'" In Black Girl Dangerous: On Race, Queerness, Class and Gender. Oak-
land, CA: BDG, 138–141.

Moody's Investors Services. 2016. "Outlook for US Higher Education Washington Higher Education Secre-
tariat." March. https://urldefense.proofpoint.com/v2/url?u=http-3A__www.acenet.edu_news-2Droom_
Documents_Moodys-2D&d=DQIFaQ&c=euGZstcaTDllvimEN8b7jXrwqOf-v5A_CdpgnVfiiMM&r=
FuC2bgPKWy3lyLSFzYGLuQ&m=ITNkhCLbCCrImEKEQruy_RRKtNaSk5U4dD06XD9cSCo&s=
VSRX0IloAxcO25CQTy5K5qP7yjmsxT39tcHo9RkGXZE&e=HEOutlook-Secretariat.pdf.

National Women's Studies Association. 2001. "What Programs Need: Essential Resources for Women's Studies
Programs." https://urldefense.proofpoint.com/v2/url?u=http-3A__www.nwsa.org_files_WhatPrograms
Need.pdf&d=DQIFaQ&c=euGZstcaTDllvimEN8b7jXrwqOf-v5A_CdpgnVfiiMM&r=FuC2bgPKWy3ly
LSFzYGLuQ&m=ITNkhCLbCCrImEKEQruy_RRKtNaSk5U4dD06XD9cSCo&s=SYKXqK6SFyEeVDC
146GWb64PH3u1U9EZqmBggwjhqvs&e=.

National Women's Studies Association. 2013. "Women's Studies Scholarship: A Statement by the National
Women's Studies Association Field Leadership Working Group." https://urldefense.proofpoint.com/v2/
url?u=http-3A__www.nwsa.org_files_2013-2DNWSA-2DTenure-2520StatementFINAL.pdf&d=
DQIFaQ&c=euGZstcaTDllvimEN8b7jXrwqOf-v5A_CdpgnVfiiMM&r=FuC2bgPKWy3lyLSFzYG-
LuQ&m=ITNkhCLbCCrImEKEQruy_RRKtNaSk5U4dD06XD9cSCo&s=rW52Ij-yIb9NFhTSmrd0t10_
nuvizpsP0zJ-eMdSBuQ&e=.

Pagowsky, Nicole, and Niamh Wallace. 2016. "Black Lives Matter! Shedding Library Neutrality Rhetoric for
Social Justice." College & Research Libraries News 76.4: 196–214.

Peterson, Kristina. 2016. "Fight Brews in House Over Use of 'Illegal Alien' by Library of Congress." WSJ: Washington Wire, April 22. https://urldefense.proofpoint.com/v2/url?u=http-3A__blogs.wsj.com_washwire_
2016_04_&d=DQIFaQ&c=euGZstcaTDllvimEN8b7jXrwqOf-v5A_CdpgnVfiiMM&r=FuC2bgPKWy3ly
LSFzYGLuQ&m=ITNkhCLbCCrImEKEQruy_RRKtNaSk5U4dD06XD9cSCo&s=vwM4kcbZ41lAo1_Xl8
gwaFg5_RWfJiCbxeUUMvpVhoM&e=22/fight-brews-in-house-over-terms-used-by-library-of-congress-
for-immigration/.

"Purdue University Libraries, Archives and Special Collections." Purdue University Libraries, Archives and
Special Collections. https://urldefense.proofpoint.com/v2/url?u=http-3A__www4.lib.purdue.edu_arch
on_index&d=DQIFaQ&c=euGZstcaTDllvimEN8b7jXrwqOf-v5A_CdpgnVfiiMM&r=FuC2bgPKWy3l
yLSFzYGLuQ&m=ITNkhCLbCCrImEKEQruy_RRKtNaSk5U4dD06XD9cSCo&s=5EqDs52aWVLm-t7
v_Mv10kt1XcLY1Kc0_mnWCYsgOeg&e=php?p=collections/controlcard.

Rockenbach, Barbara, Judy Ruttenberg, Kornelia Tancheva, and Rita Vine. 2015. Association of Research Libraries/
Columbia University/Cornell University/ University of Toronto Pilot Library Liaison Institute. Final
Report. June.

Sloniowski, Lisa. 2016. "Affective Labor, Resistance, and the Academic Librarian." Library Trends 64.4: 645–666.

University at Buffalo Libraries. "The First 20 Years of Women's Studies at UB, 1969–1989." https://urldefense.
proofpoint.com/v2/url?u=http-3A__library.buffalo.edu_archives_womens-5Fwork_history_womens-5F
studies.htm&d=DQIFaQ&c=euGZstcaTDllvimEN8b7jXrwqOf-v5A_CdpgnVfiiMM&r=FuC2bgPKWy
3lyLSFzYGLuQ&m=ITNkhCLbCCrImEKEQruy_RRKtNaSk5U4dD06XD9cSCo&s=Ll6dAWwg8tBKTe
mycaNNGKhrTU8F_Ov3U_ddY-FdSKY&e=.

University of Wisconsin–Milwaukee. 2016. "History of the UWM Women's Studies Program." March 9. https://
urldefense.proofpoint.com/v2/url?u=http-3A__guides.library.uwm.edu_WomensStudies200-2D201_
Historyoftheuwmwomensstudiesprogram&d=DQIFaQ&c=euGZstcaTDllvimEN8b7jXrwqOf-v5A_Cd
pgnVfiiMM&r=FuC2bgPKWy3lyLSFzYGLuQ&m=ITNkhCLbCCrImEKEQruy_RRKtNaSk5U4dD06X
D9cSCo&s=-UJRFxXLuhB4Za_TEkQEK6cKG7bp7nQ3ppdijgHNuHA&e=.

Utt, Jamie. 2013. "So You Want to be An Ally?" *Everyday Feminism*, November 8. https://urldefense.proofpoint.
com/v2/url?u=http-3A__everydayfeminism.com_2013_11_things-2Dallies-2Dneed-2Dto-2Dknow_&d=
DQIFaQ&c=euGZstcaTDllvimEN8b7jXrwqOf-v5A_CdpgnVfiiMM&r=FuC2bgPKWy3lyLSFzYGLuQ&
m=ITNkhCLbCCrImEKEQruy_RRKtNaSk5U4dD06XD9cSCo&s=G6tu1hPvzGVUhZEXQSqeUcd7Stk
Ma_kRw42snqiTLhc&e=.

Valenti, Jessica. 2015. "Anita Sarkeesian Interview: 'The Word "Troll" Feels Too Childish. This Is Abuse.'" *The
Guardian*, August 29. https://urldefense.proofpoint.com/v2/url?u=https-3A__www.theguardian.com_
technology_&d=DQIFaQ&c=euGZstcaTDllvimEN8b7jXrwqOf-v5A_CdpgnVfiiMM&r=FuC2bgPKWy
3lyLSFzYGLuQ&m=ITNkhCLbCCrImEKEQruy_RRKtNaSk5U4dD06XD9cSCo&s=NBEfhIQ_
GSbYQDDBkJ7-u6GdzfdOt6VfSq6qWh81j9s&e=2015/aug/29/anita-sarkeesian-gamergate-interview-
jessica-valenti.

"Winter 2016 Exhibit Highlights 40th Anniversary of Women's Studies at PSU." 2016. Portland State University
Library, January 15. https://urldefense.proofpoint.com/v2/url?u=http-3A__library.pdx.edu_winter-
2D2016–2Dexhibit-2D&d=DQIFaQ&c=euGZstcaTDllvimEN8b7jXrwqOf-v5A_CdpgnVfiiMM&r=
FuC2bgPKWy3lyLSFzYGLuQ&m=ITNkhCLbCCrImEKEQruy_RRKtNaSk5U4dD06XD9cSCo&s=
7POKutEEiH_gE2i7wet2FpH-ftIaRyJ3erz6oMEJIuo&e=highlights-40th-anniversary-of-womens-
studies-at-psu/.

LGBT Inclusive Elementary Library

JEANINE M. HUSS *and* BARBARA FIEHN

For many young children, the only access to a rich source of diverse reading material is the school library. Public library access may be difficult due to distance or other conditions. Within a school library, children can explore ideas, learn, and grow through access to inclusive fiction and nonfiction. This essay's focus is specifically on the elementary school library, presenting ideas for selection of Lesbian, Gay, Bisexual, Transgender (LGBT) themed books for the collection and building acceptance for these materials within the school and local communities. The authors hope readers beyond elementary schools will also find the information useful.

Recently, the Supreme Court has ruled in favor of gay marriage. The U.S. Departments of Education and Justice have ruled, endorsed by President Obama, that "transgender students in K–12 public schools shall be provided all privileges of their preferred gender, including sex-segregated activities and access sex-segregated facilities consistent with their gender identity" (U.S. Department of Education). Further, a number of television shows and major movies include LGBT characters (IMDb—Editors 2016), and many famous people have claimed LGBT status (Ring 2015). The American view of LGBT persons is changing. The GLAAD 2015 survey, Accelerating Acceptance, showed six out of seven Americans surveyed report less discomfort with LGBT people than was reported the previous year. Yet the education questions in the report indicated nearly one third of survey respondents were uncomfortable with LGBT content in schools. Twenty-nine percent of those surveyed would be uncomfortable finding out their child's teacher was an LGBT person; this was one percent lower than the 2014 survey. Thirty seven percent said they would be uncomfortable discovering their child had a lesson on LGBT history, the same as the 2014 survey (Goodman 2016).

The authors feel it is appropriate to use picture books with younger students and novels with older students in order to discuss many issues. The research literature supports this stand. As an example, Miller (2014) reports, "Providing LGBT novels in classrooms and libraries has proven to be an effective way to inform students and promote discussions on gender and bullying in secondary schools" (84). School libraries are particularly important for children exploring their gender, sexuality, or identity; children need to see themselves represented in books at school. Children know about their gender and sexuality from a young age. Shannon Oltmann (2016) reports in "They Kind of Rely on the Library: School Librarians Serving LGBT Students," the majority of respondents "were enthusiastic about collecting LGBT resources, noting that it is important for students to see themselves reflected in the school's resources; just as important, non–LGBT students need opportunities to learn about LGBT issues" (15). A library's heart is its collection. To maintain a healthy collection, it must meet the diversity of needs represented by all users and the school curriculum. To meet these needs the librarian must collaborate with those in the school and community who need additional guidance in working with LGBT collections.

Working with Administrators, Teachers and Parents

There are likely administrators, teachers, and parents associated with the school who are not comfortable with adding LGBT materials to the collection. Lessen this discomfort about LGBT issues by meeting each person where they are. You need to be prepared to respond to those who are uncomfortable.

- Identify allies. Contact school counselors, supportive instructors,
- Arrange assistance with both planning and presenting information.
- Use research to back up what you say. Provide reference material
- Give everyone time to listen and talk. Meetings or professionalpositive and negative views of LGBT issues.
- Examine your own biases. Discuss them aloud, so others understand your
- Create support from others. Match up people with similar cultural
- Look at families and schools as systems. Use the strength of all
- People are unique. Some people will become supportive quickly;
- Assume all adults care about children and want what is best forThe differences lie in what individuals consider best for children's growth and development.
- Consider what is best for your community and the pace at which you move

Educators' Role

The U.S. Census Bureau, U.S. Department of Education, and the U.S. Department of Health & Human Services, as well as a variety of researchers and organizations, make estimates of the number of LGBT students in public schools. There is no agreement on the numbers; however, the estimates range from three to 10 percent. These numbers indicate nearly all schools serve at least some LGBT students. In the unlikely event that a school has no self-identified LGBT students; it is likely many heterosexual students know of LGBT friends, family members, and other individuals. Martin and Murdock estimate about 80 percent of teens know someone who is LGBT (2007, xi). Therefore, educators should educate themselves about LGBT issues and incorporate best practices for LGBT inclusion in all curricula delivered in schools.

Take positive actions:

- Let others know you are supportive of LGBT rights.
- Find out what the bias issues are in your school and do what you can to provide safety for students.
- Condemn hateful acts by involving administrators, teachers, and parents to find positive solutions.

- Become part of the solution by finding ways to help wrongdoers and victims find understanding.
- Many children do not understand words used to hurt others, such as bully, gay, fag, wimpy, girly, or fairy. Assist students in learning what these words mean and how they affect others. Encourage the identification and use words that boost others, not tear them down.
- Discuss minority issues and ideas that arise as teachable moments in the classroom.
- Teach your students that acting only stereotypically masculine or feminine limits students as individuals.
- Show appreciation of students' distinctiveness. Every student deserves recognition for their contributions to the diversity of the school.
- Work with guidance counselors, social workers, and others as needed to reduce homophobia.
- Advocate for inclusion of LGBT issues in sex education courses. Curricula are available.
- Support or help students start affirming student groups.
- Make your classroom a welcoming place of inclusion.
- Integrate LGBT issues by talking about LGBT people in history, using examples of same-sex couples in math word problems, or using terminology that acknowledges different family structures and gender identities.
- Use trade books in your classroom and units that include LGBT people.
- Address letters sent home to parent or guardian as an inclusive measure.
- Encourage young children to play with kitchen sets, dress up clothes and trucks and cars, regardless of gender.
- Mention examples of LGTBQ families in discussions of families.

Collection Development Specific to LGBT Collections

Martin and Murdock (2007) provide guidelines for creating policies for collection development in their book *Serving Lesbian, Gay, Bisexual, Transgender, and Questioning Teens*. They suggest creating a non-discriminatory statement as part of a library's collection development plans, which should become a librarian's mantra. Martin & Murdock say you should "show them that you have an obligation to represent your entire community, including queer and questioning people" (2007, 66). Carefully consider the wording used in the collection development policy, make it inclusive and use words that have minimal option for misunderstanding.

Clearly state the library's mission to serve the education community, including all minorities. Use straightforward language such as: Children's print and digital materials shall represent all types of diversity, including race, ethnicity, gender expression, religious preference, family composition, ancestry, ability, sexual orientation, socioeconomic status, language fluency, and citizenship status.

Select learning resources to help students gain an awareness of our pluralistic society. A good library collection will include fiction and nonfiction, informative and entertaining materials, graphic novels, and other materials for all students. Students should see themselves and their family reflected in the collection.

Library users are of all ethnic and racial backgrounds, nationalities, socioeconomic classes, and abilities. Look for materials that include and celebrate the diversity within GLBT communities, and nonfiction biographies should include LGBT persons.

Health information is critical in all types of libraries, as mainstream information often does not account for particular risks or health complications faced by gender and sexual minorities. AIDS is still a dangerous, communicable disease, and recent materials should be included in your library collection.

Selection Criteria and Evaluation of Trade Books for LGBT Content

Collections serving children should include fiction with diverse protagonists of minorities, sexualities, gender identities, and family structures, as well as nonfiction materials for school research projects. Children are often aware of their sexuality and gender at an early age, and there are increasing numbers of families with same-gender parents. Representation of these identities and families, as well as all other identities and families, is critical for building healthy perceptions among youth.

When selecting books with LGBT content for elementary students, the authors believe it is critical for librarians and teachers to evaluate the following: the appropriateness of the book title, the characteristics, the settings, the plots, and the target audience.

Most children's literature textbooks such as *Children's Books in Children's Hands: A Brief Introduction to Their Literature* by Temple, Martinez, and Yokota (2014) now include such criteria and many suggest using standard criteria for multicultural literature, coupled with standard genre criteria for evaluation of LGBT titles. Jamie Naidoo (2012) developed extensive criteria for evaluating LGBT children's books in his book *Rainbow Family Collections: Selecting and Using Children's Books with Lesbian, Gay, Bisexual, Transgender, and Queer Content*. Naidoo's criteria are somewhat overwhelming, covering several pages. Another alternative comes from the American Library Association's Gay Lesbian Bisexual Transgendered Round Table (GLBTRT), which approves the following six simplified criteria for the quality evaluation of LGBT books. The criteria headings are from the original document, the accompanying text, however, is a summary of the original ("What to Do until Utopia Arrives: Guidelines to Evaluate the Treatment of Gay Themes in Children's and YA Literature" 2009).

- Central Characters: If the central character is LGBT, there should be no special emphasis on the sexual component of their identity. Straight main characters should demonstrate an acceptance of a parent, teacher, or best friend without destructive repercussions. The orientation of gay characters need not be explained any more than what is needed for a straight character, unless the plot demands this explanation. Portrayals of growth and development of LGBT identity should be shown as the character coping with life situations as adequately as anyone could.
- Minor Roles: Minor characters can be incidental characters such as friends, relatives, or neighbors who are LGBT. These characters should be included as a natural part of all kinds of situations developed within the story plot.
- Illustrations: Books for children should include illustrations of LGBT couples as

parents, as older sisters and brothers dating, as kids of the same sex, and as just ordinary people. They should include all races, ages, and occupations. The illustrations should not single out the LGBT characters unless appropriate to the plot.

- Degrees of Explicitness: Books for children seldom include explicitness of any kind. However, there should be realistic portrayals of affection and falling in love as there would be in a book not containing LGBT characters.
- Impact on Readers: The book should give an accurate, sympathetic picture of LGBT life in the same way it would for non-gays. Readers should learn to appreciate and not fear differences in sexual and affectional preference. The story should give young gays a clear view of the decisions facing them and show successful decision-making by all characters. The reader should see an up-front picture of gay life, not just the old caricatures.
- Author's Attitude: Any work dealing with a gay theme is prone to include clichés and preconceptions of gay character. Evaluate the writing for the inclusion of such biases.

Experienced book selectors should be adequately guided by their experience along with the above six criteria. Novice selectors or experienced ones who feel the need for more comprehensive knowledge will want to read Jamie Naidoo's book (2012). *Rainbow Family Collections* also contains extensive materials lists. In all cases, apply the use of multicultural and standard genre-appropriate criteria to all children's book selections.

Once the library has a core collection for elementary student, librarians can begin to show case the books alongside traditional and popular material.

LGBT Selection Resources

ALA GLBT Resources for Children: A Bibliography.
ALA the Rainbow Book List for GLBT books for youth 0–18.
Stonewall Book Awards, the oldest award for GLBT literature recognizes adult, young adult, and children's fiction and nonfiction.
The Lambda Literary Awards—LGBT Children's/Young Adult, individual works and collections of fiction, nonfiction, picture books, and poetry whose intended audience is young readers are all eligible.
Annual bibliographies of GLBT materials are available from the Gay, Lesbian, Bisexual, and Transgender Round Table of the American Library Association (GLBTRT).

Cataloging

Library users utilize terms they are comfortable applying to themselves when searching the catalog. Subject headings and call numbers have not always been LGBT-friendly, however, librarians have advocated for improved terminology over time. Periodically reviewing the catalog for offensive subject headings is vital; language is continually evolving, and librarians should remain current with terminology. This is particularly true for material about minority populations. The subject headings abnormal or deviant sexual behavior is no more appropriate for LGBT material, than the subject-heading alien is for noncitizens. Suggestions for better subject headings can be found using an Internet search for "GLBT Controlled Vocabularies and Classification Schemes."

Libraries have made recent efforts to reclassify call numbers to place LGBT materials among appropriate sections of the collection related to health, family, and relationships, rather than previously used classifications in psychology. Classify children's nonfiction LGBT materials in their proper places based on subject matter. Shelve children's fiction LGBT materials in areas designated other fiction materials.

Labeling

The ALA has taken a stand on the labeling of books. An Internet search using ALA Labeling will lead readers to the documents. The objection to labeling comes from use of some labels limiting access to materials for some borrowers. The most common and objectionable labeling in elementary libraries are those which indicate reading levels and are used to limit students to small portions of a collection based on the student's reading level. Genre labeling fiction books has been common for many years. These tags are often helpful to library users as are labels indicating special collections such as reference material or graphic novels.

- Identifying books with a GLBT label may prevent library users from accessing them for fear of being outed or ridiculed.
- Placing GLBT materials alongside other books and materials can help GLBT users feel welcomed. Establishing a separate section of shelving for these materials may endanger user privacy and make some students hesitant to approach them.

Challenges to the Collection

The librarian and the school administration being of one mind about challenges are helpful in building strong collections. A school board approved challenge policy in addition to a selection police is always a first line of defense. Good policy prevents the removing library materials because of a complaint and fear of controversy. The policy also provides guidance for dealing with challenges. Even with the growth in acceptance of LBGT people in American society, controversy continues when libraries display materials, present programs, and add items related to sexual orientation and gender to the collection. Excluding these resources is a form of censorship, yet the fear of a challenge deters some librarians. Objections or challenges to library materials occur, and challenges to LGBT materials are common. Before a challenge occurs, ensure school staff understands challenge procedures.

- Do not avoid a challenge by rejecting the purchase of LGBT materials. Selecting diverse materials is essential and does not represent a personal decision by the librarian. When challenges occur, the librarian should treat them as an opportunity to educate the public about the role libraries play in meeting diverse information needs in schools.
- Librarians and school administrators can also contact the ALA Office of Intellectual Freedom for help with challenges.

- Contact members of state library associations Intellectual Freedom Committees for assistance and informational resources.
- The collection development policy is the library's intellectual freedom foundation in a challenge.

Protecting Student Privacy

School libraries have both an ethical and legal obligation to maintain the privacy and confidentiality of students and staff. Privacy concepts in the ALA code of ethics and many policy statements apply to school librarians. The American Association of School Librarians (AASL) affirms the ALA privacy documents and has their own documents providing guidance on privacy and confidentiality. In addition, federal laws, such as the Family Educational Rights and Privacy Act (FERPA), state laws, and other educational organizations ethics statements direct all educators, and therefore, school librarians, to maintain student information privacy.

Being an acknowledged LGBT person within a school community has potential risks. Checking out or accessing LGBT-themed materials should not label a person as gay. School and community cultures vary widely. Educators must be mindful of curiosity, sensibilities, and peer perceptions when students exhibit an interest in LGBT materials in the library or classroom. Questioning, just curious, in or out of the closet, all members of the school community deserve safe and anonymous access to information resources.

Symons and Freeman (2015) claim LGBT patrons and their allies want their privacy protected from prying eyes. Things to consider include:

- Establish self-checkout procedures and self-service holds to increase privacy for all.
- Catalog LGBT materials with logical identifiers that enable students and faculty to locate them easily in the online catalog.
- Market LGBT materials in the same ways as other materials. Students should not have to wonder if you have these materials.
- Promote and conduct outreach to individuals who might be interested in the LGBT materials. Avoid making interested individuals come to you to ask for the material.

Conclusion

For many students, the school library is their only library. To access a public library means transportation. If children do not live within walking distance or have public transportation, there may be no way for them to get to the public library. Many parents and guardians work more than one job in order to support the family; making library trips to a distant county or city library difficult or not feasible. Some people do not live within a public library taxation area and usage fees for people outside the service area are beyond the family budget. Because of these, and similar situations, the school library is the only source of materials for learning and leisure reading. Garden (2000) reminds us "gay and lesbian kids need to read about people like themselves, just as kids in other minorities do. They need to read about ordinary people who are gay and lesbian, and like kids from other minorities, they need to read about artists, athletes, performers, educators, political figures, and other notables who come from community" (xii).

Reading is still reading, no matter the topic, culture, or experience. Educators should embrace reading as a chance to have meaningful conversations about topics that come up in books. Wanless and Crawford (2016) wrote, "Children's literature offers an engaging vehicle for generating these conversations" (9). The school library is one, if not the only, place children can access these books—"books that provide readers with opportunities to see different aspects of themselves, their communities, and the people they love" (Wanless & Crawford, 12).

Librarians need to acknowledge considerations of possible community discontent, challenges, or claims LGBT themed material is too controversial or sensitive for elementary schools. Researchers in child development, education, and literacy have found elementary children are well equipped to enjoy and understand books on varied sensitive issues. Mankiw and Strasser (2013) emphasize sensitive topics are not problems. Rather, through the process of reading books, sensitive issues are subjects to explore as part of our lives. Librarians should approach these potential concerns and controversies sensitively, gain support from school administrators and faculty. Brian Kenney, former editor-in-chief of *School Library Journal*, reminds librarians, "It takes guts to create libraries that support the needs of all our students. It takes even more guts to support collections that may attract fierce opposition. But that just happens to be our job" (Kenney 2006, u.p.). School librarians have taken up this challenge in some schools; the evidence is in library literature and school online catalogs. The authors of this essay ask the reader to consider taking up the challenge of providing quality collections build to meet the diverse needs of all students, not just for students whose information needs pose no threat of criticism.

REFERENCES

American Library Association. 2009. "Stonewall Book Awards List." Gay, Lesbian, Bisexual & Transgender Round Table (GLBTRT). https://urldefense.proofpoint.com/v2/url?u=http-3A__www.ala.org_glbtrt_award_honored&d=DQIFaQ&c=euGZstcaTDllvimEN8b7jXrwqOf-v5A_CdpgnVfiiMM&r=FuC2bgPKWy3lyLSFzYGLuQ&m=fngr1pDoVwknVsYWBR7ghRywo90PAppRzp0rRp3TO7w&s=YpU3Mnnql3wG5Tx5arecw0kwAPeXQLWlwjOlCOsoNBc&e=.
Galda, Lee, Lawrence R. Sipe, Lauren A. Liang, and Bernice E. Cullinan. 2014. *Literature and the Child*. Belmont, CA: Wadsword.
Garden, Nancy. "Foreword." In *Lesbian and Gay Voices: An Annotated Bibliography and Guide to Literature for Children and Young Adults*, by Frances Day, ix-xvi. Westport, CT: Greenwood, 2000.
Gay Lesbian Transgender Round Table. 2016. "Rainbow Book List." https://urldefense.proofpoint.com/v2/url?u=http-3A__glbtrt.ala.org_rainbowbooks_&d=DQIFaQ&c=euGZstcaTDllvimEN8b7jXrwqOf-v5A_CdpgnVfiiMM&r=FuC2bgPKWy3lyLSFzYGLuQ&m=fngr1pDoVwknVsYWBR7ghRywo90PAppRzp0rRp3TO7w&s=Aw9pwpl7RG69S94PBTcpQEb0SH7OTnkpAJWgUYK1QpQ&e=.
Goodman, Matt. 2016. "GLAAD's Accelerating Acceptance Report Provides Snapshot of Americans' Feelings about LGBT Issues." GLAAD. https://urldefense.proofpoint.com/v2/url?u=http-3A__www.glaad.org_blog_glaads&d=DQIFaQ&c=euGZstcaTDllvimEN8b7jXrwqOf-v5A_CdpgnVfiiMM&r=FuC2bgPKWy3lyLSFzYGLuQ&m=fngr1pDoVwknVsYWBR7ghRywo90PAppRzp0rRp3TO7w&s=Lv2bCx26iguAbJKavrMMn2zDscdxQkDYrOOqLmoMEJU&e=-accelerating-acceptance-report-provides-snapshot-americans-feelings-about-lgbt-issues.
IMDb-Editors. 2016. "IMDB: Memorable TV and Movie Moments in LGBT History." https://urldefense.proofpoint.com/v2/url?u=http-3A__www.imdb.com_list_ls063511182_-231&d=DQIFaQ&c=euGZstcaTDllvimEN8b7jXrwqOf-v5A_CdpgnVfiiMM&r=FuC2bgPKWy3lyLSFzYGLuQ&m=fngr1pDoVwknVsYWBR7ghRywo90PAppRzp0rRp3TO7w&s=GSZqNSGlgiKsaUjxcpZDtc7upMN1jXkuWYmZ51CXeWI&e=.
Kenney, Brian. 2006. "Do The Right Thing." *School Library Journal* 52 (1): 11.
Mankiw, S., and Janis Strasser. 2013. "Tender Topics: Exploring Sensitive Issues with Pre-K through First Grade Children through Read-alouds." *Young Children* 68 (1): 84–89.

Martin, Hillias J., and James R Murdock. 2007. *Serving Lesbian, Gay, Bisexual, Transgender, and Questioning Teens*. New York: Schuman.

Miller, Mary Catherine. 2014. "Identifying Effective Trans* Novels for Adolescent Readers." *Bookbird* 52 (1): 83–86.

Naidoo, Jamie Campbell. 2012. *Rainbow Family Collections: Selecting and Using Children's Books with Lesbian, Gay, Transgender, and Queer Content*. Santa Barbara, CA: Libraries Unlimited.

Oltmann, Shannon M. 2016. "They Kind of Rely on the Library: School Librarians Serving LGBT Students." *Journal of Research on Libraries & Young Adults* 7 (1): 1–21.

Ring, Trudy. 2015. "53 People Who Came Out This Year." https://urldefense.proofpoint.com/v2/url?u=http-3A__DQIFaQ&c=euGZstcaTDllvimEN8b7jXrwqOf-v5A_CdpgnVfiiMM&r=FuC2bgPKWy3lyLSFzYGLuQ&m=fngr1pDoVwknVsYWBR7ghRywo90PAppRzp0rRp3TO7w&s=H5MDyBTf3NIwwbsRvUJLE98KJprX4_MRMSNlrJ4s3pA&e=. https://urldefense.proofpoint.com/v2/url?u=http-3A__www.advocate.com_people_2015_12_23_53-2Dpeople-2Dwho-2Dcame-2Dout-2Dyear&d=DQIFaQ&c=euGZstcaTDllvimEN8b7jXrwqOf-v5A_CdpgnVfiiMM&r=FuC2bgPKWy3lyLSFzYGLuQ&m=fngr1pDoVwknVsYWBR7ghRywo90PAppRzp0rRp3TO7w&s=HnibBs7FtU9DNg3EH94lZjQahIAHWOeIIoh7u9gO9So&e=.

Symons, Ann K., and John "Mack" Freeman. 2015. "Serving Everyone: Welcoming the LGBT Community." *American Libraries* 46 (6): 30–30.

Temple, Charles A., Miriam G. Martinez, and Junko Yokota. 2014. *Children's Books in Children's Hands*. New York: Pearson.

"Toolkit for 'Out at Last': Teaching Tolerance—Diversity, Equity and Justice." 2016. https://urldefense.proofpoint.com/v2/url?u=http-3A__www.tolerance.org_toolkit_toolkit-2Dout-2Dlast&d=DQIFaQ&c=euGZstcaTDllvimEN8b7jXrwqOf-v5A_CdpgnVfiiMM&r=FuC2bgPKWy3lyLSFzYGLuQ&m=fngr1pDoVwknVsYWBR7ghRywo90PAppRzp0rRp3TO7w&s=j7pGbuslxReLil69hdGNA1xPV22zDUVBCGaR2JwIZEo&e=.

"U.S. Departments of Education and Justice Release Joint Guidance to Help Schools Ensure the Civil Rights of Transgender Students: U.S. Department of Education." 2016. https://urldefense.proofpoint.com/v2/url?u=http-3A__Ed.Gov&d=DQIFaQ&c=euGZstcaTDllvimEN8b7jXrwqOf-v5A_CdpgnVfiiMM&r=FuC2bgPKWy3lyLSFzYGLuQ&m=fngr1pDoVwknVsYWBR7ghRywo90PAppRzp0rRp3TO7w&s=womNXd_KnuCEa0mYpQKwfhrHLWyvs7BtOSE0YvxACZ8&e=. https://urldefense.proofpoint.com/v2/url?u=http-3A__www.ed.gov_news_press-2Dreleases_us-2Ddepartments-2Deducation-2Dand-2Djustice-2Drelease-2Djoint&d=DQIFaQ&c=euGZstcaTDllvimEN8b7jXrwqOf-v5A_CdpgnVfiiMM&r=FuC2bgPKWy3lyLSFzYGLuQ&m=fngr1pDoVwknVsYWBR7ghRywo90PAppRzp0rRp3TO7w&s=h5CpTtwYappRaiFSUZLbqiOAkOF5jyY3PiYLGE9f8o0&e=-guidance-help-schools-ensure-civil-rights-transgender-students.

Wanless, Shannon B., and Patricia A. Crawford. 2016. "Reading Your Way to a Culturally Responsive Classroom." *Young Children* 71 (2): 8–15.

"What to Do Until Utopia Arrives: Guidelines to Evaluate the Treatment of Gay Themes in Children's and YA Literature." 2009. Gay, Lesbian, Bisexual & Transgender Round Table (GLBTRT). https://urldefense.proofpoint.com/v2/url?u=http-3A__www.ala.org_glbtrt_popularresources_utopia&d=DQIFaQ&c=euGZstcaTDllvimEN8b7jXrwqOf-v5A_CdpgnVfiiMM&r=FuC2bgPKWy3lyLSFzYGLuQ&m=fngr1pDoVwknVsYWBR7ghRywo90PAppRzp0rRp3TO7w&s=wSaekcW6kFapTxln8jATe_Hq3MO_e_zgoGJDktoYqmE&e=.

Reaching LGBTIQ Teens
through Comics and Graphic Novels

Lisa Morgan

LGBTIQ (Lesbian, Gay, Bisexual, Transgender, Intersex, Questioning) teens represent just one of many populations libraries serve—one that is often overlooked in terms of both collection and programming. The common disregard for the needs of LGBTIQ teens, whether from fear of public criticism or the assumption that they are not representative of the community, is a disservice to the teens and the library community as a whole. LGBTIQ teens are particularly vulnerable to a number of mental health and social problems resulting from their marginalized status in society. Libraries have the potential to become lifelines for these teens but this is only possible through a conscious effort to meet their needs and make them feel welcome in library spaces. This essay will showcase LGBTIQ voices in comics and graphic novels and offer suggestions for their use in engaging and supporting LGBTIQ teens in libraries. I will consider the issues facing these teens and the ways in which libraries can support them through collection and programming efforts.

Issues Facing LGBTIQ Teens

The teen years can be tough for anyone. The pressure of fitting in with peers while at the same time forging one's own identity is a challenge many teens face. Feelings of isolation, loneliness, and low self-esteem are hallmarks of the teenage experience. These negative feelings are often magnified for LGBTIQ teens who often experience homophobia. In *Growing Up LGBT in America*, the Human Rights Campaign (2012) identified the difficulties teens encounter at home, in school, and in the community. Their survey of more than 10,000 LGBT teens ages 13–17 found that the primary challenges were related to the teens' gender and sexual identity. The most significant problems facing the teens included non-acceptance of family members, bullying, and a fear of their sexual orientation being revealed. A sense of social isolation persists among LGBTIQ teens as they navigate a society that discriminates against them and marginalizes them because of their sexual identity. These challenges have a significant impact on the physical and emotional well-being of LGBTIQ teens. This same population of teens is more vulnerable to homelessness and suicide and experience higher rates of drug and alcohol use (Higa et al. 2014). Supportive social environments can offset these challenges and contribute to a greater sense of self-acceptance and overall well-being for LGBTIQ teens. Libraries are uniquely positioned to provide such an environment.

Libraries can foster supportive environments in a number of ways. Perhaps the most obvious way to support LGBTIQ teens is to include materials in the collection they can relate to. In addition to providing entertainment value, books contribute to teens' identity formation. Regardless of their sexual or gender identity, teens seek characters similar to themselves (Martin & Murdock). Books that reflect teens' lived experiences show them that they are not alone. It is especially important for LGBTIQ teens to see positive representations of themselves in books since this is sometimes the only affirmation they receive. Books offer teens "portrayals of what it means to be queer—a way to describe what they feel, to affirm that it is normal" (Martin and Murdock 2007, 17).

Libraries can also establish inclusive policies and practices that demonstrate a commitment to providing a safe, welcoming environment for LGBTIQ teens. Something as simple as avoiding gendered language—for example "sir" or "ma'am"—when addressing patrons or posting LGBTIQ community information lets teens know that they are welcome and will be supported in the library. Regularly incorporating LGBTIQ materials in library displays—as opposed to a singular focus on Pride month—validates teens' experiences and shows an ongoing dedication to meeting their needs. Likewise, responding to homophobic language and behavior in the library lets teens know that homophobia will not be tolerated. LGBTIQ teens who experience homophobia and marginalization at home or school can thrive in a library that provides them with positive experiences through books, programs, or simple, day-to-day social interactions. This essay considers using a specific collection—comics and graphic novels—to support LGBTIQ teens in libraries.

Online Resources for Helping LGBTIQ Teens in Your Library

- Open to All: Serving the GLBT Community in Your Library (American Library Association Gay, Lesbian, Bisexual, and Transgender Round Table)
- Safe Space Kit: A Guide to Supporting Lesbian, Gay, Bisexual, and Transgender Students in Your School (Gay, Lesbian & Straight Education Network)
- It Gets Better Project
- The Trevor Project

Why Comics?

The graphic format is a compelling one that holds great appeal for teens. The dramatic impact of the visual image allows readers to connect with the material on a deeper level. McCloud (1994) describes our engrossment with cartoon images in terms of "amplification through simplification" (30). Abstract images in comics focus on simple, specific details in such a way that magnifies the overall emotional impact on the reader. Also contributing to the heightened emotional impact of graphic texts is the concept of closure. Closure is what allows readers to deduce what happens from one panel to the next in a comic book or, as McCloud puts it, to "observ[e] the parts but perceiv[e] the whole" (63). Readers must be active participants in this process. The more a reader is invested in a story, the greater the emotional impact (Watts 2015).

The universality of many cartoon images draws us into the story and facilitates easy identification with characters. We are able to see ourselves represented directly on the page. For LGBTIQ teens, seeing characters similar to themselves in comics and graphic novels can be a powerful source of self-affirmation. The current trend in graphic texts toward more diversity in content and creators opens up the possibility for more LGBTIQ teens to see their experiences celebrated and validated. As Allison (2014) notes, "what has been marginalized is brought to the center and given a privileged place in these stories" (74).

LGBTIQ Voices in Comics

LGBTIQ representation in American comics is a fairly recent development. Comics have been a lightning rod for controversy since their debut in the 1930s. Early critics were concerned that comics would be a negative influence on children, hampering their reading abilities and corrupting their behavior. Dr. Frederic Wertham, a New York psychiatrist, was one of the most vocal opponents. Wertham launched a crusade against comic books and drew national attention to the issue with calls for legislation banning the sale of comics to children. While the government failed to enact legislation, Wertham's efforts did lead to the 1954 creation of the Comics Code Authority. The Comics Code was a self-regulatory code of conduct adopted by the Comics Magazine Association of America in an effort to address the concerns being raised by critics. Comics that adhered to the Code's broad regulations—there were 41 provisions, many related to sex—prohibiting "immoral" content received the Seal of Approval indicating their suitability for young readers (Nyberg). The restrictions of the Code implicitly precluded LGBTIQ content from appearing in mainstream comics.

A thriving market of underground comics emerged in the 1960s and 1970s in response to the strict censorship enacted by the Code. Independently produced and distributed, these comics were free to explore social issues such as gay and women's rights. As a result, the "queer comix" movement was born. This movement represented "a wholly new and unique space where LGBTQ youth could, for once, express themselves and speak out freely about social issues directly impacting the LGBTQ community" (McCabe). The influence of the Comics Code began to decline in the 1970s and ultimately ended in 2011 when the last two mainstream publishers (DC and Archie) left the Comics Code Authority. Modern comics and graphic novels feature more LGBTIQ characters than ever before. And while there is still much work to be done to increase representation, LGBTIQ teens at least have more opportunities to see themselves directly in the pages.

The following titles represent some of the most highly recommended contemporary comics and graphic novels featuring LGBTIQ content for teens. It is not intended to be an exhaustive list, but rather a jumping off point for starting or enhancing your library's collection.

LGBTIQ Graphic Memoirs:

- *Fun Home: A Family Tragicomic* (Alison Bechdel)
- *Honor Girl* (Maggie Thrash)
- *Tomboy* (Liz Prince)
- *Pedro & Me: Friendship, Loss, and What I Learned* (Judd Winick)
- *Awkward and Definition; Likewise* (Ariel Schrag)

LGBTIQ Comics and Graphic Novels:

- Batgirl *(Cameron Stewart, Brendan Fletcher, Babs Tarr)*
- *Lumberjanes* (Noelle Stevenson, Shannon Watters, Kat Leyh, Carolyn Nowak, Brooke Allen)
- *Harley Quinn* (Amanda Conner, Jimmy Palmiotti, Chad Hardin, John Timms, Jed Dougherty)
- *Midnighter* (Steve Orlando, Aco, Hugh Petrus, Alec Morgan, Stephen Mooney)
- *Black Panther* (Ta-Nehisi Coates, Brian Stelfreeze, Laura Martin)
- *Kevin Keller* (Dan Parent)
- *Young Avengers* (Kieron Gillen, Jamie McKelvie)
- *Catwoman* (Genevieve Valentine, Garry Brown, Lee Loughridge)
- *Wandering Son* (Shimura Takako, Matt Thorn)
- *Love & Rockets* (Jaime Hernandez)
- *Skim* (Mariko Tamaki, Jillian Tamaki)
- *Nimona* (Noelle Stevenson)
- *Blue is the Warmest Color* (Julie Maroh)
- *Scott Pilgrim* (Bryan Lee O'Malley)
- *The Sandman* (Neil Gaiman)
- *Smile* (Raina Telgemeier)

Developing a LGBTIQ Comics and Graphic Novel Collection

Graphic texts are simply a different format of material and thus should be treated like any other part of a library collection. The collection development practices and procedures already in place for traditional materials can be used to build a LGBTIQ comics and graphic novel collection. A collection development policy that specifically states a variety of formats will be collected and diverse viewpoints will be represented will serve as a strong foundation upon which to build a LGBTIQ comics and graphic novel collection for teens. Graphic texts often suffer from the perception that they are "lesser" forms of literature and therefore do not belong in library collections. In fact, that argument was a contributing factor in the development of the Comics Code. A collection policy that supports the inclusion of multiple formats indicates a library's commitment to meeting its patrons' diverse needs and provides justification when comics and graphic novels are challenged. The next section will address the issue of challenges in greater detail.

Comics and graphic novels are experiencing a period of incredible growth and popularity in libraries. The largest direct distributor of comics and graphic novels in the United States—Diamond Book Distributors—reported a 17 percent increase in publisher sales to libraries in 2015 (Batten 2016). This increased popularity is reflected in the professional resources librarians rely on for evaluation and selection of materials for library collections. Professional journals and magazines—including *Library Journal, School Library Journal, The Horn Book Magazine, Voice of Youth Advocates (VOYA), Kirkus Book Reviews*, and *Publishers Weekly*—now regularly review comics and graphic novels. Another useful resource is the Young Adult Library Services Association (YALSA) annual list of Great Graphic Novels for Teens. While these sources are valuable tools for selecting comics and graphic novels, they do not categorize titles by content and are therefore limited in usefulness when it comes to identifying titles with LGBTIQ content. For that, librarians can turn to a handful of LGBTIQ-specific resources.

Lambda Literary promotes LGBTQ literature through various programs supporting writers. The annual Lambda Literary Awards includes a "Graphic Novel" category and the book review section of their website covers "Illustrated" titles, including comics and graphic novels. The American Library Association (ALA) presents an annual Rainbow Book List—a bibliography of books with significant LGBTQ content and which recognizes graphic novels and graphic nonfiction. The GLAAD Media Awards honor all types of media—including "Outstanding Comic Book"—for their fair, accurate representations of the LGBTQ community. Finally, ALA's Gay Lesbian Bisexual Transgender Round Table maintains GLBT Reviews—a website devoted to LGBT book and media reviews. The site can be easily searched for comics and graphic novel reviews.

In addition to the professional library journals and the LGBTIQ-specific resources mentioned above, there are several online sites devoted to comics and graphic novels. The following provide a wealth of information, including reviews, and are valuable tools for developing or enhancing your LGBTIQ comics and graphic novel collection for teens.

Online Comics Resources:

- No Flying, No Tights
- Comics Worth Reading
- Diamond Bookshelf
- Comic Book Resources
- Book Riot Comics
- The Mary Sue
- Comics Alliance
- The Comics Journal
- Graphic Novel Reporter

Dealing with Materials Challenges

When developing an LGBTIQ comics and graphic novel collection for teens librarians must be prepared for potential criticism of the material. Graphic texts are particularly vulnerable to censorship attempts because of their visual nature (Baur and Foust 2014). The power of the image that pulls a teen completely into a story is the same power that threatens someone who disagrees with the content of that image. Comics and graphic novels routinely appear on the ALA's annual Frequently Challenged Books list. A challenge occurs when an individual or group attempts to restrict or remove access to library materials because they object to the content. In 2014, three of the top ten books on the list were comics or graphic novels. Books featuring LGBTIQ content are also frequent targets of challenges. Four of the top ten challenged books in 2015 cited "homosexuality" as a reason for the challenge. Given the frequency with which both graphic texts and LGBTIQ materials are challenged, it stands to reason that a collection combining the two will face some criticism.

The potential for criticism over LGBTIQ materials should not deter librarians from including them in collections. In fact, failing to do so represents a form of censorship. Excluding materials to avoid conflict is "censorship by omission" (Alexander and Miselis 2007) and violates the ALA professional standards requiring librarians to provide resources to all members of the community. The professional standards are based on the Library Bill of Rights. Adopted in 1939 and amended several times since, the Library Bill of Rights is a set of principles founded on the ideas of intellectual freedom—the right to read—and equal access to information. The ALA Intellectual Freedom Committee has crafted several interpretations that provide more specific guidance on the application of the principles in library practice. One of these interpretations, "Diversity in Collection Development," outlines librarians' professional responsibility to include in collections content that reflects a diversity of issues, including those of a sexual nature. Another, "Access to Library Resources and Services Regardless of Sex, Gender Identity, Gender Expression, or Sexual Orientation," highlights the librarian's duty to resist attempts to exclude materials for content dealing with gender identity or sexual orientation. The inclination to avoid controversy is understandable, but the ALA makes clear the role of librarians in meeting the information needs of all community members by providing a variety of resources representing multiple perspectives. The fear of challenges should not deter us from doing our job of serving LGBTIQ teens.

Instead of trying to avoid criticism, libraries would be better served by positioning themselves to effectively handle it. There are several things libraries can do to equip themselves for dealing with challenges to library materials. Having written policies in place is a crucial first step. A collection development policy that outlines the library's guidelines for selecting materials as well as the policies and procedures for dealing with challenges is the best defense. The collection development policy affirms the library's position on intellectual freedom by spelling out its commitment to open access to information in a variety of formats and featuring diverse perspectives. In addition to having written policies in place, it is important that library staff and board members are aware of and understand them. Regular customer service training on how to deal with sensitive matters such as challenges will help staff effectively handle them when the need arises.

The ALA offers a wealth of information and resources to help libraries deal with challenges to materials. On the ALA website librarians will find strategies for communicating effectively, fielding complaints, and talking with the media. Sample questions and answers demonstrate useful language for addressing challenges. Additionally, young adult librarians will find tips geared specifically toward them—a necessity when dealing with materials that are often a lightning rod for controversy. Another great resource—especially when working with a graphic text collection—is the Comic Book Legal Defense Fund (CBLDF). CBLDF is a non-profit organization devoted to "protecting the First Amendment rights of the comics medium." The organization provides legal support for cases involving First Amendment rights and advocates against unconstitutional legislation affecting comics. CBLDF also directly supports libraries in dealing with challenges to comics and graphic novels. Their extensive website offers "a daily news blog on First Amendment issues, a large and growing resource section with case files and documents on the history of comics censorship, and tool kits for artists, readers, and librarians about their First Amendment rights" (Comic Book Legal Defense Fund 2016). Being prepared for potential challenges will go a long way toward lessening the impact when they do occur. As they say, an ounce of prevention is worth a pound of cure.

Online Resources for Dealing with Challenges

- *Strategies and Tips for Dealing with Challenges to Library Materials* (American Library Association)

- *Dealing with Challenges to Graphic Novels* (National Coalition Against Censorship, the Comic Book Legal Defense Fund, and the American Library Association)
- Freedom to Read Foundation
- Comic Book Legal Defense Fund
- National Coalition Against Censorship

Programming with an LGBTIQ Comics and Graphic Novel Collection

Library programming featuring comics and graphic novels offers a great opportunity for engaging with teens. One option is a LGBTIQ Comic Book Club. A comic book club offers several avenues for connecting with teens—through discussions of art, pop culture, and storytelling. This type of club is no different from other book clubs except for the LGBTIQ issues that will be part of the discussion. Establishing ground rules about respecting participants is crucial. Teens need to know that they can speak openly in a safe space without fear of bullying or taunting. For many LGBTIQ teens, the library may be the only place they can speak freely about the issues affecting them. It should be noted that even though this program is designed for LGTBIQ teens it is a great opportunity for those who do not identify as such to learn about the issues affecting their peers and become supporters. Another option is a program that gives teens a chance to create a graphic autobiography. The program could explore notable LGBTIQ graphic memoirs and bring in presenters to help the teens with the production aspects of the project such as illustration and storytelling. LGBTIQ teens would have the opportunity to practice self-expression—a key element of identity formation—in a supportive environment.

Passive programming—programming that does not require direct interaction with library staff—is another way to reach LGBTIQ teens. Examples of passive programming include book displays and themed booklists. There are several benefits to this type of programming. In addition to freeing up staff time, it offers a way to engage teens who might not be able to attend programs as well as those who are uncomfortable asking for help. Librarians may assume that LGBTIQ teens are not part of the local community because they do not ask for materials reflecting their experience. However, as I mentioned above, many LGBTIQ teens have experienced homophobia and may be hesitant to reveal their sexual orientation in an interaction with library staff. Passive programming is a way to support teens who may not be open about their sexual orientation. Including LGBTIQ titles in book displays and booklists lets teens know that the library carries materials relevant to their experiences. Doing so on a regular basis instead of only during Pride month shows the library's commitment to supporting LGBTIQ patrons and helps normalize material that is too often marginalized. The same applies to graphic texts—including them in book displays and booklists is a way to counteract the stigma they carry of being "lesser" literature.

Conclusion

Libraries exist to serve all members of the community not just the visible ones. A library collection should include a wide range of voices and experiences reflective of the broader society (Calkins 2014). Providing access to LGBTIQ materials is crucial to the well-being of teens. Seeing their lives reflected back to them can give them hope in the face of despair. Comics and graphic novels offer a powerful way of engaging LGBTIQ teens in the library. They can be vehicles for self-affirmation and self-expression. Library programming featuring graphic texts can help minimize the feelings of isolation common to LGBTIQ teens. Librarians would be well served to set aside their fear of criticism and embrace the principles of inclusion and access set forth in the Library Bill of Rights. By doing so, the library becomes a lifeline for LGBTIQ teens who may have no other source of support.

REFERENCES

Alexander, Linda B., and Sarah D. Miselis. 2007. "Barriers to GLBTQ Collection Development and Strategies for Overcoming Them." *Young Adult Library Services* 5 (3): 43–9.

Allison, Marjorie C. 2014. "(Not) Lost in the Margins: Gender and Identity in Graphic Texts." *Mosaic* 47 (4): 73–97. doi:10.1353/mos.2014.0042

Batten, Tom. 2016. "Picture the Possibilities." *Library Journal* 141 (11): 30–34.

Baur, Jack and Amanda Jacobs Foust. 2014. "Banned Books Week Celebrates Comics." *American Libraries Blog.* https://americanlibrariesmagazine.org/blogs/the-scoop/banned-books-week-celebrates-comics/.

Calkins, Emily. 2014. "The Right to Read: The How and Why of Supporting Intellectual Freedom for Teens." *In the Library with the Lead Pipe.* http://www.inthelibrarywiththeleadpipe.org/2014/the-right-to-read-the-how-and-why-of-*supporting-intellectual-freedom-for-teens*/.

Comic Book Legal Defense Fund. 2016. "Education." http://cbldf.org/about-2/.

Higa, Darrel, Marilyn J. Hoppe, Taryn Lindhorst, Shawn Mincer, Blair Beadnell, Diane M. Morrison, Elizabeth A. Wells, Avry Todd, and Sarah Mountz. 2014. "Negative and Positive Factors Associated with the Well-Being of Lesbian, Gay, Bisexual, Transgender, Queer, and Questioning (LGBTQ) Youth." *Youth and Society* 46 (5): 663–87. doi:10.1177/0044118X12449630.

Human Rights Campaign. 2012. Growing up LGBT in America: At Home, at School, and in the Community. Washington, D.C.: Author. http://www.hrc.org/files/assets/resources/Growing-Up-LGBT-in-America_Report.pdf.

Martin, Hillias J., Jr., and James R. Murdock. 2007. *Serving Lesbian, Gay, Bisexual, Transgender, and Questioning Teens: A How-To-Do-It Manual for Librarians.* New York: Neal-Schuman.

McCabe, Caitlin. 2016. "How the Comics Code Laid the Foundation for LGBTQ Comix." *Comic Book Legal Defense Fund,* http://cbldf.org/2016/06/how-the-comics-code-laid-the-foundation-for-lgbtq-comix/.

McCloud, Scott. 1994. *Understanding Comics: The Invisible Art.* New York: William Morrow.

Nyberg, Amy Kiste. 2016. "Comics Code History: The Seal of Approval." *Comic Book Legal Defense Fund.* http://cbldf.org/comics-code-history-the-seal-of-approval/.

Watts, Pam. 2015. "The Social Justice League." *Teaching Tolerance* 49: 54–7.

Women and Wikipedia

Diversifying Editors and Enhancing
Content through Library Edit-a-Thons

THERESE F. TRIUMPH *and* KIMBERLEY M. HENZE

Our case study will describe a series of women-themed Wikipedia edit-a-thons hosted by the University of North Carolina–Chapel Hill (UNC-CH) Libraries in the spring of 2015. The authors will discuss the outcomes of two specific edit-a-thons for women artists and scientists; explain some of the benefits of hosting an edit-a-thon; and share resources, tips, and advice for librarians seeking to host their own edit-a-thons. The events, which bring together people interested in creating, developing, and enhancing Wikipedia articles, are an attempt to address the absence of women entries, the lack of credible sources, and the dearth of women editors.

Wikipedia was created in 2001 as an open, collaborative, digital repository of knowledge with content furnished by volunteer editors (Wikipedians), who create, edit, and update entries. As of January 2016, Wikipedia had 27.5 million named user accounts with a core unit of 115,000 regular editors (Wikipedia "Number of Editors" 2016). The online encyclopedia's greatest strength is its ability to harness the wisdom of the masses and proffer accessible and far-reaching content, but the credibility, reliability, and citability of that information has historically made for wary librarians and educators. Students, however, have not been as averse to the resource. In fact, a 2014 study found that 98.6 percent of undergraduates at participating Midwest public universities used Wikipedia as an information source (Kim, Sin, and Yoo-Lee 2014). Wikipedia's user base extends beyond college students, though, and is evidenced by the source's rank as the seventh most visited site on the Internet, both in the United States and across the globe (Alexa 2016).

The online encyclopedia is editable by anyone who learns the online protocol of the site, so librarians are becoming part of the movement to enhance and bolster Wikipedia's content by holding "edit-a-thons," which bring together people interested in creating, developing, and enhancing Wikipedia entries in a collaborative and social way. Specifically, a Wikipedia edit-a-thon is an event held to welcome new populations to the editing community, create or amend critical information, and in the process expand the pool and diversity of editors and articles. A library-hosted event emphasizes the importance of research best practices while engaging multiple literacy skills and highlighting the excellent library resources available. Edit-a-thons enable librarians to connect with professors, students, or student groups on campus and directly support research and outreach by providing relevant, reliable resources, writing funding grants, planning and hosting the event, articulating the value of an edit-a-thon to stakeholders, providing reference and subject specialists for participants, organizing workflow during the event, and analyzing results afterward.

Edit-a-thons then emerge not only as a space for educating users on information and digital literacy, but also on the disciplinary, gendered, and historical biases of information. While men and women use the site in nearly equal numbers at 56 percent of men and 50 percent of women in the United States (Zickuhr and Rainie 2011), a 2011 survey found that only 8.5 percent of editors were female (Pande 2011). When those numbers came to public attention, there was a movement to bring women to the editing community and women's issues to article content (Cohen 2011). A low percentage of female participants introduces systemic gender bias into the encyclopedic content: biographical articles on historically significant women and articles on what are traditionally viewed as women's issues are often fewer in number, biased in content, and shorter in length. Wikipedia participants witness first-hand the pervasiveness of these issues in contemporary culture, and in the process of creating and revising content, they become "information activists," a skill which they can apply to various other outlets in their occupational, digital, and educational lives.

Case Studies

Art+Feminism

The Sloane Art Library at UNC-CH partnered with a university graduate student group, the Art and Museum Library and Information Student Society (AMLISS), to hold a node event of the international Art+Feminism Wikipedia Edit-a-thon, based at the Museum of Modern Art in New York (Wikipedia "UNC Art+Feminism" 2015). In 2015, the second annual international event was held over the weekend of International Women's Day and brought together 1,500 participants in 74 node edit-a-thons across seventeen countries and four continents, united under the hashtag #artandfeminism. Unfortunately, the weekend of March 8, 2015, corresponded to UNC-CH's academic spring break, when many students leave campus. In an effort to involve as many participants as possible, we decided to hold our event in April, alongside three other UNC-CH and one Duke University edit-a-thon, under the umbrella #wikiNC.

The event was thus held on the evening of April 7 in the Sloane Art Library. We utilized the library instruction space for a basic Wikipedia tutorial before moving to the main library for collaborative work. Editors made use of the extensive UNC-CH art resources for research, including the Archive of North Carolina Woman Artists, from which we pulled our local list of articles to be edited or created. Online resources gathered by the librarians were put on the Wikipedia meetup page for participants' easy access.

The edit-a-thon was open to UNC-CH students, staff, faculty, and the Wikipedia community. The UNC-CH Art+Feminism edit-a-thon had a small but mighty core of 13 undergraduate, graduate, staff, and faculty participants, augmenting or creating 13 Wikipedia articles on North Carolina women artists.

Women in Science

The UNC-CH Kenan Science Library and two graduate groups, Women in Science and Engineering (WISE) and Women in Computer Science (WICS), held an edit-a-thon to add women scientists to the online encyclopedia (Wikipedia "UNC Women in Science" 2015). Our edit-a-thon was held in April, to coincide with several other UNC-CH edit-a-thons and the North Carolina Science Festival. In addition to bolstering the credibility of Wikipedia, the science librarians were interested in connecting with the science students, showing them the many resources available through the library, and cultivating/enhancing women in the science, technology, engineering and mathematics (STEM) fields. We extended an invitation for this event to all campus members and the local Wikipedia community. In addition, the science librarian invited Rachel Swaby, the author of *Headstrong: 52 Women Who Changed Science—and the World* (2015), to the edit-a-thon and included her book in the event's resources. Though Swaby was unable to attend in person, she publicized the edit-a-thon online. The event even attracted the remote participation of University of Michigan chemistry post-doc, whose research includes Wikipedia edit-a-thons (Moy, Locke, Coppola and McNeil 2015).

The event was held on April 16 in the library, utilizing the classroom for the editing tutorial taught by the graduate students and the library space for group collaboration and editing purposes. The science librarian collected both print resources on UNC-CH women faculty from the Wilson Library Special Collections, and online resources, which were put on the Wikipedia meetup page for participants' easy access.

There was a diverse turnout of undergraduate and graduate students, faculty, and non–UNC attendees totaling 33 people. We edited or created 21 Wikipedia web pages about women scientists, which are noted on the Women in Science meetup page, "Event Outcomes."

How to Host an Edit-a-Thon

Hosting an edit-a-thon may seem a little daunting, especially for those new to web editing, but conveniently, Wikipedia and its Wikimedia division have tutorials, guidelines, and teaching materials geared to supporting edit-a-thons (Wikipedia "How to Run an Edit-a-thon" 2016). Reaching out to local editors and the surrounding Wikipedia groups is a great way to become a more proficient editor and to attract "professional" editors to attend your event. Edit-a-thons can vary in size, from small research groups to large all-campus events. Additional support can be found by partnering with student groups, professors, or local organizations.

Picking a Theme

The first step is to pick a theme or topic for the edit-a-thon. Take into consideration a particular community's interests as well as the strengths of a library's collection. UNC-CH has phenomenal research collections, which were assembled as both inspiration and research tools for participants. The Archive of North Carolina Women Artists, for example, was the guiding blueprint for prioritizing which articles we augmented and created at the Art+Feminism edit-a-thon. The University Archives in Wilson Library's Special

Collections collects all college department publications, which also proved a great resource for identifying women science faculty.

However, library collections don't have to be the sole basis for a theme; prospective edit-a-thon hosts can look to the community's own history or interests. Colorful, yet little-documented, local histories with important women leaders or unique traditions are great themes, as they can serve as a point of commemoration and can keep the community invested in the event. Similarly, if there's a particular women's interest cause that's close to the community, there may be organizations or alliances with whom a library could partner.

Funding

When it comes to funding, the most important thing to remember is that the edit-a-thon can be adjusted to fit any library's parameters: even if that means a no-cost event. At a bare-bones level, a completely virtual event with streamed instruction sessions and a collaborative Wikipedia meetup page is an option, too. To have a more involved event, perhaps with guest speakers, food, event swag, or a rented larger venue, there are a number of funding options host libraries might pursue. First, look into funding options specifically for edit-a-thons like Wikimedia DC, which has rolling grant funds available through a simple application. However, if you're working from within a larger institution, keep in mind that administrators may have to process grant funding applications.

Another option for women's studies events might be to partner with an academic Women's or Gender Studies department, local women's interest nonprofits, or museums. One 2015 Art+Feminism node event was a collaboration between the art group Fembot, *Ms.* magazine, USC Annenburg School for Communication and Journalism, and the University of Oregon's Center for the Study of Women in Society (Wikipedia "Ms. Fembot" 2015).

Benefits

In order to maximize or clearly express the need for funding to stakeholders at an institution, there are several important points to mention. Edit-a-thons have meaningful benefits as practices of women's and gender studies programs, training in information and digital literacy, and service to the greater community. First, women's issues illuminate the social construction of gendered roles in society, how those roles have evolved over time, and how to be critically attentive to these and other intersectionalities to promote an ethical climate of positive change. This knowledge, already an invaluable part of academic departments and special interest groups, should extend to a library context as well.

Second, informed and ethical citizenship in the twenty-first century involves a set of skills that enable individuals to recognize, access, evaluate, incorporate, use, and ethically understand information critically in its textual, digital, visual, or fluid forms (ACRL 2015). Edit-a-thons foster this literacy because they provide opportunities for students and patrons to witness the backend system of an information resource, create new information themselves, and engage with other creators, all in an environment of critical production, collaborative meaning-making, and information activism.

Third, most—if not all—libraries have an outreach mission to engage their patrons;

promote research, scholarship, or creativity; and enhance the livelihoods of a local, national, or global community. UNC-CH Libraries' Vision, for example, is to "be a leader among academic research libraries in meeting users' evolving knowledge-creation and knowledge management needs" and to "define and integrate new library roles, practices, partnerships, and technologies in achieving this vision" (UNC Libraries 2016). Edit-a-thons align with these values because they facilitate community engagement, critical perspectives, collaborative research, and the production of knowledge.

Event Planning

Begin planning the edit-a-thon by establishing tasks and delegating jobs. This includes the development of a Wikipedia meetup page, the establishment of an event location, and the scope of the event. A meetup page can be designed as the central location for all of the event-planning information. As more information is developed, the site can include the edit-a-thon participants as they sign up, the available research resources, a list of the event topics with existing Wikipedia pages, those that need pages, helpful editing tutorials, and other resources.

Planning should also include the availability of Internet access for all participants, the location and setup of the edit-a-thon, how and where to hold an instruction session for first-time editors, and recruiting experienced Wikipedians to help newly minted editors during the event. Parking, administration permissions, and security issues need to be addressed, too. If food is to be supplied, location of the food, paper goods, and cleanup should be identified.

The night of the UNC-CH events, signs and balloons were used to distinguish the event locations and both edit-a-thons began with a thirty-minute instruction session on how to edit in Wikipedia, followed by several hours of editing. Experienced editors had nametags identifying their skill and were available to help others. The libraries were set up with various spaces for collaboration and quiet work; print resources were readily available and to treat the participants, food was provided and several raffles were held of donated gifts.

Promoting Your Event

In order to maximize edit-a-thon attendance and outreach, thoughtful and effective promotions can be accomplished very economically. The Wikimedia meetup page will allow other Wikipedia editors in the community to be alerted (for free) to the event and can be used as the main resource page. Additionally, we coordinated our efforts with three other academic library edit-a-thons to cross-promote, build awareness in the area, and share advice and successes. Apart from our events, colleagues also held, during the month of April, an American Indian History in North Carolina edit-a-thon, an African American Soldiers in U.S. Wars edit-a-thon, and a Women at Duke edit-a-thon.

A poster designed by the University Library, the libraries' websites, and each event's meetup page offered individual event details but also cited events at participating libraries. Social media for all events were united under the hashtag #wikiNC, which we used to promote events beforehand, to live-update social media during the events, and to post results/offer resources after the events. We also encouraged participants to post their thoughts and photos with the shared hashtag. Catering to our user base, many of the edit-a-thons made Facebook events as well, which the other libraries shared on their own pages.

Other sources of publicity included outreach to graduate groups on campus, faculty, and university listservs. Faculty outreach is a powerful rallying source because, depending on curricula and teaching schedules, edit-a-thons can be integrated into a student assignment, extra credit opportunity, or annual departmental event. Free food or swag are popular incentives and can be catered to an event's theme or resources. The Art+Feminism edit-a-thon was featured in the student newspaper, *The Daily Tar Heel*; while this coverage came subsequent to the event, we're hoping that the publicity will boost awareness for the next iteration (Chou 2015).

Finding (or Making) Your Experts: Train the Trainer

For those new to Wikipedia's citation system, attribution policies, writing style, markup, and backend interface, the thought of teaching others these procedures might feel like the blind leading the blind. Luckily, the Wikipedia community has built and gathered extensive resources for all levels of researcher, editor, and edit-a-thon host.

First, most metropolitan areas have local Wikipedia experts, ready with advice, training, or clarification about running an edit-a-thon smoothly and teaching participants how to create enduring and productive articles and edits. Making a Wikimedia meetup page allows for these local volunteers to reach out and contact you.

Even if local Wikipedia experts attend the event, the event hosts will still need onsite know-how to provide training, answer participants' questions, and troubleshoot any problems as they arise. Building this base of competent editors is made very manageable by the plethora of Wikipedia tutorials on every part of the editing process, written for trainer and trainee alike (Wikipedia "Tutorial" 2016). Welcome to Wikipedia is a good place to start for building expertise (Wikipedia "Welcome" 2015). At our Art+Feminism edit-a-thon, our Wikipedia trainers were library science graduate students who had been working with the Wikipedia system for some time and were able to adapt their research-instruction-session muscles to teaching participants how to edit.

Apart from Wikipedia expertise, it's also beneficial to have content specialists for assisting with the discovery, evaluation, use, and attribution of the research material for the theme. Luckily, this is the substance of librarianship, so a library edit-a-thon already has a base of skilled research instructors to help. Both the Art+Feminism and Women in Science edit-a-thons used a combination of reference and subject-specialist librarians along with graduate students in art history and science. In addition, professors, practitioners, or professionals of a topic can serve as content experts, providing insight into the topic alongside librarians.

Organizing Participants

In order to best prepare for the event and coordinate new users, some sort of organized registration of participants is needed. Conventionally in edit-a-thon practice, the announcement of the event and the organization of participants take place on a Wikimedia meetup page. To sign up, participants create a username and make a first edit on the meetup page in order to add their names to the registration section of the page. The advantage of this first edit is that users complete an editing task before the event and are thus introduced, on a basic level, to Wikipedia editing systems. This also ensures there will not be any technical difficulties from Wikipedia's standard limit on the number of usernames created from a single IP address during a short period of time, for example, during the edit-a-thon. Note, this restriction can be circumvented by having a Wikipedian with "account creator status" at the event (Wikipedia "Requests for Permission" 2016).

At the same time, it is worth considering meet-up pages might not be the best sole registration method. Advertising on a meetup principally reaches already-experienced Wikipedians, and new- or non-users might experience difficulty or confusion registering without any assistance. If using a meetup page, be certain to include (and highlight) detailed and clear directions for editing the page in correspondence with participants. For some—digital natives in particular—the registration method might feel like standard practice, but if a goal of hosting an edit-a-thon is to welcome new editors into the Wikipedia environment in an open, fully supportive, and easily accessible setting, meetup pages might not be the best option. The Art+Feminism event used a multi-site registration option, with both a meetup page and a Facebook event page open for participants to sign up. Tutorials, overviews, and lists of articles to edit can also be pushed out through multiple platforms.

During the event, you'll need to manage the list of articles that users can edit, are currently editing, or have completed through some sort of collaborative information system that is able to stay current and be visible to all users. There are myriad ways to do this, and when choosing which method is best, be sure to consider your user base. If an edit-a-thon has many participants new to technology, an analog organization system might be best. For example, the Women in Science event used a centrally located board with post-its to keep track of articles. The Art+Feminism event used an in- and out-box system with files on local artists. If a user base is more adept at technology, a system like Google Docs or live-editing the edit-a-thon meetup page may be easier options for keeping track of articles.

Analyze Your Results

There are two parts to analyzing the success of the edit-a-thon: how did the edit-a-thon impact Wikipedia and how successful was the edit-a-thon event. First, analyzing the impact of the edit-a-thon can be done by reviewing all edits made via the participants' usernames. Since Wikipedia editing is open to all, searching a username's contributions can provide a detailed list of all edits made by each participant. An edit review is very helpful if the edit-a-thon is used as part of a class for grading purposes or funded research for verification of work accomplished. In addition, reviewing the edits can identify any concerns or discrepancies noted on the "talk" page of a newly edited/created Wikipedia page. A "talk" page is visible by clicking the tab at the top of a page and reviewing any questions, concerns, or comments posted by other editors about the edits on the page (Wikipedia "Talk Pages" 2015). If social media was employed, searching for a specific hashtag can be useful in determining the reach of the event, too.

Second, the success of the event according to the participants can be conducted by surveying the participants at the end of the event. These participant comments are useful for reporting on the event to sponsors/administrators, and they can help to improve future edit-a-thons and be used to promote additional edit-a-thons.

Summary

Wikipedia edit-a-thons are a potent opportunity for librarians to advance information literacy and engage with their communities, while raising awareness and correcting the contemporary gender biases of our society. With our UNC-CH edit-a-thons as successful case studies, we've outlined strategies and considerations for selecting a theme, securing funding, articulating benefits, planning the space, promoting the event, finding/making Wikipedia experts, organizing participants, and analyzing event results. As a last point, we'd like to assert that these events are collaborative learning spaces for everyone involved: experienced editors, librarians, and participants all learn from each other, which makes for a productive, positive experience and return-editors. Remember that you can have fun with this and with each edit, the world's largest free and open encyclopedia becomes a little more critically and ethically attentive to women's interests.

Finally, we want to thank our fellow UNC-CH librarians Angela Bardeen, Mireille Djenno, and Emily Jack; librarians Kelly Wooten from Duke and Heather Gendron from Yale; and library science graduate student Amelia Holmes, who mentored, conducted, and participated in the development of the multiple edit-a-thons across the UNC-CH and Duke campuses. Thank you also to Judy Panitch and Tanya Fortner, UNC-CH Libraries, for their publicity.

References

Alexa. 2016. "How Popular Is Wikipedia.org?" Last modified February 15. http://www.alexa.com/siteinfo/wikipedia.org.

Association of College and Research Libraries (ACRL). 2015. "Framework for Information Literacy for Higher Education." Chicago: American Library Association. http://www.ala.org/acrl/standards/ilframework.

Chou, Jun. 2015. "Feminists, Artists Unite for Wikipedia 'Edit-a-thon.'" *The Daily Tar Heel*, April 8. http://www.dailytarheel.com/article/2015/04/feminists-artists-unite-for-wikipedia-edit-a-thon.

Cohen, Noam. 2011. "Define Gender Gap? Look Up Wikipedia's Contributor List." *New York Times*, January 30. http://www.nytimes.com/2011/01/31/business/media/31link.html?_r=2&src=busln.

Kim, Kyung-Sun, Sei-Ching Joanna Sin, and Eun Young Yoo-Lee. 2014. "Undergraduates' Use of Social Media as Information Sources." *College and Research Libraries* 75, no. 4: 442–457.

Moy, Cheryl L., Jonas R. Locke, Brian P. Coppola, and Anne J. McNeil. 2015. "Improving Science Education and Understanding Through Editing Wikipedia." *Journal of Chemical Education* 87, no. 11: 1159–1162.

Pande, Mani. 2011. "Shedding Light on Women Who Edit Wikipedia." *Wikimedia Blog*, July 15. http://blog.wikimedia.org/2011/07/15/shedding-light-on-women-who-edit-wikipedia/.

Swaby, Rachel. 2015. *Headstrong: 52 Women Who Changed Science—And the World*. New York: Broadway.

UNC Libraries. 2016. "Mission Statement." Accessed February 16. http://library.unc.edu/about/mission/.

Wikipedia. 2015. "Ms. Fembot Edit-a-thon." Last modified November 25. https://en.wikipedia.org/wiki/Wikipedia:Ms._Fembot_Edit-a-Thon.

_____. 2015. "Talk Pages." Last modified May 14. https://en.wikipedia.org/wiki/Wikipedia:Tutorial/Talk_pages.

_____. 2015. "UNC Art+Feminism." Last modified April 8. "https://meta.wikimedia.org/wiki/Meetup/UNC/Art_%2B_Feminism_2015.

_____. 2015. "UNC Women in Science." Last modified April 20. https://meta.wikimedia.org/wiki/Meetup/UNC/Women_in_Science.

_____. 2015. "Welcome to Wikipedia." Last modified November 3. https://en.wikipedia.org/wiki/Wikipedia:Welcoming_committee/Welcome_to_Wikipedia.

_____. 2016. "How to Run an Edit-a-thon." Last modified January 26. https://en.wikipedia.org/wiki/Wikipedia:How_to_run_an_edit-a-thon.

_____. 2016. "Number of editors." Last modified February 8. https://en.wikipedia.org/wiki/Wikipedia:Wikipedians.

_____. 2016. "Requests for Permission: Account Creator." Last modified February 18. https://en.wikipedia.org/wiki/Wikipedia:Requests_for_permissions/Account_creator/Administrator_instructions.

_____. 2016. "Tutorial." Last modified February 1. https://en.wikipedia.org/wiki/Wikipedia:Tutorial.

Zickuhr, Kathryn, and Lee Rainie. 2011. "Wikipedia, Past and Present." *Pew Internet & American Life Project*. January 13. http://www.pewinternet.org/files/old-media//Files/Reports/2011/PIP_Wikipedia.pdf.

Behind Every Great Protagonist Is a Woman

Gender Imbalances in Popular Fiction and How to Correct Them

Jessica Zellers

Like many young girls, I avidly followed the adventures of Meg Murry, the awkward heroine of Madeleine L'Engle's science fiction novel *A Wrinkle in Time*. Since its 1963 publication, the book has fired the imagination of young readers, showing them how an ordinary young woman could save the world, not just with the power of love but with the power of science. More than fifty years later, the book continues to inspire; no less a figure than Chelsea Clinton praised it, very publicly, in the speech to introduce her mother Hillary Clinton at the Democratic National Convention (Clinton 2016).

The book that went on to become a classic initially struggled to find a home, having been rejected by dozens of publishers because of its unconventional protagonist: back then, nobody wrote female leads in science fiction stories (Hunt 2005). The idea seems outré today, with some of the most popular science fiction books starring female characters such as Katniss Everdeen (*The Hunger Games)* and Beatrice Prior *(Divergent)*—and, in film, with characters such as Furiosa *(Mad Max)* and Rey *(Star Wars: The Force Awakens)*.

Women have gained greater visibility in fiction than other marginalized groups. Any mainstream bookseller or public librarian knows that it is far easier to locate stories prominently featuring women and girls than to find stories prominently featuring, for instance, people of color, people with disabilities, or people from religious or cultural minorities.

This common-sense assertion is confirmed by a few quick searches in NoveList, a database of popular fiction and nonfiction titles. A search for "women" yields 122,166 results; "deafness" yields 244 results; "Hindus" yields 143 results. These examples are used not to accurately describe the presence or absence of marginalized groups in popular reading materials, but to illustrate that stories about women tend to be far more accessible than stories about other marginalized groups.

And that is the problem. In literature as in society, women have made dramatic advances—but because it is comparatively easy to connect readers with books about women and girls, we forget that there's an imbalance. We become complacent, not recognizing that equality is still a long way down the road.

In this essay, I argue that women are underrepresented in adult popular fiction, based on a collection analysis of the Leisure Reading area at Western Carolina University, a regional comprehensive university in the University of North Carolina system. I discuss why this underrepresentation needs to be corrected, and I offer ways for librarians to bring balance to their collections.

Background and Methodology

Hunter Library of Western Carolina University serves over 10,000 students, primarily undergraduates. Located in a prominent spot near the main entrance of the library is the Leisure Reading area, a small but thriving collection of popular fiction and nonfiction. Six library faculty and staff select titles in accordance with Hunter Library's Collection Development policy, which calls for books that are meant to be read purely for pleasure, and not in support of curriculum or research.

To make their purchasing decisions, book selectors depend on common collection development tools such as professional reviews, respected amateur reviews, bestselling status, book buzz in the media, awards lists, and patron recommendations. It should be noted, however, that the Leisure Reading collection represents a small portion of the budget and investment of staff time. Consequently, selectors tend toward "sure bets," that is, books that have high potential for popularity. They do not scour the corners of the internet, hunting for obscure or out-of-print gems.

Thus the Leisure Reading collection mostly comprises mainstream, recent, and core/classic titles. Graphic Novels, regardless of genre, are shelved together, while the remaining books are shelved in one of five genres: Horror, Science Fiction and Fantasy, Mystery/Thriller, Romance, or Nonfiction. Books that do not fit easily into these categories (historical fiction or commercial fiction, for instance) are shelved in the closest-fitting genre.

To understand the representation of women among protagonists in popular adult fiction, I considered four sections: Graphic Novels, Horror, Science Fiction and Fantasy, and Mystery/Thriller. I excluded Nonfiction because my study was limited to fiction, and I excluded Romance, because it is the one genre that offers an abundance of female protagonists, almost by definition (the exception being the male-male subgenre). Within Graphic Novels, Horror, and Science Fiction and Fantasy, I performed a content analysis of every tenth book. Within Mystery/Thriller, I performed a content analysis of every fifth book, to compensate for a small sample size.

In each book I analyzed, I recorded the sex of the leading one or two protagonists, noting whether they were male or female. Books with three or more protagonists, or books with protagonists of uncertain sex, were accounted for in a third category, "Uncertain/Ensemble." To identify the protagonists and determine their sex, I looked at jacket copy, paying special attention to pronouns.

Results and Discussion

Out of 79 books analyzed, there were 88 protagonists, of whom 50 (57 percent) were male, 26 (29 percent) were female, and 12 (14 percent) were uncertain or ensemble.

Sex of Protagonist in 79 Popular Adult Fiction Novels

Protagonists	Male	Female	Uncertain/Ensemble
Graphic Novels	19	3	5
Horror	11	6	3
SF/F	11	8	4
Mystery/Thriller	9	9	0
Totals	50	26	12

The results are clear: male protagonists are represented far more often than female protagonists, at a rate of nearly two to one. In fact, male protagonists are represented more than female protagonists, protagonists of uncertain sex, and ensemble casts combined.

These are disheartening numbers. Women make up half the population in real life, but less than a third of the population among protagonists in fiction. Moreover, women are far more likely than men to read books or literature (Bohne and Triplett 2015, 68). A woman selecting any given novel will, statistically speaking, wind up with a story from the perspective of a male lead. She will find characters of her own sex represented as sidekicks or subplots, not as the heroes.

The need to see oneself in fiction is critical, a point illustrated by Nigerian novelist Chimamanda Ngozi Adichie in her TED Talk "The Danger of a Single Story," in which she recalls her first attempts at writing fiction. As a seven-year-old girl, she naturally modeled her stories after the ones she was familiar with, books about American and English children: "All my characters were white and blue-eyed, they played in the snow, they ate apples, and they talked a lot about the weather, how lovely it was that the sun had come out" (Adichie 2009). She did not see her own experiences, her own culture, her own geography.

And to an extent, this is appropriate. Fiction would be a dull affair if it presented only the familiar. Novels are powerful precisely because they can put readers in the minds of characters who look, think, live, and act differently than ourselves. Avid readers know this intuitively, and several studies have confirmed that reading engenders empathy; see, for instance, the work of Carnegie Mellon neuroscientists who monitored the neural activity of people reading *Harry Potter and the Sorcerer's Stone* (Wehbe et al. 2014).

But it goes without saying (or ought to) that we need to be able to see ourselves in the stories we read. Able-bodied, cisgendered, heterosexual white American males are extremely well-represented in fiction. These readers can easily find protagonists who are at least superficially similar to themselves in novels—but on the flip side, they cannot so easily find marginalized groups featured prominently. And members of those marginalized groups, of course, must work harder to find books that represent their own experiences.

But How Did This Happen?

Librarians are not singlehandedly responsible for the homogeneity of the books on their shelves. Responsibility must be shared among the other players in the literary ecosystem, including authors, agents, editors, publishers, and booksellers. We can only purchase and promote the books the market provides to us. The market is vast, however. Not even considering self-published books, there are hundreds of thousands of titles published in the United States every year.

Because it's impossible to keep up with the sheer volume of titles, those who work in libraries to collect and to market books depend on tools such as awards lists. Particularly when budgets are small and each dollar must be justified, these tools can be wonderful time-savers, and they can help us feel confident that we are wisely spending our money.

Unfortunately, there's a steep bias against diversity in the common collection development tools. Nicola Griffith (incidentally, the author of *Hild*, a novel starring a bisexual female saint) looked at fifteen years' worth of data from the Pulitzer Prize, Man Booker Prize, National Book Award, National Book Critics' Circle Award, Hugo Award, and Newbery Medal. "When women win literary awards for fiction it's usually for writing from a male perspective and/or about men," she concludes. "The more prestigious the award, the more likely the subject of the narrative will be male" (Griffith 2015).

Giffith looks at prestigious awards given to books about women; in a similar vein, Kamila Shamsie considers recommendations of books *by* women. While it is important to recognize that women can successfully write male protagonists (see J.K. Rowling's Harry Potter) and that men can successfully write female protagonists (see Stieg Larsson's Lisbeth Salander, she of the dragon tattoo), Shamsie's findings raise a serious eyebrow. She looked at five years of book recommendations in *The Guardian*, amounting to 162 works of fiction. Of those books, 56 percent of male reviews chose only books written by men, while 32 percent of female reviewers chose only books written by women.

"If male writers are more likely than women writers to value books by writers of their own gender," asks Shamsie, "what does that mean for judging panels, for book blurbs, for the championing of lesser-known writers by better-known writers? What, in short, does it mean for our literary culture?" (2015). What it means for literary culture, and what it means for librarians, is that gender bias pervades the tools we depend on to do our jobs. Whether this bias is intentional or unintentional, personal or institutional, is beside the point. Gender bias does exist, and it affects the tools that librarians use to make their professional decisions.

The answer is not to discard those tools. Even if librarians wanted to dismiss traditional resources such as awards lists and reviews on the grounds of bias, they would be hard pressed to find comparable replacements. Books selectors and readers' advisors need external information to be able to do their jobs. Even if a prestigious award such as the Pulitzer Prize tends to skew toward white male authors, Pulitzer winners still ought to be collected. They are superb books according to various objective and subjective measures. Furthermore, traditional awards sometimes go to marginalized voices, as happened with the 2016 Nebula Awards, which were dominated by women and people of color.

Instead, the answer is to be mindful of biases. Gender imbalances among protagonists in popular adult fiction collections will inevitably happen otherwise. Collection development librarians, even those with the best of intentions, will build a collection that over-represents male protagonists, unless they take deliberate steps to prevent it.

How to Fix Gender Disparity

Librarians can follow some or all of these steps to work towards gender parity on their shelves:

Demonstrate the Problem

Though most people who work with popular fiction are aware of the lack of diversity in books with regard to race and sexual orientation, the gender disparity among protagonists is much less apparent. Reviewing either the literature (scholarly or popular) can bring the problem into relief, but even then, some people will be reluctant to believe the problem exists in their own library. This is an understandable response: an accusation of sexism in the collection feels like a criticism of both personal and professional integrity.

Furthermore, it would be a poor use of staff time and money to correct a problem that does not exist. "Well, everyone knows it's a problem, it's common knowledge" is a weak justification for undertaking a project. Administrators want to see evidence before committing to a project, and collection development librarians want to see evidence that their current practices are resulting in a gender imbalance.

So, the first task is to take a random sample of the popular adult fiction collection. A sample of ten or even twenty percent of the books is feasible for very small collections, such as those typically found in academic libraries. For larger collections, a smaller percentage is fine, as long as the books in the sample are truly random. An easy way to do this is to look at the first book on every shelf, for instance, or the first book on every other shelf.

Library staff can perform the analysis. Alternately, volunteers or Friends of the Library can analyze the books. The job title doesn't matter, as long as the person performing the analysis can use the available clues (chiefly, dusk jacket copy) to identify the sex of the protagonist(s). This is usually straightforward, though in some cases, as with Ann Leckie's gender-bending science fiction novel *Ancillary Justice*, the "other" category will come into play. And when there are more than two or three protagonists, analyzers will be best served by an "ensemble" category, as with Alan Moore's *The League of Extraordinary Gentlemen*, which, despite the title, prominently features a female lead (and quite a few men who could hardly be called "gentle," but I digress).

An optional category for analysis is book genre. If genre information is easily obtainable, by dint of shelving or spine stickers, this is well worth recording. This granular analysis can guide future book selection decisions. In my library, for instance, the greatest sexual disparity between protagonists is in graphic novels, while the mystery/thriller section is perfectly balanced.

Bear in mind that women protagonists are the norm in romance and erotica novels, which may partially cloak a gender bias in the larger collection. Take this into account and, after the hash marks are tallied, see if the data points to a significant sex imbalance in either direction. If so, continue below with Step 2.

Develop a More Balanced Collection

If you've identified gender gaps in your fiction collection, take steps to correct the problem. A quick infusion with one-time money would be a great start, but the more important goal is to incorporate changes in your long-term strategy. Ordering a few novels with female protagonists is a bandage. Changing the underlying system is a cure.

To change that underlying system, book selectors and collection developers can take conscious steps to supplement their standard resources by consulting reviews and publications that emphasize women's writing:

- The Book Smugglers. With an emphasis on Young Adult and Speculative Fiction, The Book Smugglers review site frequently showcases books with female protagonists.
- VIDA. Dedicated to illuminating and decreasing the imbalance of critical attention paid to women writers, VIDA provides resources to help with the discovery of books by women writers.
- [Fill in blank] for Women. An internet search for "books for women" will usually reveal titles with books about women's issues, or books in genres such as romance that reliable feature female protagonists. This is a good start, but a robust library collection will feature female protagonists in all genres, not just in niche sections. Try searching for "science fiction for women" or "graphic novels for women," for instance.
- In addition to internet searching, try keyword searching reviews, either in review journals or in your book vendor's interface, if it offers reviews. Possible searches include "female hero," "woman protagonist," "heroine," etc.
- If you have access to the NoveList database, you can search for "strong female," one of the descriptors used for book characters.

Selectors can incorporate some or all of these resources into their standard process for selecting titles.

Promote Books with Female Protagonists

You don't have to wait for your collection to achieve gender parity to start promoting female heroes. You can increase the visibility of women protagonists using the books that already exist.

- Display a book with a female protagonist face-out on the shelf
- Do a book display of female protagonists
- Do a rotating display of female protagonists by genre. Do Historical Fiction in January, Fantasy in February, Thrillers in March, etc.
- Booklists and displays that feature female protagonists are great, but don't forget to include them in other sorts of themed groups, like Beach Reads or Urban Fiction.
- Whatever you do, don't limit yourself to Romance, Erotica, and Women's Fiction. Readers already know to expect female protagonists from these genres, and it does a disservice to imply that women are heroes only in this one corner of fiction. Women also fight aliens, stop ticking bombs, undergo midlife crises, defeat demons, and ride into the sunset.
- Don't forget to recommend books with female protagonists to male readers. They can handle it. Really.

Track Your Results

As with any project, you'll want to evaluate your results. After implementing changes in collection development to work toward parity, wait for a period of time to elapse, perhaps six or twelve months. Then perform another content analysis. Considering only new acquisitions will show the most dramatic changes; if that's not feasible, take a sample of the whole collection, but be aware that results may be too subtle to notice. Transforming the character of an entire collection can take years.

Conclusion

Females take the starring role in adult popular fiction far less often than males. While women are represented or overrepresented in a few corners that cater almost exclusively to female readers, most noticeably in the romance genre, men are much more likely to be the heroes of novels.

These findings may be surprising. Thanks to conference panels, professional journals, scholarly articles, and campaigns such as We Need Diverse Books, there's strong awareness that the book world is stubbornly homogeneous with regard to race, sexual orientation, religion, and physical ability. What's less well known is that women are underrepresented as protagonists.

The encouraging news is that this problem is fixable. Because of systemic and historical biases, books with female protagonists do not always receive their due representation in the tools used by collection development librarians, such as awards lists and prestigious review sources—but the books are out there. Women have been starring in novels since at least 1688, when Aphra Behn wrote *Oroonoko*. The market is filled with entertaining, high-quality books starring women. We as librarians simply need to commit to collecting and promoting them.

REFERENCES

Adichie, Chimamanda Ngozi. "The Danger of a Single Story." Speech, TEDGlobal from Oxford, United Kingdom, July 23, 2009.
Bohne, Silber, and Tim Triplett. *A Decade of Arts Engagement: Findings from the Survey of Public Participation in the Arts, 2002–2012*. Washington, D.C.: National Endowment for the Arts, 2015. Accessed August 3, 2016. https://www.arts.gov/sites/default/files/2012-sppa-feb2015.pdf
Clinton, Chelsea. "Introduction to Hillary Clinton." Speech, Democratic National Convention from Philadelphia, PA, July 28, 2016.
Griffith, Nicola. 2015. "Books About Women Don't Win Big Awards: Some Data." Accessed August 4, 2016. https://nicolagriffith.com/2015/05/26/books-about-women-tend-not-to-win-awards/.
Hunter, Karen. 2005. "Madeleine L'Engle." *Madeleine L'Engle* (9781429813945) 1. *Biography Reference Center*, EBSCO*host*. Accessed August 2, 2016.
Shamsie, Kamila. 2015. "The Year of Women." Accessed August 4, 2016. http://www.thebookseller.com/insight/year-women.
Wehbe, Leila, Alona Fyshe, Tom Mitchell, Brian Murphy, Partha Talukdar, and Aaditya Ramdas. 2014. "Simultaneously Uncovering the Patterns of Brain Regions Involved in Different Story Reading Subprocesses." *PLOS ONE*. Accessed August 4, 2016. http://dx.doi.org/10.1371/journal.pone.0112575.

Spreading Girl Germs
Sources on Third-Wave Feminism in Collaborative Librarianship

ANNA W. CULBERTSON *and* LAUREL BLISS

Since it is largely the actions of men that comprise recorded history, Women's Studies is a discipline that relies heavily on primary sources and various types of gray literature to call to memory people, eras, and events. Add to this the expanding idea of what it means to be a woman and the challenges of pushing society to embrace gender fluid identities, and the need for access to documentation is even more critical. It is stunning to consider that mainstream acceptance of transgender people would not even begin to take place until the current millennium. Caitlyn Jenner, former Olympic gold medalist who revealed her new name and use of female pronouns in 2015, is now perhaps the most highly publicized transgender person on record. The Michigan Womyn's Music Festival, noted for its controversial women-born-women-only policy, concluded its final run in August 2015—another major stride in the same year. Although LGBT studies as a stand-alone discipline is increasingly being established in colleges and universities around the world, the onset of third-wave feminism in the early 1990s was instrumental in promoting a widespread call for tolerance and inclusion of all gender identities.

Zines and other underground publications that harken back to the Riot Grrrl Movement are an increasingly popular format collected by libraries and archives around the world, and are likewise used more and more in teaching and scholarship. They also provide a superior range of subjective experiences to accompany circulating scholarly literature holdings developed by subject librarians concerned with sex and gender. This essay will examine the collaborative efforts of a Women's Studies librarian and a Special Collections librarian at San Diego State University, as they aim to provide a critical approach to scholarship in third-wave feminism by developing collections and teaching students to utilize both primary and secondary sources in their research. We will first briefly examine the background of Women's Studies at SDSU and the program's current range of scholarship, and describe the roles of each librarian, respectively. Then we will explore the history and development of the library's *Zines and Minicomics Collection* and its role in research, instruction and outreach.

The Women's Studies Curriculum at SDSU

The Women's Studies program at SDSU began in 1970, and was the first such program in the country. The department itself was founded in 1975. Current courses are research-intensive and interdisciplinary in scope, focusing primarily on modern and contemporary issues affecting perceptions of gender. One frequently taught upper division course, WMNST 590 Feminist Thought, explores readings of feminist theory in historical perspective, with attention to contemporary debates in feminist scholarship. In WMNST 530 Women's Movements and Activism, students look at women's movements worldwide and examine women's diverse social/political strategies within local, national, and global contexts. Another popular course, WMNST 375 Sex, Power, and Politics, addresses topics such as leadership and ideology, power and authority, and the women's movement as a political movement. Doing an in-depth analysis of third-wave feminism is an important component of each of these courses.

A key role for the subject librarian is supporting the Women's Studies curriculum through development of the book and media collection. This means monitoring what is being taught, taking note of the research interests of the teaching faculty, and responding, when possible, to purchase requests from faculty. The collecting focus is on secondary literature suitable for undergraduates and the purchase of films that directly support an individual class. However, relevant primary materials published in book format are keenly sought after as well.

One of the challenges in shaping the book collection lies in the interdisciplinary and global focus of the program. Many publications fall within the broad subject parameters, and would be of interest to students and faculty. This is where knowledge of the curriculum comes into play. In addition, budgetary limitations and lack of an approval plan for purchases mean that the subject librarian must individually select titles, which is a time-consuming process. Having a robust interlibrary loan cooperative within San Diego does help researchers quickly and easily borrow books, relieving some of the pressure to have a perfect book collection here at SDSU.

An emerging area of developing the book collection is focusing on obtaining publications by faculty members. This serves two purposes: it increases the visibility of SDSU as a research institution and it supports the curriculum, as faculty are likely to teach in the same areas they do research in.

Special Collections and University Archives at SDSU holds a considerably broad range of printed books and documents supporting topics in women's studies. Since SDSU was one of the first universities in the country to offer a degree in Women's Studies, we are fortunate to offer an exceptional range of archival resources for this area of study. Not only do we house the papers of the Women's Studies Department, but we also hold archival collections of various individuals and local organizations. Some highlights include the papers of Bonnie Zimmerman, Professor Emeritus and one of the nation's top lesbian scholars, and the papers of Gracia Molina de Pick, former student, feminist, Chicana activist and educator. In addition, we hold the records of the San Diego chapter of National Organization for Women (NOW) and the Center for Women's Studies and Services, the first women's center in Southern California.

One of the earliest rare books in the collection that supports the study of women is a 1591 German translation of Jean Bodin's *De la Démonomanie*, a treatise on witchcraft and sorcery that advocates the tactical use of extreme torture on suspected witches, among other topics. We also own the first American edition of Mary Wollstonecraft's *A Vindication of the Rights of Women* (1792), numerous Victorian etiquette books, postcards promoting women's suffrage, numerous second-wave periodicals, feminist science fiction novels, and an early Olympia Press edition of Valerie Solanas' *SCUM Manifesto*. These examples are simply intended to illustrate the *range* of materials in the collection, while our overall holdings are vast.

However, one collection that stands out amongst all resources as unique in format, content and historical context is our Zines and Minicomics Collection. Originally created in 2002 and formerly known as the West Coast Zines Collection, this expansive array of do-it-yourself publications includes but is not limited to topics in all areas of identity politics as well as punk rock, anarchism, activism, alternative lifestyles, creative writing, humor, and popular culture. One of its strongest concentrations is in feminism, with titles dating back to the Riot Grrrl movement of the early to mid–1990s as well as contemporary publications representing the ongoing legacy of third-wave feminism. Courses incorporating third-wave feminist thought into the syllabi are taught across several departments, including Women's Studies, LGBT Studies, English and Comparative Literature, History, Art, Chicana/o Studies and Latin American Studies. Our diverse campus curriculum offers an exceptional range of opportunities for interdisciplinary exposure to this unique, non-traditional format of library resources.

A Timely Reorganization Project

Over the past two years, the Zines and Minicomics Collection has been subject to a major reorganization project aimed at improved access and a better representation of its scope. Its initiation was timely, as zines have recently gained much traction on campus across the curriculum, in research, and in personal interest amongst students. A brief background of this project will help illustrate how we are now better equipped to use the collection in library instruction, reference and outreach. The project was prompted in part by the recognition that "West Coast" did not adequately represent the current range of materials in the collection—there are, in fact, zines from all over the world included. In addition, combining the collection with a concentration of minicomics that was identified in another collection seemed appropriate. Minicomics are self-published or small press comics that often take somewhat of a crossover format in relation to zines. The distinction between zines and minicomics is hotly debated on the Web, but in order to streamline access to similar materials (and avoid getting sucked into semantic debates), the decision was made to combine the two. Zines often contain comic art and many minicomics resemble zines in format and content, both being mediums for reflection on life, politics, personal struggles and so on. The mixed-media experience of the combined genres also sets an interesting course for research in any number of areas.

Another major reason for the reorganization project is that the collection is described in a finding aid that has been haphazardly tagged over the years by numerous contributors using inconsistent terminology. For instance, a keyword search for "feminism" would reveal, say, 29 entries, while a keyword search for "feminist" would reveal 36. While any good search strategy begins by varying search terms to produce the most comprehensive list of results possible, this should also not needlessly frustrate the researcher. A controlled vocabulary with consistency in tagging enables the researcher to feel confident that they have successfully exhausted their options. However, zine librarians have long recognized the inadequacies of pre-existing content standards and controlled vocabularies for describing zine content. In a chapter about cataloging zines for the recent Library Juice publication, *Informed Agitation: Library and Information Skills in Social Justice Movements and Beyond*, Jenna Freedman and Rhonda Kauffman write about the need to "[inform] and [empower] library workers with subject expertise in zines (or another Special Collections area) to do their own cataloging" (Freedman and Kauffman 2014, 221).

For these reasons, I decided to begin the project using a popular online resource amongst zine librarians—the Zine Thesaurus of Subject Terms developed by the Anchor Archive Zine Library in Halifax, Nova Scotia. The list is impressively comprehensive especially in regards to identity politics and contains excellent coverage of cross-references. In the occasional event that a term representing any of our zine content does not appear in the ZTST, we keep a running document of those terms that serves as a local addendum to the list. This part of the reorganization project remains in process, as I am currently exploring separate resources for categorizing the minicomics, but for the purpose of supporting research in third-wave feminism, we are now well prepared.

A final step in the reorganization project involves the physical re-housing of zines. They were previously organized in folders stored in archival storage cartons—a method that offers the best possible preservation environment for the materials, but the worst possible browsability. The solution to this draws inspiration from zine libraries and infoshops around the country that store their collections in magazine files. Archival pamphlet files perform in this same way, enabling improved browsability in an acid-free storage environment, with particularly old, rare or fragile zines enclosed in polyester sleeves for added support. The zines are still stored in the secure stacks area of Special Collections, but the result is a much more efficient environment for identifying zines for use in library instruction.

The difference this project has made on library instruction is tangible. My first instruction session at SDSU was, conveniently, for a Women's Studies course on third-wave feminism, and my unfamiliarity with the collection coupled with the inconsistent tags in the finding aid resulted in a grueling level of preparation work. This experience largely prompted my initiation of the entire reorganization project. Librarians and users alike are now able to search effortlessly across the finding aid for zines on any topic, including those in women's studies as well as countless others across the curriculum. The finding aid also links to the ZTST, recommending its consultation for more in-depth searches. The visual serendipity of browsing enabled by the new storage method further facilitates internal identification of zines for library instruction, research assistance, digital projects and exhibits.

Towards an Institutional Priority of Mainstreaming

At SDSU, Special Collections has been historically run as an independent operation. Class visits have been direct point-of-need arrangements that have only occasionally involved subject librarians. Collection development is usually done internally, as is all research and curation of exhibits and digital collections. This has inevitably resulted in siloed views and efforts. Historically, the Women's Studies curriculum has not been served nearly as often by Special Collections as is ideal, considering the range and extent of related resources we own. We aim to change this by working overall to mainstream Special Collections functions, and, together on a smaller scale, by coordinating our instructional efforts as subject librarian for Women's Studies and Special Collections librarian. By demonstrating successful collaborations, we can serve as an example for others within our library and across the profession.

The idea of "mainstreaming" has gained much attention in recent years as an essential transition for the survival of Special Collections departments. In 2013, the Association of Research Libraries (ARL) published an important issue of *Research Library Issues* dedicated to the topic of mainstreaming Special Collections. The issue features case studies in all aspects of special collections librarianship, from collection development to instruction, with an overall goal, according to introductory author Lisa R. Carter, of emphasizing how "efforts to align, integrate, and centralize Special Collections can drive transformative change that enables the whole library to meet its teaching, learning, and research mission and become an effective partner in advancing the scholarly record" (Carter 2013, 4). While a few years old, this collection of case studies is worthy of mention as it is the most comprehensive publication in the field to date that evidences a paradigm shift towards mainstreaming Special Collections functions.

Suddenly, everyone in the special collections world has moved beyond discussions of access and openness to wholeheartedly embrace holistic library service goals. This shift in approach generates increased interest amongst subject librarians in co-teaching instruction sessions that combine primary and secondary source research methods. It has also lead to a more collaborative approach to the creation and maintenance of instructional materials such as our research guides, which had traditionally been solely the purview of the subject specialist. Now, each guide includes an "SDSU Special Collections" section that focuses on materials in manuscript and archival collections, print collections, and graphic and ephemera collections that might be of interest to researchers in that particular subject area.

A Two-Pronged Approach to Instruction

In the traditional setting, the subject librarian is responsible for providing general instruction sessions to Women's Studies classes. These course-based sessions are often tied to specific research assignments. These assignments frequently address contemporary gender issues such as sexual violence on college campuses, the role of women in politics, or women's rights organizations in other countries. Assignments also explore historical topics like the careers of important feminist theorists or third-wave feminism. In these instances, the instructor is most interested in having their students find a few books and articles on their topic. Some sessions address forming strategies for finding primary material within the main book collection. These include tips on what keywords to use in a search of the library's catalog, and how to interpret a bibliographic record to determine if it does contain relevant primary sources. In the past, the Special Collections librarian has also stepped in to demonstrate primary source research, and this has been effective in many cases.

The library's instruction steering group has been exploring ways to flip the traditional classroom library instruction sessions. A flipped model would allow students to work through tutorials, videos, and online quizzes on their own, helping them gain mastery of basic research skills before entering a library classroom. Time spent with a librarian could then focus on higher level skills that directly relate to their assignment and to the course's student learning outcomes. In a Special Collections setting, this would mean that at a minimum, students would enter the reading room already knowing about policies and procedures, and would be comfortable searching our finding aid database for materials related to their research topic.

When time permits and the format is appropriate for the assignment, it is ideal for the two librarians to collaborate within Special Collections, with sources such as zines, alternative publications, ephemera and departmental records spread out on the tables. This affords the students an opportunity for hands-on engagement with materials while learning how to locate secondary and primary sources. Such a format provides an atmosphere conducive to contextualization of topics through direct exposure to related documents. Furthermore, it facilitates a more tangible assessment of student learning outcomes, which we develop in the library from an information literacy perspective in addition to supporting the outcomes developed across academic departments and courses.

In the fall semester of 2015, a new comparative literature course called the Social Politics of Indie included a focus on DIY and the birth of the Riot Grrrl movement. The Zines and Minicomics Collection provides a unique multi-generational representation of Riot Grrrl because it includes not only zines that were created in the moment of the movement, but also those created in the last twenty years or so since. Zine-making remains a popular form of indie publishing today and we receive regular contributions to the collection by current zinesters as well as donors that acquire zines locally and regionally.

One fairly broad criticism of the Riot Grrrl movement was its failure to acknowledge people of color. Since the Zines and Minicomics Collection includes so many zines created in the movement's wake, it represents third-wave feminism and other gender studies issues from the further-marginalized perspectives of zinesters of color. In light of the controversy in early 2015 surrounding the Brooklyn Zine Fest's decision to exclude a panel on Black Lives Matter (Alam 2015; Brooklyn Zine Fest 2015), collections that pick up the slack, so to speak, will continue to be invaluable in academia for their commitment to inclusivity. As diversity is an institutional priority outlined in our own current strategic plan, the professor of the course, likewise, was excited to bring this emphasis to the topic.

The session began with a demonstration of how to search the finding aid database, followed by a brief history of zines and an introduction to the Riot Grrrl and Queercore movements that arose out of the straight, white male stranglehold on the punk scene. Numerous significant titles, people and events were identified and the aforementioned people of color controversy was discussed. At the end of the session, the students learned how to fold their own eight-page zine from one sheet of paper, which better equipped them for their zine-making assignments and provided them with their own copy of a zine made by librarians on how to properly cite zines. The response to the session from the students and the professor alike was overwhelmingly positive. Students were prompted not only to be more experimental in their zine-making assignments but also to start exploring zine collecting and making on their own. Several of the students have since approached both me and the professor about starting a zine club on campus. The power that the idea of expression through self-publishing has over the students is tangible and moving.

Community Engagement as a Collection-Building Tool

Another component of the "Social Politics of Indie" course that promoted student engagement and connectivity was an invited guest that has been actively involved in the San Diego zine-making network for over a decade. Kim Schwenk, one of the founding members of Grrrl Zines A-Go-Go, spoke to the class about her organization and how to participate in the local zinester community. Incidentally, GZAGG was fundamental in the formation of the original West Coast Zines Collection at SDSU. One of the organization's early members, Elke Zobl, also founder of the Grrrl Zine Network, began working with a former Special Collections department head in 2002 to solicit zine donations to the collection. The collection has since grown to include thousands of zines, including ongoing contributions by authors of their own publications as well as donations from individuals and other zine libraries around the country. SDSU, in turn, has recently begun donating duplicates to the newly established zine collection at San Diego Public Library. GZAGG continues to give lectures and lead workshops all over the region today, and regularly donates zines to the collection at SDSU.

A popular (and unfortunate) misconception about zines in academic collections is that they are only available to enrolled students and serious scholars. In a recent piece in The Guardian about Papercut Zine Library in Somerville, Massachusetts, volunteer Adrienne Naylor expresses her concern for zines being funneled into collections at academic institutions where access procedures are prohibitive. While she perhaps rightfully identifies such environments as "not necessarily the best at providing the kind of access embodied by a zine ethos" (Fleischer 2015), Naylor's comment is based on assumptions of a generalized and somewhat outdated nature that special collections in academic libraries everywhere have been actively at work to overturn for years now. As a state institution housing public records, SDSU's Special Collections is open to the public. Access is granted to anyone with any valid photo identification, which is recorded confidentially and only for purposes of tracking theft. Nothing else is required—no letters of introduction and no proof of academic status or campus affiliation. This is not to say that we seek to invalidate such perceptions, but that such press makes our own need for improved community outreach and engagement all the more evident.

Conclusion

Where do we go from here? The inevitable result of increased outreach and instruction using zines is already evidenced by increased demand and especially more donations. One major challenge will be finding a balance. Our ultimate goal is widespread use of zines—not just in the Women's Studies curriculum but across all programs—through collaborative collection development, instruction and outreach. However, we also want to see the collection used on the broadest level possible, including by the community. Limited staffing—there is currently one librarian and one staff person in Special Collections that manage the Zines and Minicomics Collection—and limited time are two obstacles to propelling explosive growth and use.

Instruction demand is also a challenge. Some subject areas generate so much need for library instruction that all other duties are nearly paralyzed during the spring and fall semesters. This is frequently the case for the Special Collections librarian, who provides instruction across numerous colleges and departments. By exploring ways to adapt the flipped classroom model to library instruction, the subject librarian and Special Collections librarian anticipate more time to collaborate in the classroom. We are also discussing opportunities to restructure traditional arrangements in which classes visit the library twice in the semester so that the visits are no longer separate and distinct. This format allows for more in-depth engagement with classroom activities and experiments and ample time remaining for quality follow-up discussions. We are extremely motivated by the possibilities opened up by active collaborative engagement with the collection. In time, we aim to provide the best possible description and access to the vast array of topics contained in zines and a maximum level of scholarly and creative output across campus and the region.

REFERENCES

Alam, Jordan. 2015. "White Out: Erasure of the Black Lives Matter Panel and People of Color from the Brooklyn Zine Fest: The Cowation." *White Out*. April 17. http://thecowation.blogspot.com/2015/04/white-out-at-brooklyn-zine-fest.html.

"Brooklyn Zine Fest #BlackLivesMatter / POC Visibility Controversy." 2015. *POC Zine Project*. April 21. http://poczineproject.tumblr.com/post/117008340204/brooklyn-zine-fest-blacklivesmatter-poc.

Carter, Lisa R. 2013. "Special at the Core: Aligning, Integrating, and Mainstreaming Special Collections in the Research Library." *Research Library Issues: A Report from ARL, CNI, and SPARC* 283: 1–5. http://publications.arl.org/rli283/.

Fleischer, Evan. 2015. "Someone to Share Your Experience: Zine Library Perseveres in the Internet Age." *The Guardian*. November 11. http://www.theguardian.com/culture/2015/nov/11/someone-to-share-your-experience-zine-library-perseveres-in-the-internet-age.

Freedman, Jenna, and Rhonda Kauffman. 2014. "Cutter & Paste: A DIY Guide for Catalogers Who Don't Know About Zines and Zine Librarians Who Don't Know About Cataloging." In *Informed Agitation: Library and Information Skills in Social Justice Movements and Beyond*, ed. Melissa Morrone, 221–244. Sacramento, CA: Library Juice. Accessed November 10, 2015. ProQuest ebrary.

Foreign Governments and International Organizations
Web Resources for Women's Studies

KAREN EVANS

The lives of women vary dramatically throughout the world; some women live in democratic countries with access to education, employment, health care, and the freedom to make decisions about their lives. Other women struggle to survive in countries besieged by war or live in patriarchal societies with strict rules governing their behaviors and choices in life.

This essay explores several of the issues women face; some are universal such as equality in pay and employment. Other issues may fall under a broad heading of violence against women, but can be considered cultural such as honor killings or genital mutilation. However these cultural actions are becoming an issue for western countries as immigrants arrive and want to retain their homeland ways and not totally assimilate into western societies.

The first part of the essay focuses on websites providing information on topics pertinent to women. The second part concentrates on recognized government websites detailing programs and resources for women. A section on discussing uncomfortable topics, such as honor killings or trafficking completes the essay.

General Resources on women is the first topic heading, providing access to websites covering general or multi subject resources on women. Subject headings after General Resources are alphabetized and provide information on a variety of topics. The other subject headings for this essay are: Female Genital Mutilation (FGM); Health, Sexual and Reproductive Rights; Honor/Honour Killings; International Women's Day; Statistics and Facts; Trafficking; Violence Against Women.

Websites

General Resources

Peace Corps: Global Issues: Gender Equality and Women's Empowerment.[1] The site explores issues of gender including equality, violence, empowerment, and parity. A vocabulary of gender terms (women's empowerment, gender gap) provides clarification on their meaning. A link to lesson plans for teachers who want to use the information in a classroom is provided.

United Nations (UN): Global Issues: Women.[2] This site provides an overview of actions the UN has taken for and about women. Some of the topics include violence against women, the Commission on the Status of Women, and the Convention on the Elimination of All Forms of Discrimination Against Women (CEDAW). Links within the site provide access to additional information and resources.

United Nations (UN): Global Issues: Women: Related Links.[3] Provides numerous links on topics including UN bodies, legal instruments, news, conferences and events, UN family and gender issues, and violence against women.

United Nations (UN): Sustainable Development Programme: Gender Equality.[4] The Gender Equality program provides information on gender and climate change and gender and sustainable development. Our Stories relates ways in which women are working to change their environment, including women artisans in upper Egypt, women in Niger working to fight sand encroachment, and young women being encouraged to join the police force in Timor-Leste. Additional sections include programs and initiatives, one called Unite to End Violence Against Women. In Focus, Related News, and Our Perspective contribute additional information about this United Nations program.

United Nations (UN): Women.[5] Links provide information on UN Women (guiding documents, accountability), what they do (economic empowerment, ending violence against women), where they are (Africa, Middle East, Asia), how they work (intergovernmental support, training, global coordination), partnerships, news, and a digital library complete the site. The site explains the many roles of the United Nations concerning women throughout the world.

United Nations (UN): Women: Commission on the Status of Women.[6] Provides a brief history of the commission, current news, and multi-year programs the commission is involved in. Numerous links provide access to additional information on resolutions and sessions of the Commission on the Status of Women.

Female Genital Mutilation (FMG)

United Kingdom (UK): Health and Social Care Information Centre.[7] The Health and Social Care Information Centre provides databases on female genital mutilation. The site covers how the data is collected and measured, patient identifiable data, patient objections, and publications.

United Kingdom (UK): National Health Service: Female Genital Mutilation.[8] The National Health Service site defines the four types of FGM: clitoridectomy, excision, infibulation, and additional harmful procedures. The immediate and long term physical effects of the mutilation are listed, along with psychological and mental health issues. A link provides access to organizations providing assistance for those who have been subjected to the procedures or are worried they may become a victim. Information on reversing FGM is provided, along with information on why this procedure is performed on women. The site also provides a statement opposing FGM women can print and carry with them at all times. The National Health Service suggests females print and carry a copy with them; particularly when they travel to their home countries. Leaflets are also available in several languages explaining what female genital mutilation is. This is a very comprehensive site on the topic, offering numerous resources to professional health workers and the general public.

United Nations (UN): Population Fund: Female Genital Mutilation: Frequently Asked Questions.[9] This United Nations site defines and explains female genital mutilation. Additional information and resources are available in a variety of sections on the website. News, resources, publications, videos, and links provide a wealth of resources on the topic.

World Health Organization (WHO): Media Centre: Female Genital Mutilation.[10] Provides key facts and general information on the procedures that make up female genital mutilation. The site explains who is at risk for these procedures along with the cultural and social factors associated with performing FGM. The World Health Organization has posted an international response to FGM on this site, including their work with the UN and UNICEF. Links provide access to information on stopping and preventing female genital mutilation worldwide.

Health, Sexual and Reproductive Rights

Amnesty International: Women's Health, Sexual, and Reproductive Rights.[11] Sections on getting involved, updates on women's health, sexual, and reproductive rights around the world. Video spotlight, feature, and amplify your voice provide additional information on causes and concerns in the world.

International Planned Parenthood: Sexual and Reproductive Health and Rights-The Key to Gender Equality and Women's Empowerment.[12] Report on the sexual and reproductive rights of women. The first focus of the report includes the sexual and reproductive health and rights, and the social development of girls and women.

The second focus is on the sexual and reproductive health and rights and women's economic participation and the last concentration is on sexual and reproductive health and rights and women's participation in public rights of women and political life. The report also includes an executive summary and recommendations.

International Women's Health Coalition.[13] Their mission is to advance the sexual and reproductive rights of women and adolescents. The coalition works to advance global policy, create young leaders, and partner with local groups in Asia, Africa, the Middle East, and Latin America. Their priorities include ending early forced marriage, sexual health education, safe and legal abortions, and advancing the rights of adolescent girls.

United Nations (UN): Human Rights: Office of the High Commissioner: Sexual and Reproductive Health and Rights.[14] Fact sheets (some in Spanish) cover several topics, including HIV/AIDS Abortion Contraception and Family Planning Violence against Women Maternal Mortality and Morbidity Lesbian, Gay, Bisexual, and Transgender and Intersex Highlights of events and statements (right to sexual and reproductive health), studies, reports and papers (inquiry report on contraception ban in Manila), and related links on topics such as Human Rights Related to Maternal and Child Health provide resources and information on a variety of issues.

United Nations (UN): Population Fund: Family Planning.[15] The Family Planning site provides an overview on the importance of family planning and how it saves lives, empowers women, and provides economic benefits. Several pages of news provide links to read about concerns focused on family planning. Publications, resources, and videos on family planning provide access to numerous resources for users.

United Nations (UN): Population Fund: Sexual and Reproductive Health.[16] Similar to the United Nations Family Planning site, this site provides an overview of sexual and reproductive health, including key concerns and a life cycle approach. News (Ending Fistula: After 66 Years of Living with Fistula, a Malawian Woman Finally Receives Repair Surgery), publications (Girlhood, Not Motherhood), resources (Adolescent Sexual and Reproductive Health), and selected links (Family Planning, Midwifery) complete the site.

UN Women: Gender Equality and AIDS.[17] Six buttons on the right side of the website will lead you to information on Resources (tool, subject, region), stories, news, links, events (past and upcoming), and participate (contribute, receive updates or RSS feed, share website). What's New and In the News provide current information on women and AIDS.

World Health Organization (WHO): Global Health Observatory (GHO): Women and Health.[18] The site provides access to a data repository, reports (Global Health Risk, World Health Statistics), country statistics, a map gallery by theme (Alcohol and Health, Road Safety), and Standards. Also available are GHO Themes on a variety of topics, including Health Systems and Infectious Diseases. A wealth of information is available on this site.

World Health Organization (WHO): Sexual and Reproductive Health.[19] The Sexual and Reproductive Health website provides resources on a variety of health topics (abortion, sexually transmitted diseases), cross-cutting issues (gender rights, best practices), Ebola, global strategies, partnerships, and advocacy. A What's New section highlights current work being done in sexual and reproductive areas, guidelines, and opportunities. A list of publications includes information on health topics such as abortion or contraception. Information is also organized by type (guides, training materials), language (French, Spanish, English), and research.

World Health Organization (WHO): Ten Top Issues for Women's Health.[20] A list of the top ten health issues facing women include cancer, HIV, sexually transmitted diseases, and violence against women. Each entry provides information on why the issue is considered a top ten by the World Health Organization.

Honor/Honour Killings

Honor killings are committed against women by family members. The women can be any relation within the family; a mother, sister, daughter, or aunt. The act is committed as a way to bring honor back to the family because of an act involving the female. The act can be the female wanting to obtain an education, wanting to date someone her family does not approve of, or refusing an arranged marriage. A female can also be the victim of an honor crime if she is the victim of rape.

British Broadcasting Corporation (BBC): Honour Crimes.[21] The BBC provides an introduction to the issue, how prevalent the problem is in the United Kingdom, and globally. Links provide access to a Q&A about honor killings and BBC news articles on the issue.

Honour Based Violence Awareness Network (HBVA): Honor Based Violence Awareness Network.[22] The site provides a Q&A about honor violence and honor killings. The section on honor based violence includes a historical overview, the situation today, types of honor violence (forced abortion, forced marriage, abduction, honor suicide or killing), regional information, and statistical data. Training information and a library provide further resources.

Preliminary Examination of so-called "Honour Killings" in Canada.[23] Provides information on honor killings outside of Canada and within the borders of Canada. The site also provides information on several murders considered to be honor killings in Canada; the age of the victim is not a factor as attested to with the honor murder of a five year old daughter. Additional resources include the history of honor killings, the psyche of honor killing, victim, perpetrator and accomplice profiles. The site concludes with the sociocultural influences of honor killings. There is an extensive reference list for further information.

International Women's Day

Amnesty International: 6 Reasons Why We Still Need International Women's Day.[24] Amnesty International provides six reasons why an International Women's Day is needed throughout the world. The six reasons listed with an explanation are: Women and girls cannot get abortions; Girls continue to be forced into marriage; Marital rape is not always considered rape; Women are sentenced to jail because of stillborn births; Survivors of forced sterilization have not received justice; Women are sexually harassed in public places.

International Women's Day.[25] Provides information on creating activities for International Women's Day. If you need ideas, several activities from the 2016 event are listed for your perusal. Resources and events and activities are available to help you plan an event. You can register to pledge for parity (ensuring global gender parity), and receive information on upcoming events and ideas for International Women's Day.

United Nations (UN) Women: International Women's Day.[26] While the majority of the website discusses events for the 2016 International Women's Day; two sections of this site make it worth viewing. Photo Essay: A Day in the Life of Women highlights women from around the world and the activities they perform. The second section is the interactive Timeline: Women's Footprint in History. The timeline highlights women and their activities from 400 BC with Agnodice, who was considered the first female gynecologist to 2016 and Loveness Mudzuru and Ruvimbo Tsopodzi, who took their government to court over child marriages.

Statistics and Facts

The World Bank: Female Population.[27] Provides female population information for the world from 1996 to 2015. Additional statistics are available for topics including fertility and birth rates, contraceptives, live expectancy at birth, and maternal mortality.

United Nations (UN): Statistics Division: The World's Women 2015: Trends and Statistics.[28] Eight chapters cover population and families, health, education, work, power and decision making, violence against women, environment, and poverty. Information on each topic is about a page long, with a graphic to illustrate various facts and statistics. For example, the graphic for power and decision making includes the number of women in parliaments, executive branches, and the judiciary. The chapters and/or data can be downloaded. The site also includes a section on developing ways to obtain and understand gender statistics better in the future.

UN Women: Facts and Figures: Economic Empowerment: Benefits of Economic Empowerment.[29] Entries discuss the benefit of females in the workplace, from faster economic growth to female education helping to decrease child mortality rates. Numerous ways in which women are not equal to men in the workforce are listed, including the fact that women work more without pay in areas of caring for family member, maintaining a home and childcare.

Trafficking

European Parliamentary Research Blog: Trafficking in Women.[30] Information is provided on trafficking in Europe and the world. Three sections report on the overviews of human trafficking, analysis of the problem, and stakeholder views. Each section contains links to the reports listed.

United Nations Office on Drugs and Crime (UNODC): Human Trafficking.[31] The UNODC provides a definition and the elements of (what happens, how it happens and why) human trafficking. A FAQ section provides answers to the most commonly asked questions about the topic. A section also explains why human trafficking is considered a criminal act. Human trafficking is considered different from migrant smuggling, and the website explains the difference between the two activities involving humans.

Violence Against Women

Amnesty International: Support the International Violence Against Women Act (IVAWA).[32] According to this site, one in three women in the world will be a victim of abuse in her lifetime. Amnesty International describes the types of violence are subjected to and the aim of the IVAWA to thwart the violence. Background information on violence is provided along with a FAQ about the IVAWA. Links provide ideas to become involved with the cause and take action to support the International Violence Against Women Act.

UN Women: Infographic on Violence Against Women.[33] The infographic provides information on violence against women including the different types of violence (physical, sexual, psychological), human trafficking and exploitation, female genital mutilation (FGM), and child marriage.

World Health Organization (WHO): Violence Against Women.[34] WHO provides a fact sheet on violence against women, including the scope of the problem involving violence against women, risk factors, the health consequences, and the impact of the violence against women on children. Prevention and response and the WHO response to the violence are also described. Links lead to publications and related information on the topic.

Governments

Australian Government: Department of Foreign Affairs and Trade.[35] Highlights work by the Office of Ambassador for Women and Girls, including empowerment, ending violence and discrimination, end trafficking of women and girls, and improve the participation of women in leadership areas. Links lead to publications on the areas of gender equality and women's empowerment.

Australian Government: Office of the Prime Minister and Cabinet: Office for Women.[36] This office works to progress gender advancement in the offices of the Australian government. Their 3 priorities include strengthening the economic security and work participation of women, more women in leadership positions, protecting women and children from violence. Information is provided on current initiatives, including leadership, economic security, and safety. Resources and the latest news provide additional information.

Australian Suffragettes.[37] A fascinating look at the struggle for the right of women to vote in Australia. From describing the term "suffragette" to the actions it took for women to be granted the right to vote, this is a fascinating look at how the women in one country worked for a right against some interesting prejudices. Several useful links, from Australian suffragettes to women and voting in Australia complete the site.

Japan: Ministry of Foreign Affairs: Women's Issues: Women's Empowerment and Gender Equality.[38] Information is provided on the National Action Plan on Women, Peace, and Security, including the establishment of the national plan.

Kingdom of Belgium: Foreign Affairs, Foreign Trade and Development Cooperation: Gender and Women's Rights.[39] Provides information on actions Belgium has taken with the United Nations and the European Union to combat discrimination against women. Links provide access to United Nations and European Union information on women.

New Zealand: Ministry for Women.[40] Four areas are profiled where the New Zealand government works to improve the lives of women: education and training, safety, leadership, and utilizing women's skills. An extensive list of publications are available on a wide variety of topics relating to women and gender.

Sweden: Feminist Foreign Policy.[41] According to the website, equality between women and men is a fundamental right. Links provide access to feminist foreign policy, sexual and reproductive health rights, and what feminist foreign policy can do. Sweden states it has the first feminist government in the world, and provides information on how the government is working to ensure gender equality.

United Kingdom (UK): Living Heritage: Women and the Vote.[42] The site provides a vast array of information concerning women and voting in the United Kingdom. The site provides an overview of the process, plus information on key dates, furthering your research, contemporary context, expert interviews, and resources from the parliamentary collection.

Sensitive Subjects in the Classroom

Discussing sensitive topics in a classroom can be a delicate situation. Do you employ trigger warnings (advising students that topics may be discussed which could upset them) for your students? Do you plunge into the topic without any boundaries or guidelines for the students? Below are links to educational facilities with resources on discussing sensitive topics in the classroom. Some of the topics discussed in the links include civility in the classroom, creating a safe place in the classroom, ground rules for class discussions, and adding information to syllabi.

Indiana University Bloomington: Center for Innovative Teaching and Learning: Facilitating Discussion of Sensitive Issues.[43] The University of Sheffield: Learning and Teaching Services: Teaching Sensitive or Controversial Topics[44] University of California at Berkeley: Center for Teaching and Learning: Sensitive Topics in the Classroom.[45]

Conclusion

There are a multitude of websites available about women and women's issues. This essay provides a sample of the resources available on pertinent topics related to women. Using the parameters of non-governmental organizations and foreign countries limited the amount of entries for this essay. There are numerous other resources available electronically and in print on the topics discussed in this essay, including trafficking of women and girls, sexual health and birth control, honor killings and female genital mutilation, gender equality, and much more. Take the time to learn about the issues facing women in the world, and the actions of so many pushing for women to be recognized as human beings with the right to determine their own lives and make their own decisions.

NOTES

1. https://urldefense.proofpoint.com/v2/url?u=http-3A__www.peacecorps.gov_wws_articles_global-2Dissues-2Dgender-2Dequality-2Dand-2Dwomens-2Dempowerme_&d=DQIFaQ&c=euGZstcaTDllvimEN8b7jXrwqOf-v5A_CdpgnVfiiMM&r=FuC2bgPKWy3lyLSFzYGLuQ&m=Wx8wtCjAH2175SRLZVtUTKGMCRheTUtLvY2TlBGueqc&s=bdNu7PtB4Z0NU-3WfiYhY9xEI39EufDRG05yHdDidJc&e=

2. https://urldefense.proofpoint.com/v2/url?u=http-3A__www.un.org_en_globalissues_women_&d=DQIFaQ&c=euGZstcaTDllvimEN8b7jXrwqOf-v5A_CdpgnVfiiMM&r=FuC2bgPKWy3lyLSFzYGLuQ&m=Wx8wtCjAH2175SRLZVtUTKGMCRheTUtLvY2TlBGueqc&s=uFOdc8ipEAxpn-Qf4r77HeLbYIeUfZTVFFuL_x3OF80&e=

3. https://urldefense.proofpoint.com/v2/url?u=http-3A__www.un.org_en_globalissues_women_links.shtml&d=DQIFaQ&c=euGZstcaTDllvimEN8b7jXrwqOf-v5A_CdpgnVfiiMM&r=FuC2bgPKWy3lyLSFzYGLuQ&m=Wx8wtCjAH2175SRLZVtUTKGMCRheTUtLvY2TlBGueqc&s=OEEg51N4Q707nJgq_5CVKEdHCXLugiA5sMGh75IairM&e=

4. https://urldefense.proofpoint.com/v2/url?u=http-3A__www.undp.org_gender_&d=DQIFaQ&c=euGZstcaTDllvimEN8b7jXrwqOf-v5A_CdpgnVfiiMM&r=FuC2bgPKWy3lyLSFzYGLuQ&m=Wx8wtCjAH2175SRLZVtUTKGMCRheTUtLvY2TlBGueqc&s=9x1OD56OYGjSFmEHc87Gf5UMUMtwdZi_rHb4XHNjW7k&e=

5. https://urldefense.proofpoint.com/v2/url?u=http-3A__www.unwomen.org_en&d=DQIFaQ&c=euGZstcaTDllvimEN8b7jXrwqOf-v5A_CdpgnVfiiMM&r=FuC2bgPKWy3lyLSFzYGLuQ&m=Wx8wtCjAH2175SRLZVtUTKGMCRheTUtLvY2TlBGueqc&s=krzidAZQQczpFlzLH5wd2yJTWjV-6MrTxxl3jzezrlA&e=

6. https://urldefense.proofpoint.com/v2/url?u=http-3A__www.unwomen.org_en_csw&d=DQIFaQ&c=euGZstcaTDllvimEN8b7jXrwqOf-v5A_CdpgnVfiiMM&r=FuC2bgPKWy3lyLSFzYGLuQ&m=Wx8wtCjAH2175SRLZVtUTKGMCRheTUtLvY2TlBGueqc&s=wwxOoU6QbXnQLZBuFUYVWdoZrssdl_VVHVK-_xccGdU&e=

7. https://urldefense.proofpoint.com/v2/url?u=http-3A__www.hscic.gov.uk_fgm&d=DQIFaQ&c=euGZstcaTDllvimEN8b7jXrwqOf-v5A_CdpgnVfiiMM&r=FuC2bgPKWy3lyLSFzYGLuQ&m=Wx8wtCjAH2175SRLZVtUTKGMCRheTUtLvY2TlBGueqc&s=3TKlWrenocnVtFszOL6AYcXIQ1V9eHM3KmlH6v9GH3o&e=

8. https://urldefense.proofpoint.com/v2/url?u=http-3A__www.nhs.uk_conditions_female-2Dgenital-2Dmutilation_Pages_Introduction.aspx&d=DQIFaQ&c=euGZstcaTDllvimEN8b7jXrwqOf-v5A_CdpgnVfiiMM&r=FuC2bgPKWy3lyLSFzYGLuQ&m=Wx8wtCjAH2175SRLZVtUTKGMCRheTUtLvY2TlBGueqc&s=bcBZ7F46gabnFYonXXnRIn5rn2OEAftpj4M25rbikVM&e=

9. https://urldefense.proofpoint.com/v2/url?u=http-3A__www.unfpa.org_female-2Dgenital-2Dmutilation&d=DQIFaQ&c=euGZstcaTDllvimEN8b7jXrwqOf-v5A_CdpgnVfiiMM&r=FuC2bgPKWy3lyLSFzYGLuQ&m=Wx8wtCjAH2175SRLZVtUTKGMCRheTUtLvY2TlBGueqc&s=Z4Gf5iNYi7A2HpXABC0xCUkVkRTamCfYH4jobFtq9p4&e=

10. https://urldefense.proofpoint.com/v2/url?u=http-3A__www.who.int_mediacentre_factsheets_fs241_en_&d=DQIFaQ&c=euGZstcaTDllvimEN8b7jXrwqOf-v5A_CdpgnVfiiMM&r=FuC2bgPKWy3lyLSFzYGLuQ&m=Wx8wtCjAH2175SRLZVtUTKGMCRheTUtLvY2TlBGueqc&s=sk_GTVxFAzl1Md8ETy9gkxPJ-eKgR-BK8GcJtVKNUyY&e=

11. https://urldefense.proofpoint.com/v2/url?u=http-3A__www.amnestyusa.org_our-2Dwork_issues_women-2Ds-2Drights_women-2Ds-2Dhealth-2Dsexual-2Dand-2Dreproductive-2Drights&d=DQIFaQ&c=euGZstcaTDllvimEN8b7jXrwqOf-v5A_CdpgnVfiiMM&r=FuC2bgPKWy3lyLSFzYGLuQ&m=Wx8wtCjAH2175SRLZVtUTKGMCRheTUtLvY2TlBGueqc&s=lA-athvMUu1pA34cm0ZZtnSQNSlnoabIF1UvNL61wF0&e=

12. https://urldefense.proofpoint.com/v2/url?u=http-3A__www.ippf.org_sites_default_files_2020-5Fgender-5Fequality-5Freport-5Fweb.pdf&d=DQIFaQ&c=euGZstcaTDllvimEN8b7jXrwqOf-v5A_CdpgnVfiiMM&r=FuC2bgPKWy3lyLSFzYGLuQ&m=Wx8wtCjAH2175SRLZVtUTKGMCRheTUtLvY2TlBGueqc&s=39IhoYogQpl1zvuGSB0iWSjrav35PZl_madV3C8V9ok&e=

13. https://urldefense.proofpoint.com/v2/url?u=https-3A__iwhc.org_&d=DQIFaQ&c=euGZstcaTDllvimEN8b7jXrwqOf-v5A_CdpgnVfiiMM&r=FuC2bgPKWy3lyLSFzYGLuQ&m=Wx8wtCjAH2175SRLZVtUTKGMCRheTUtLvY2TlBGueqc&s=1KVdruQrIiZdzUEOQ2NWVEaAqiQk309O0OFFcI8OMqw&e=

14. https://urldefense.proofpoint.com/v2/url?u=http-3A__www.ohchr.org_EN_Issues_Women_WRGS_Pages_HealthRights.aspx&d=DQIFaQ&c=euGZstcaTDllvimEN8b7jXrwqOf-v5A_CdpgnVfiiMM&r=FuC2bgPKWy3lyLSFzYGLuQ&m=Wx8wtCjAH2175SRLZVtUTKGMCRheTUtLvY2TlBGueqc&s=0xREMJZYAuwKf4QEqF3f4ItUFaNTjFnQc3eJ6qcewPw&e=

15. https://urldefense.proofpoint.com/v2/url?u=http-3A__www.unfpa.org_family-2Dplanning&d=DQIFaQ&c=euGZstcaTDllvimEN8b7jXrwqOf-v5A_CdpgnVfiiMM&r=FuC2bgPKWy3lyLSFzYGLuQ&m=Wx8wtCjAH2175SRLZVtUTKGMCRheTUtLvY2TlBGueqc&s=sJNZwLHVFQqJBnypyYw8lZuM3Lehd10BjbZ9JvplK_4&e=

16. https://urldefense.proofpoint.com/v2/url?u=http-3A__www.unfpa.org_sexual-2Dreproductive-2Dhealth&d=DQIFaQ&c=euGZstcaTDllvimEN8b7jXrwqOf-v5A_CdpgnVfiiMM&r=FuC2bgPKWy3lyLSFzYGLuQ&m=Wx8wtCjAH2175SRLZVtUTKGMCRheTUtLvY2TlBGueqc&s=EQmN29mR2gKCmEOyfaecNY4wxxF4RRSrbgmCklj2Uxk&e=

17. https://urldefense.proofpoint.com/v2/url?u=http-3A__www.genderandaids.org_&d=DQIFaQ&c=euGZstcaTDllvimEN8b7jXrwqOf-v5A_CdpgnVfiiMM&r=FuC2bgPKWy3lyLSFzYGLuQ&m=Wx8wtCjAH2175SRLZVtUTKGMCRheTUtLvY2TlBGueqc&s=irRJvOt00kNiMaHXiFprqp4hItvV2XpWi2cI1bbmiYw&e=

18. https://urldefense.proofpoint.com/v2/url?u=http-3A__www.who.int_gho_women-5Fand-5Fhealth_en_&d=DQIFaQ&c=euGZstcaTDllvimEN8b7jXrwqOf-v5A_CdpgnVfiiMM&r=FuC2bgPKWy3lyLSFzYGLuQ&m=Wx8wtCjAH2175SRLZVtUTKGMCRheTUtLvY2TlBGueqc&s=RLFYgxfvNh-keqRb41X4HgyTRT-3-b7sTwhr_D9tW9c&e=

19. https://urldefense.proofpoint.com/v2/url?u=http-3A__www.who.int_reproductivehealth_en_&d=DQIFaQ&c=euGZstcaTDllvimEN8b7jXrwqOf-v5A_CdpgnVfiiMM&r=FuC2bgPKWy3lyLSFzYGLuQ&m=Wx8wtCjAH2175SRLZVtUTKGMCRheTUtLvY2TlBGueqc&s=qvjTgScGQ8YkcIBiQMwtzwdMsjgTovVsg_Y-l0EOj-U&e=

20. https://urldefense.proofpoint.com/v2/url?u=http-3A__www.who.int_life-2Dcourse_news_commentaries_2015-2Dintl-2Dwomens-2Dday_en&d=DQIFaQ&c=euGZstcaTDllvimEN8b7jXrwqOf-v5A_CdpgnVfiiMM&r=FuC2bgPKWy3lyLSFzYGLuQ&m=Wx8wtCjAH2175SRLZVtUTKGMCRheTUtLvY2TlBGueqc&s=STSbH4ot0427B4bOYQceDDgeSWVKwJPjfqANbhjZs08&e=

21. https://urldefense.proofpoint.com/v2/url?u=http-3A__www.bbc.co.uk_ethics_honourcrimes_&d=DQIFaQ&c=euGZstcaTDllvimEN8b7jXrwqOf-v5A_CdpgnVfiiMM&r=FuC2bgPKWy3lyLSFzYGLuQ&m=Wx8wtCjAH2175SRLZVtUTKGMCRheTUtLvY2TlBGueqc&s=ChUPAWthM-ZN0fRcmh_MQl8nH_82NYUCVzTkaQilrAI&e=

22. https://urldefense.proofpoint.com/v2/url?u=http-3A__hbv-2Dawareness.com_faq_&d=DQIFaQ&c=euGZstcaTDllvimEN8b7jXrwqOf-v5A_CdpgnVfiiMM&r=FuC2bgPKWy3lyLSFzYGLuQ&m=Wx8wtCjAH2175SRLZVtUTKGMCRheTUtLvY2TlBGueqc&s=TG97kom6mZ4l2X1-e0RkxT76yLEMuTbJBXiBq4u9YAE&e=

23. https://urldefense.proofpoint.com/v2/url?u=http-3A__www.justice.gc.ca_eng_rp-2Dpr_cj-2Djp_fv-2Dvf_hk-2Dch_p1.html&d=DQIFaQ&c=euGZstcaTDllvimEN8b7jXrwqOf-v5A_CdpgnVfiiMM&r=FuC2bgPKWy3lyLSFzYGLuQ&m=Wx8wtCjAH2175SRLZVtUTKGMCRheTUtLvY2TlBGueqc&s=Lb4hzWxWXdzVIUBDF2ZTCj4t9o4F5vjNq-UkHrCb6Vw&e=

24. https://urldefense.proofpoint.com/v2/url?u=https-3A__www.amnesty.org_en_latest_campaigns_2016_03_6-2Dreasons-2Dwhy-2Dwe-2Dstill-2Dneed-2Dinternational-2Dwomens-2Dday_&d=DQIFaQ&c=euGZstcaTDllvimEN8b7jXrwqOf-v5A_CdpgnVfiiMM&r=FuC2bgPKWy3lyLSFzYGLuQ&m=Wx8wtCjAH2175SRLZVtUTKGMCRheTUtLvY2TlBGueqc&s=IiimyOgTNrS1kM1DraculNq2pMxMcSAlW-oX3zkf8uo&e=

25. https://urldefense.proofpoint.com/v2/url?u=https-3A__www.internationalwomensday.com_&d=DQIFaQ&c=euGZstcaTDllvimEN8b7jXrwqOf-v5A_CdpgnVfiiMM&r=FuC2bgPKWy3lyLSFzYGLuQ&m=Wx8wtCjAH2175SRLZVtUTKGMCRheTUtLvY2TlBGueqc&s=WRC2LWJ4snHPZ_NI3PJeUAWmC2XnLMalLliFQRal6Xo&e=

26. https://urldefense.proofpoint.com/v2/url?u=http-3A__www.unwomen.org_en_news_in-2Dfocus_international-2Dwomens-2Dday&d=DQIFaQ&c=euGZstcaTDllvimEN8b7jXrwqOf-v5A_CdpgnVfiiMM&r=FuC2bgPKWy3lyLSFzYGLuQ&m=Wx8wtCjAH2175SRLZVtUTKGMCRheTUtLvY2TlBGueqc&s=9zJvqFusk22Tw_r4dRZhn1ZBlvaqM572MG7f9DwVaw4&e=

27. https://urldefense.proofpoint.com/v2/url?u=http-3A__data.worldbank.org_indicator_SP.POP.TOTL. FE.ZS&d=DQIFaQ&c=euGZstcaTDllvimEN8b7jXrwqOf-v5A_CdpgnVfiiMM&r=FuC2bgPKWy3lyLSFzYGL uQ&m=Wx8wtCjAH2175SRLZVtUTKGMCRheTUtLvY2TlBGueqc&s=0XpshNYkFSNx3Zz5xNiyOppdvHP 437Zx7uIHL4hdoFk&e=

28. https://urldefense.proofpoint.com/v2/url?u=http-3A__unstats.un.org_unsd_gender_worldswomen. html&d=DQIFaQ&c=euGZstcaTDllvimEN8b7jXrwqOf-v5A_CdpgnVfiiMM&r=FuC2bgPKWy3lyLSFzYGLu Q&m=Wx8wtCjAH2175SRLZVtUTKGMCRheTUtLvY2TlBGueqc&s=7Dyi0caT_ghOX0ERcDE13ovnVk2GJ6 oKQ3sE_S2zBSQ&e=

29. https://urldefense.proofpoint.com/v2/url?u=http-3A__www.unwomen.org_en_what-2Dwe-2Ddo_ economic-2Dempowerment_facts-2Dand-2Dfigures&d=DQIFaQ&c=euGZstcaTDllvimEN8b7jXrwqOf-v5A_ CdpgnVfiiMM&r=FuC2bgPKWy3lyLSFzYGLuQ&m=Wx8wtCjAH2175SRLZVtUTKGMCRheTUtLvY2TlBG ueqc&s=IfsgOxIkfqVMMMQjBwjqCzsOGgsZVi0RiTGUVy4wmBA&e=

30. https://urldefense.proofpoint.com/v2/url?u=https-3A__epthinktank.eu_2015_11_25_trafficking-2Din-2Dwomen-2D2_&d=DQIFaQ&c=euGZstcaTDllvimEN8b7jXrwqOf-v5A_CdpgnVfiiMM&r=FuC2bgP KWy3lyLSFzYGLuQ&m=Wx8wtCjAH2175SRLZVtUTKGMCRheTUtLvY2TlBGueqc&s=xSRbF3-XB_C0mjp 0ZnnWX1Ai2hZh-4tKZTNlG7x6Umg&e=

31. https://urldefense.proofpoint.com/v2/url?u=https-3A__www.unodc.org_unodc_en_human-2Dt rafficking_what-2Dis-2Dhuman-2Dtrafficking.html&d=DQIFaQ&c=euGZstcaTDllvimEN8b7jXrwqOf-v5A_ CdpgnVfiiMM&r=FuC2bgPKWy3lyLSFzYGLuQ&m=Wx8wtCjAH2175SRLZVtUTKGMCRheTUtLvY2TlBG ueqc&s=QfX3jEPMHFpbqU25f6qiVUbZRdNQ2wGV55lN9icyxgE&e=

32. https://urldefense.proofpoint.com/v2/url?u=http-3A__www.amnestyusa.org_our-2Dwork_issues_ women-2Ds-2Drights_violence-2Dagainst-2Dwomen_international-2Dviolence-2Dagainst-2Dwomen-2Dact &d=DQIFaQ&c=euGZstcaTDllvimEN8b7jXrwqOf-v5A_CdpgnVfiiMM&r=FuC2bgPKWy3lyLSFzYGLuQ& m=Wx8wtCjAH2175SRLZVtUTKGMCRheTUtLvY2TlBGueqc&s=63GqCIjL9o6Y6c_QkeUs53x5rn-r31WE_ H59pCl0txo&e=

33. https://urldefense.proofpoint.com/v2/url?u=http-3A__www.unwomen.org_en_digital-2Dlibrary_ multimedia_2015_11_infographic-2Dviolence-2Dagainst-2Dwomen&d=DQIFaQ&c=euGZstcaTDllvimEN8b 7jXrwqOf-v5A_CdpgnVfiiMM&r=FuC2bgPKWy3lyLSFzYGLuQ&m=Wx8wtCjAH2175SRLZVtUTKGMCR heTUtLvY2TlBGueqc&s=ZgwD-CKCgY_zbU0LcbJUxSAAikOrE0fmzZYU9vp5Xjc&e=

34. https://urldefense.proofpoint.com/v2/url?u=http-3A__www.who.int_topics_gender-5Fbased-5Fvio lence_en_&d=DQIFaQ&c=euGZstcaTDllvimEN8b7jXrwqOf-v5A_CdpgnVfiiMM&r=FuC2bgPKWy3lyLSFz YGLuQ&m=Wx8wtCjAH2175SRLZVtUTKGMCRheTUtLvY2TlBGueqc&s=uOrWBtEJBFrsIHwR-3hEx93Q 6PsCqMbKgpM_8Hw2ZPw&e=

35. http://dfat.gov.au/international-relations/themes/gender-equality/pages/gender-equality.aspx

36. https://urldefense.proofpoint.com/v2/url?u=https-3A__www.dpmc.gov.au_office-2Dwomen&d= DQIFaQ&c=euGZstcaTDllvimEN8b7jXrwqOf-v5A_CdpgnVfiiMM&r=FuC2bgPKWy3lyLSFzYGLuQ&m= Wx8wtCjAH2175SRLZVtUTKGMCRheTUtLvY2TlBGueqc&s=e9cObEkC2n3ouwCJoqPa2fqwDAo0dK9pL0_ gmKi4gIg&e=

37. https://urldefense.proofpoint.com/v2/url?u=http-3A__www.australia.gov.au_about-2Daustralia_ australian-2Dstory_austn-2Dsuffragettes&d=DQIFaQ&c=euGZstcaTDllvimEN8b7jXrwqOf-v5A_CdpgnVfii MM&r=FuC2bgPKWy3lyLSFzYGLuQ&m=Wx8wtCjAH2175SRLZVtUTKGMCRheTUtLvY2TlBGueqc&s= Ai7KUS9qVKsYP1vEFQOaCHwgzqewKgPLYun8zjDOMME&e=

38. https://urldefense.proofpoint.com/v2/url?u=http-3A__www.mofa.go.jp_fp_pc_page23e-5F000181. html&d=DQIFaQ&c=euGZstcaTDllvimEN8b7jXrwqOf-v5A_CdpgnVfiiMM&r=FuC2bgPKWy3lyLSFzYGLu Q&m=Wx8wtCjAH2175SRLZVtUTKGMCRheTUtLvY2TlBGueqc&s=FA4QHDkAxt1B0_xqaoXyGwCxCvRu 7KogxilQA-5l7Ek&e=

39. https://urldefense.proofpoint.com/v2/url?u=http-3A__diplomatie.belgium.be_en_policy_policy-5Fareas_human-5Frights_specific-5Fissues_gender-5Fand-5Fwomen-5Frights&d=DQIFaQ&c=euGZstcaTDll vimEN8b7jXrwqOf-v5A_CdpgnVfiiMM&r=FuC2bgPKWy3lyLSFzYGLuQ&m=Wx8wtCjAH2175SRLZVtUT KGMCRheTUtLvY2TlBGueqc&s=Hk4bHtv9DDRoirchnqQMjRuxe98F0O7lqFUmLLifEFw&e=

40. https://urldefense.proofpoint.com/v2/url?u=http-3A__women.govt.nz_&d=DQIFaQ&c=euGZstca TDllvimEN8b7jXrwqOf-v5A_CdpgnVfiiMM&r=FuC2bgPKWy3lyLSFzYGLuQ&m=Wx8wtCjAH2175SRLZ VtUTKGMCRheTUtLvY2TlBGueqc&s=XV7MI8gT0DZrJUhTTLiZi2bjZFwdi0KktJmRWpQSA84&e=

41. https://urldefense.proofpoint.com/v2/url?u=http-3A__www.government.se_government-2Dpolicy_ feminist-2Dforeign-2Dpolicy&d=DQIFaQ&c=euGZstcaTDllvimEN8b7jXrwqOf-v5A_CdpgnVfiiMM&r= FuC2bgPKWy3lyLSFzYGLuQ&m=Wx8wtCjAH2175SRLZVtUTKGMCRheTUtLvY2TlBGueqc&s=KKr12 P0isA-UK0IPYwsEUSZPPKyff4UCvwzaaiND9UA&e=

42. https://urldefense.proofpoint.com/v2/url?u=http-3A__www.parliament.uk_about_living-2Dheri tage_transformingsociety_electionsvoting_womenvote_&d=DQIFaQ&c=euGZstcaTDllvimEN8b7jXrwqOf-v5A_CdpgnVfiiMM&r=FuC2bgPKWy3lyLSFzYGLuQ&m=Wx8wtCjAH2175SRLZVtUTKGMCRheTUtLvY2 TlBGueqc&s=zM4j1jM9IWbcrIFqEVf0_SEcm-G3kIcku5VMTd0kiac&e=

43. https://urldefense.proofpoint.com/v2/url?u=http-3A__citl.indiana.edu_resources-5Ffiles_teaching-2Dresources1_teaching-2Dhandbook-2Ditems_discussion-2Dsensitive-2Dissues.php&d=DQIFaQ&c=euGZ

stcaTDllvimEN8b7jXrwqOf-v5A_CdpgnVfiiMM&r=FuC2bgPKWy3lyLSFzYGLuQ&m=Wx8wtCjAH2175SR
LZVtUTKGMCRheTUtLvY2TlBGueqc&s=A6BHSOd7KkU0nIDCQH2Pw0B_VUlwpGglOyQoOp0YX-
Y&e=

44. https://urldefense.proofpoint.com/v2/url?u=http-3A__www.facultyfocus.com_articles_effective-
2Dclassroom-2Dmanagement_top-2D10-2Dtips-2Dfor-2Daddressing-2Dsensitive-2Dtopics-2Dand-
2Dmaintaining-2Dcivility-2Din-2Dthe-2Dclassroom_&d=DQIFaQ&c=euGZstcaTDllvimEN8b7jXrwqOf-
v5A_CdpgnVfiiMM&r=FuC2bgPKWy3lyLSFzYGLuQ&m=Wx8wtCjAH2175SRLZVtUTKGMCRheTUtLvY2
TlBGueqc&s=6Eg9UmCMOikXaPn5l2_-5EdgFPboZ_OFbFWRCxme-jU&e=

45. https://urldefense.proofpoint.com/v2/url?u=http-3A__teaching.berkeley.edu_sensitive-2Dtopics-
2Dclassroom&d=DQIFaQ&c=euGZstcaTDllvimEN8b7jXrwqOf-v5A_CdpgnVfiiMM&r=FuC2bgPKWy3lyL
SFzYGLuQ&m=Wx8wtCjAH2175SRLZVtUTKGMCRheTUtLvY2TlBGueqc&s=NDy2bIyPNXfv3LohcETvp
eiQs_N_webJz_OGzl0MZ7A&e=

U.S. Government Resources on Women and Women's Issues

KAREN EVANS

The United States federal government publishes a wealth of material for and about women. This essay will highlight several of the sources. Sources were located using the Google search engine and a variety of search terms. Some of the terms used include U.S. government and women; U.S. federal government and women, and U.S. federal government resources about women. Searches were also performed using the above terms and topics (sexual assault, finances, etc.). General Resources begins the essay; that section contains links to websites with multi-topic information. Otherwise, the entries are listed alphabetically by topic.

The entries are not an exhaustive list of information. Additional information is available from the U.S. federal government on many of the sites listed in this essay. Furthermore, many topics not found in this essay (education, immigration) have resources specifically for women. You are encouraged to search the U.S. government websites for additional information and resources on women. Topics for this essay include General Resources; Employment, Retirement, and Financial Security; Health and Reproductive Care for Women; Military: Current and Veterans; Statistics; Violence and Women; Women's History

General Resources

U.S. Department of Labor: Federal Agency Resources for Women (https://www.dol. gov/wb/otherfedagencies.htm). The U.S. Department of Labor site provides links to several sources with information for women. Among the sites profiled are the U.S. Commission on Civil Rights, U.S. Department of Agriculture, U.S. Department of State, and the U.S. Small Business Administration.

U.S Department of State: Office of Global Women's Issues (http://www.state.gov/s/ gwi). Several links provide information and videos on the importance of women's issues in a global society. Among the topics profiled are artisan enterprise, early and forced marriages, election season, and gender based violence. Access is also provided to additional resources including events, newsletters, and global programs.

White House Council on Women and Girls (https://www.whitehouse.gov/

administration/eop/cwg/resources). Information on resources for women and girls is provided. Links lead to information on financial literacy, government jobs, resources for women veterans, community service and more. Featured reports include Women and Girls in Science, Technology, Engineering, and Math; Women and Girls of Color: Addressing Challenges and Expanding Opportunity, and American Jobs Act: Impact for Women.

Employment, Retirement and Financial Stability

Social Security: Women (https://www.ssa.gov/people/women/). Information provided for women under various circumstances; working, brides, new mothers, wives, divorced, caregivers, and widows. Each topic supplies pertinent information. The link for working women has a brochure explain social security, how it is calculated, your benefits, when to apply, and how to contact a Social Security office. There is also a benefits planner and a retirement estimator.

The White House: Your Right to Equal Pay (https://www.whitehouse.gov/issues/equal-pay). The site provides information on equal pay for women and why equal pay is a right of women. Four sections provide information on understanding the basics of equal pay, know your rights for equal pay, get the resources, and take action. A link provides access to the report Fifty Years after The Equal Pay Act.

United States Department of Labor: Audience: Find It! By Audience: Women (https://www.dol.gov/general/audience/aud-women). The Department of Labor provides information on women in the work force. Resources are also provided on women in the military and women veterans. Federal laws and regulations offer information on workplace violence, rights after a mastectomy, qualified domestic relations orders, and other information. Publications include Women and Retirement Savings and A Woman's Place is in the Mines.

USA.gov: Retirement (https://www.usa.gov/retirement). Offers information on retirement, including how to save, preparing for retirement, pensions, civil service retirement, public service and volunteering. Each section provides links to additional information.

Health and Reproductive Care for Women

CDC: HIV Among Women (http://www.cdc.gov/hiv/group/gender/women/index.html). Provides information on HIV in women, including Fast Facts, Living with HIV, and Prevention Challenges. The site also includes several ventures the CDC is involved in to assist in preventing HIV in women. Among the ventures are funding to organizations and health departments, campaigns, and research. A bibliography, fact sheets, and additional organizations provide a wide area of resources.

Center for Disease Control and Prevention (CDC): Women's Health (http://www.cdc.gov/women/index.htm). Numerous resources are available for women concerning health issues. Some of the resources include The Women's Health Initiative, Healthy Living, and Leading Causes of Death. New at CDC includes Zika and Pregnancy, STD Awareness, Smoker's Stories, and Prediabetes awareness. Related links cover numerous issues such as cancer prevention and control, healthy weight, reproductive health, and violence prevention.

CDC: Women's Reproductive Health (http://www.cdc.gov/reproductivehealth/WomensRH/index.htm). The CDC site on reproductive health includes information on preconception health, contraception, depression, hysterectomy, infertility, menopause, and other issues women can face. Each topic contains a link that provides additional information on the topic. For example, depression covers postpartum depression, the symptoms of depression, and treatments.

National Institute of Mental Health: Women and Mental Health (http://www.nimh.nih.gov/health/topics/women-and-mental-health/index.shtml). The site presents information on the different types of mental illness affecting women. Among the topics covered are anxiety disorders, bipolar, depression, and eating disorders. Related information links lead to more information on medications, risk of suicide with some mental illnesses and information on postpartum depression. Featured publications and research on women's mental health is also available.

U.S. Department of Veterans Affairs: PTSD: Women (http://www.ptsd.va.gov/public/PTSD-overview/women/). According to the website, women can experience PTSD differently than men. Information is provided on trauma, sexual assault, and trauma related to combat situations. The sections provide a range of information; the section on sexual assault contains a definition of the term, who commits sexual assault, how often assaults happen, and what happens to a victim after an assault. The site details the feelings many victims experience, including anger, depression, shame, social problems, and substance abuse. Sexual assaults can also lead to PTSD in the victims. Combat related trauma covers traumatic stress in women veterans, women's mental health services in the VA, and rape of women in a war zone.

U.S. Food and Drug Administration: For Women (http://www.fda.gov/ForConsumers/byAudience/ForWomen/default.htm). Several topics are covered on this site, including heart health, drug trials, medication, breast implants, and tips for caregivers. A section on women's health programs includes food safety for moms-to-be and the take time to care program. A variety of ways to stay informed with information from the site include free publications, e-mail alerts, and updates. Some of the programs are also available in Spanish.

U.S. National Library of Medicine (https://www.nlm.nih.gov/medlineplus/women.html). The website presents a very long list of health topics affecting women in alphabetical order. From abdominal pregnancy to women's health checkup; this site covers the majority if health issues women can face. Entries start with a summary of the topic and progress to a start here section where readers will find links to additional sites and information on the topic. Additional information includes the latest news, diagnosis and tests, treatments and therapies, related issues, clinical trials, statistics and research, journal articles, find an expert, and patient handouts complete the resources available. This site provides an extraordinary amount of information on each health topic. Some information is also available in Spanish.

Women's Health.gov: Healthy Aging (http://www.womenshealth.gov/aging/). Information is presented on an assortment of issues facing women as they age. Diseases and conditions, caregiving, wellness, staying active, falls, and mental health are some of the topics covered on this site. Each topic provides material, including news on the topic, links to additional publications, organizations and websites for assistance and more knowledge about the topic.

Women's Health.gov: Mental Health (http://www.womenshealth.gov/mental-health/). The mental health section of Women's Health.gov provides an important resource on mental health and women. Pregnancy, menstruation, infertility, nutrition, and exercise are some of the topics covered that can impact mental health. Additional information is available on what to do if you need help, preventing suicide, and women veterans and mental health. Fact sheets provide information on other sources, including caregiver stress, binge eating, and stress and health.

Military: Current and Veteran

Women in the Army (https://www.army.mil/women/). A site on women in the United States Army. From News (Army opening armor and infantry to women) and videos (advising the Afghan army, earning the Ranger tab). Related links include the U.S. Army Women's Museum, and DOD Women's History Month. Three resources for veterans include Experiencing War: Women of Four Wars, Center for Women Veterans, and Women Veterans Health Care.

U.S. Department of Defense: Women's History Month (http://archive.defense.gov/home/features/2015/0315_womens-history/). This site is packed with information about women in the military, from a picture of women in the U.S. Marine Corps Women's Reserve in 1918 to a timeline of women's involvement from 1775 to 2015 in the military. Profiles, videos, news stories and an infographic titled By the Numbers: Women in the U.S. Military contribute to making this a fascinating site on women in the U.S. military.

U.S. Department of Veterans Affairs: Center for Women Veterans (http://www.va.gov/womenvet/). Coordinates health care, benefits, and programs for women. One section highlights women who served, from women who served in Vietnam to the death of one of the oldest female veterans in the United States. Links provide information on women veterans as a population group, FAQs, and a historical perspective on women veteran's issues. Information is provided on outreach, benefits, burials and memorials through the Women Veterans Program.

U.S. Department of Veterans Affairs: Women Veterans (http://www.benefits.va.gov/persona/veteran-women.asp). Information is provided on a variety of benefits, including disability, pension, education and training, healthcare, vocational rehabilitation, employment, and burial. Information and a link (including a webinar) are available for women who are survivors of military sexual trauma (MST).

Statistics

Bureau of Justice Statistics: Stalking (http://www.bjs.gov/index.cfm?ty=tp&tid=973). Defines stalking victims and the actions that constitute stalking. General information is provided on stalking laws, but all states have laws against stalking and can differ according to the state's definition. Links lead to publications and products on stalking. Included in this section are statistics on stalkers (age, race) and stalking victims.

Centers for Disease Control and Prevention: Contraceptive Use (http://www.cdc.gov/nchs/fastats/contraceptive.htm). Contraceptive use statistics can be found on this site; from the number of women using birth control to the type of method being used.

The site also provides statistics on teenagers and sexual activity, contraceptive use, and child bearing.

Centers for Disease Control and Prevention: National Center for Health Statistics: Women's Health (http://www.cdc.gov/nchs/fastats/womens-health.htm). Data is provided on a number of topics, from the health status (healthy, not healthy) to alcohol use, level of obesity, smoking, hypertension, physical activity, health insurance coverage, and cause of death.

United States Department of Labor: Data and Statistics: Women in the Labor Force (https://www.dol.gov/wb/stats/stats_data.htm). The latest annual data on women in the workforce can be found on this site. Additional data include occupations, mothers and family, women veterans, and earnings. Infographics are available on equal pay, working mothers in the U.S., Hispanic women in the labor force, and breaking down the gender wage gap. Linked resources include data on earnings and the labor force.

United States Department of Labor: Data & Statistics: Women in the Labor Force (https://www.dol.gov/wb/stats/stats_data.htm). The infographic provides data on numerous aspects of women at work. Eight sections provide statistics and information on: Latest Annual Data (women of working age, unemployment, and earnings); Facts over Time (women in the labor force, participation in selected occupations); Occupations (most common, highest and lowest paying); Mothers and families (selected labor force characteristics, births in past twelve months); Women veterans (unemployment, employment by sector); Earnings (over time, age, occupation); Additional links provide access to publications and resources on earnings and the labor force.

Women's Health.gov: Statistics (http://www.womenshealth.gov/statistics/). Information is provided on many topics, including: pregnancy, sexually transmitted diseases, violence and abuse, mental health and minority health. Understanding statistics is part of this site; providing assistance to users in grasping the information presented. A link to features (National Center for Health Statistics) and Quick Health Data Online provide supplemental data for users.

Violence and Women

United States Department of Justice: Office on Violence Against Women (https://www.justice.gov/ovw). Information about the office and its areas of focus on women and violence are available for users. Selected publications, news, and resources to identify and prevent gender bias are available. An action center provides links to campus sexual assault and finding help for victims of violence—including domestic and dating violence, sexual assault, and stalking.

Women's Health.gov: Violence Against Women (http://www.womenshealth.gov/violence-against-women/). Subjects available on this website include: Am I being abused?; get help for violence; laws on violence against women; types of violence against women; mental health effects of violence; help end violence against women. Fact sheets include resources on date rape drugs, sexual assault, depression and female genital cutting.

Women's Health.gov: Violence Against Women: Human Trafficking (https://www.womenshealth.gov/violence-against-women/types-of-violence/human-trafficking.html). This site is part of the larger Women's Health.gov: Violence Against Women and focuses on human trafficking. A definition of trafficking is followed by ways a person may be trafficked and what may happen to them. Links are provided to additional information and resources on trafficking humans, including Fact Sheet: Sex Trafficking, Federal Anti-Trafficking Efforts, and Fact Sheet: Victim Assistance.

Women's Health.gov: Female Genital Cutting (http://womenshealth.gov/publica tions/our-publications/fact-sheet/female-genital-cutting.html). This site uses a Q&A for-mat to provide information on more than 12 questions about female genital cutting or female genital mutilation. Questions include what is female genital cutting, what are the different types of cutting, where is it done, and why is it performed? A worthwhile site for answers on this topic.

Federal Bureau of Investigation: Reaching Out about Female Genital Mutilation (https://www.fbi.gov/news/stories/2016/may/fbi-reaching-out-about-female-genital-mutilation/fbi-reaching-out-about-female-genital-mutilation). Female genital mutilation (FGM) is illegal in the United States and the Federal Bureau of Investigation has provided a website with information on what they are doing to combat FGM in the United States. Resources are included on this site for further information.

Women's History

Kids.gov: Women's History Month Lesson Plan (https://kids.usa.gov/teachers/les son-plans/history/womens-history/index.shtml). In addition to the multitude of websites the U.S. government has for adults, they also have websites geared toward children. The Women's History Month Lesson Plan has a variety of exercises for children which provide resources and information on Women's History Month. Pertinent information to assist teachers in using the site include the objective, standards, time required and grade level. Activities are provided along with suggested questions for the students to answer. Five resources, including the Smithsonian Education Women's History Teaching Resources are available for additional information and resources.

Library of Congress: Women Come to the Front (http://www.loc.gov/exhibits/wcf/). Two essays are included in this site, War, Women, and Opportunity and Seeds of Change. Eight women are profiled on the website; Clare Boothe Luce, Janet Flanner, and May Craig are among the women profiled. A small section after each biography provides pho-tos of the women and links to articles or additional information about them. One woman was decorated twice for military bravery and had a comic book created about her adven-tures.

Library of Congress: Women of Protest: Photographs from the Records of the National Woman's Party (https://www.loc.gov/collection/women-of-protest/about-this-collection/). This collection highlights the National Woman's Party and their actions for suffrage in the United States. Over 440 digitized photographs illustrating the actions women took for suffrage include parades, hunger strikes and imprisonment. A historical overview of the party, a timeline, information on the leaders, tactics for their campaign, and photographs of the women who were arrested for the cause make this a fascinating glimpse into the history of women working for suffrage. Several pictures are of women arrested; the photos give a glimpse into their motivation and provide information on the woman, including notes about her, her education and the number of times she was arrested (one woman was arrested five times).

The National Archives: Archives Library Information Center: Women (http://www.

archives.gov/research/alic/reference/womens-history.html). The Archives Library Information Center has created a resource on women in the United States. Some of the items include bibliographies (women's history, pathfinder for women's history research in the National Archives and Records Administration Library), African-American Women's Resources (African American Women Writers of the 19th Century, Claiming their Citizenship: African American Women from 1624–2009), Biographies (Distinguished Women of Past and Present, Biographies of Women in Science), Politics and Women (Center for American Women and Politics, Women and Social Movements in the United States, 1600–2000), Suffrage (The 19th Amendment, Not For Ourselves Alone: The Story of Elizabeth Cady Stanton and Susan B. Anthony), and Women and the Military (Fly Girls, Military Resources: Women in the Military). Other Resources on the Web provides links to resources on many other topics, including Civil War Women, Gifts of Speech: Women's Speeches From Around the World and the Real Rosie the Riveter Project.

National Park Service: Places Where Women Made History (https://www.nps.gov/nr/travel/pwwmh/index.htm). The National Park Service has created a travel itinerary for those interested in historical places in the United States highlighting women's history in the United States. This site has information on 74 sites in New York and Massachusetts. The site provides a numbered map, clicking on a number will allow you to access information about the site. Number 6 on the tour is the home of Susan B. Anthony in Rochester, New York. A page of information is provided on Anthony, including pictures of her home and partner Elizabeth Cady Stanton. If one prefers, a list of sites in New York and Massachusetts is available with links to information on the site. A bibliography of reading materials and websites is available, with print resources listed in categories of general, reference, biographical, and young readers.

National Park Service: Women of the Gold Rush (https://www.nps.gov/klgo/learn/historyculture/women.htm). Women were a part of the Klondike Gold Rush from 1897 to 1898. They came from all walks of life to find their treasure and change their lives. The National Park Service profiles 4 women who went to the Klondike to search for gold. The profiles are vivid and allow us an entry into life during the gold rush in Alaska.

United States House of Representatives: History, Art & Archives: The Women's Rights Movement, 1848–1920 (http://history.house.gov/Exhibitions-and-Publications/WIC/Historical-Essays/No-Lady/Womens-Rights/). A detailed history of the Women's Right Movement is found on this site is provided through five essays, including I'm No Lady; I'm a Member of Congress, On the National Stage, and A Changing of the Guard. Member profiles are available for the female members of Congress. Historical data is available for many areas, including women of color in Congress, women representatives and Senators by Congress, 1917 to the present, women who have chaired Congressional committees, 1923 to the present, and women who became cabinet members and United States diplomats. This site provides a wealth of information on women in the United States Congress.

Conclusion

From women staking their claim in the Klondike Gold Rush to women veterans of several wars, these sources illustrate the wealth of information about women in this country, exemplifying the determination, grit, and desire women exhibited in numerous ways to build this country and obtain the equality they deserved in American society.

Collaboration
Women Remaking American Political Culture

VINCE LEE

Overview and Introduction

Culminating with a keynote delivered by NPR White House correspondent Tamara Keith, the one-day Women's History symposium was created and hosted through a collaboration by the University of Houston Library's Carey C. Shuart Women's Archive and Research Collection, Department of History, and the Women's, Gender & Sexuality Studies Program. The purpose of the symposium was threefold: highlighting the resources available for research within the Shuart Women's Archive, drawing academic attention to topics that have been under-studied: there is currently a dearth of existing scholarship on Houston and Texas women and there are abundant topics awaiting discovery for would be authors and researchers, and offering an outreach opportunity to potential donors and community members on materials they possess that could be added to the Shuart Women's Archive through the Attic Roadshow Drive.

The symposium illustrated that it is not only a collaboration among panelists, and the women within the grassroots community affecting change and remaking the political landscape, but a collaboration among departments, faculty, archivists, and benefactors all having the singular vision of creating an event that would build momentum not only for the archives in collection building going forward but be self-sustaining in bringing awareness within the community of the types of materials currently available for research. Parsons states in his introduction, "A conference or symposium is a chance to be exposed to new studies and ideas, to meet leaders in the academic field or those just starting, to form collaborations, to develop new projects and build research teams, and to give or receive mentoring advice" (Parsons, 2015).

It's often said that to raise a child or to attempt a significant undertaking it takes a village. Nowhere is this truer than in planning for and creating Women's history symposium. Roberts states in her booklet, "A symposium is first and foremost a 'people project.' Whether you are dealing with volunteers, presenters, sponsors, speakers, or attendees, you will always need to do three things: (a) draw 'em in, (b) keep 'em there, and (c) get 'em back next year. The key to achieving this is leadership. Everyone wants to be well led, whether they are volunteers or paid staff" (Roberts 2013). However, before the collaboration can begin it has to originate from someone willing to take a risk and having the vision and courage to start something. That someone was Carey C. Shuart, founder and benefactor of the Women's Archives that bears her name at the University of Houston Libraries Special Collections.

Through Shuart's advocacy for the idea of a symposium, she enlisted the help of the Director of development at the College of Liberal Arts and Social Sciences (CLASS) in organizing a planning committee to make this happen. This occurred in early in February of 2015. Additionally, Shuart would underwrite portions of the symposium and partner with the Alice Kleberg Reynolds Foundation and Melanie Gray in sponsorship of the event.

Purpose

"An event is a planned gathering with purpose" (Dowson and Bassett 2014). The initial purpose of hosting the one-day women's symposium was to leverage the event and draw attention to the Carey Shuart Women's Archive. By raising awareness of the archival collections and resources available we are communicating not only to faculty and students of the University of Houston but the surrounding community that these resources are available for their use. Through the excitement and momentum generated from the event, we wanted to build our archival collections through community and scholarly outreach by working with the community and prospective donors letting them know that they have materials which we want for the archives. To accomplish this we created fliers and marketing to let attendees know what we were interested in and that we would like to talk with them about their materials.

Planning

The success or failure of any symposium lies in the pre-planning, planning, and logistics phase that lead up to the big event. As partners and within our planning committee we had to ask ourselves that most important question-why have a women's symposium? Of course one question would lead to another. What did we hope to achieve as a result of the event? Who are we targeting as an audience? How were we going to put all this together in eight months' time? We were approached with the initial idea by the Director of Development for the College of Liberal Arts and Social Sciences (CLASS).

The draft proposal we were presented with outlined that the one-day women's history conference hosted in collaboration with the Carey C. Shuart Women's Archive and Research Collection, UH Women's, Gender & Sexuality Studies, the UH Department of History, Houston HerStory, Houston Public Media, and other Houston community organizations would be held in Rockwell Pavilion and the Student Center on the main campus of the University of Houston. The draft also outlined that the events are geared for a variety of audiences both from the university and the community. The initial draft and vision for the program was that there would be four different types of events: two panels with academic papers; one panel with Living Archives interviews of activist women; a luncheon talk by an academic scholar; and an evening keynote address.

However, after subsequent meetings the planning committee deemed that the event needed to be streamlined due to the duration of the event and logistics involved. Instead there would be three different types of events: one panel with Living Archives interviews of activist women in political roles who made policy; two panels with academic papers; and an evening keynote address. The Living Archives panel which would kick things off in the afternoon would take the place of the initial talk of the academic scholar to consolidate time and avoid redundancy.

As the planning committee were charged by Carey to plan and host the symposium preferably in the fall of 2015. The actual date was later ultimately set for October 14, 2015. We arrived at this date based on a host of logistical factors namely, the availability of venues to be reserved, avoiding scheduling conflicts with other events at the beginning of the fall term, and available dates for our initial list of panelists and keynote speaker. Once this date was penciled in we realized this would give us about 8 months to plan and execute the elements of the symposium. This was not much time considering we still had to decide who we wanted as our panelists and keynote speaker and secure them for the event, not to mention who were our contingency plan of backups in the event our initial choices couldn't make it. On top of that there was the matter of compiling a guest list of our targeted audience, as well the marketing and communications component of making the public aware of the symposium.

This in turn brought up a question for cost for the event? Should we charge for admission or would this be free? If it is free then free for whom? If we charged who would we charge and what is a reasonable amount? The planning committee did feel that with the costs involved and if we wanted guests to be vested in the process, then an amount should be charged to make sure that they would show up. We had settled on $20 for the general public to attend the keynote and the reception to the keynote. It is more than a nominal amount to help defray costs associated with expenses, honorariums, and marketing that are associated with the event, but the amount is not prohibitive that guests would balk at attending. Attendance to the keynote and reception would remain free to UH faculty and students. The two afternoon panels would be free for faculty, students, and the public except for the Barbara Karkabi Living Archives event in which the general public is charged $10.

Venue

As a result of our discussions on targeted audience and who to invite, we had to decide the appropriate venue for the symposium. Will this be held at one location or multiple locations? Initially we had thought that we would host all events at the Rockwell Pavilion located at the M.D. Anderson Library. The benefits of this were that it would be in the library, in close proximity to the Carey Shuart Women's Archive, and the location is centralized on campus. Everyone (faculty, students, and visitors) would know or could be directed to the location. However, the planning committee decided that the keynote being a ticketed event with a reception for the speaker should be held at a more formal venue that would allow VIPs and sponsors to mingle with the speaker prior to the keynote. Also, as the attendance was anticipated to be around 150 guests, the venue should be able to accommodate large seating and have great acoustics for a recording. Based on these criteria, the planning committee settled on the University of Houston Student Center Theater. The theater was also centralized on campus and in close proximity to the M.D. Anderson Library. After the afternoon events and panels concluded the audience could easily make their way next door for the pre-symposium reception and then the evening keynote over at the Student Center.

Marketing and Communication

Communication and marketing of the event was three-pronged. To invite guests and interested parties to the Symposium we had to compile a mailing list. These would include campus partners, donors, faculty from other junior and community colleges within the Greater Houston area, and local women's activist groups. We also had Dr. Nancy Young, professor of history, contact the media for coverage of the event. One of the contacts was Marisa Ramirez, media representative at the University of Houston, who interviewed Dr. Young. From that interview was a news release published on the UH News and Events site promoting the day long symposium with key facts and information.

A symposium publicity postcard was also designed by a staff member of CLASS. The postcard was created with a prominent photo of keynote speaker Tamara Keith along with a schedule of the day's panels and events. The postcards were shared both electronically through emails and listservs and physically distributed at campus locations. They were also distributed in packets to attendees on the day of the event.

Additionally, an "Attic Roadshow" flier and questionnaire was designed as a community outreach tool for our campaign to the community to grow the Shuart Women's Archive. This drive would expand the holdings of the Shuart Archives through further acquisitions and donations from interested community members and organizations looking for a home to place their papers or records. Additionally the questionnaire and flier provides examples of the types of materials in which the archives collect and also a survey for guests to fill out on the types of materials they may have along with contact information for follow-up by a consultant.

Finally, having tackled marketing through the traditional venues and covering our bases through mass mailings, media, fliers, and postcards, the planning group realized that it was important to create a website dedicated to the symposium for a number of reasons. First, the website is a marketing and communications tool. Its design and interface would provide information an attendee would want to know about the event. Second, the website reaches a greater audience and much more quickly through the internet than mass mailings, fliers, and media announcements could hope to do. This is because a website is persistent and present on the web as long as it is hosted and maintained. It doesn't depend on timing of a news release which someone may have missed depending on when it was announced through the media. The website encounters no physical limitations of fliers. It's not dependent on the quantity printed up or distributed nor is there any fear of having enough on hand or running out. Links to a website can be embedded on other sites and shared through emails and social media that go out.

Third, there is an online audience that simply uses the internet to find news, information, and events that they access on their smartphones, laptops, or desktops. Andrew McLoughlin, in the book *The Future of Events and Festivals*, underscores this development by stating, "Smart phone technology is indirectly prescribing the future direction of event design and interaction with audiences and furthermore stakeholders in a wider context. The global popularity and use of smart phones and burgeoning innovative technologies are expediting ingenious ways of engaging audiences worldwide" (McLoughlin 2015). Having a website created and dedicated for the sole purpose of the symposium makes the odds greater that they will come across this information.

Fourth, and perhaps most importantly, having a website allowed us to design and embed our Attic Roadshow Questionnaire online using Google Forms. Responses submitted from the online questionnaire would go to me as the administrator of the form and I would be notified via my Gmail account. I also would have information of the prospective donor and contact to follow-up with regarding their materials for the Shuart Women's Archive.

Fortunately, I was able to setup a website for the symposium in rather short time by enlisting the help of UH Libraries Web Services. Since our own web services had already created what are known as extended sites off of their web services projects page, all they needed to do was assign and configure a page for me with some introductory content on the symposium. From there I was able to login to the site add additional pages and content along with tabs: About, Schedule, Location, Attic Roadshow, Questionnaire, and Sponsors. All this was done quickly and easily, in about 45 minutes to an hour on the preconfigured templates that were available for each page. I just had to provide title, content, and images where necessary for each page and order them in a way that would make intuitive sense to the user. Because web services created and maintained the site and this was all done in house within the UH Library, there was no cost involved in purchasing a domain name or paying a hosting site to maintain it.

The Big Day

The big day of the symposium occurred on Wednesday, October 14, 2015. A registration table was set up complete with fliers and postcards for the event as well as name tags for guests and speakers, along with a cash box for admissions. For the Attic Roadshow table we placed our fliers with questionnaires for guests to take and to disseminate. On an easel next to the table was a prominent signboard of the Attic Roadshow to let guests know who we were and what we were all about. We also had a smaller sign on the table offering three tours of the Shuart Women's Archive at scheduled intervals during the day (11:10 a.m., 1:10 p.m., and 5:10 p.m.). The table was staffed both by myself and my graduate assistant as consultants for the Attic Roadshow Drive answering any questions that guests may have.

Also, in keeping with the theme of the symposium, we setup two display cases of select materials from the Carey Shuart Women's Archives on women and politics and women and activism. These were from various archival collections such as the Houston Gorilla Girls, Lynn Randolph, Houston Area Now, Nikki Van Hightower, Harris County Women's Political Caucus, and Minnie Fisher Cunningham to name but a few collections. The purpose of the displays were to highlight materials from the collection related to the theme of the symposium. The displays would also provide an opportunity for conversation with prospective donors to give illustrative examples of materials the archive collects and to talk about materials which they may have in their attics, garages, and storage.

The lineup for the symposium kicked off at 11:30 am with the Barbara Karkabi Living Archives Series entitled: "The Body Politic: How It Matters When Women Make Public Policy." The panelists for this session were: Sue Lovell (member at-large, Houston City

Council 2006–2012), Amber Anderson Mostyn (founder of Mostyn Law), Aimee Mobley Turner (president, League of Women Voters-Houston), Sue Walden ($$, Carly Fiorina presidential campaign); and it was moderated by Nancy Sims of the University of Houston.

This was then followed by an Academic Panel, "Race, Ethnicity and Activism," from 2 to 3:15 p.m. The papers presented were authored by Cynthia Orozco (Eastern New Mexico University), "Adela Sloss Vento: Mexican American Civil Rights Activist and Political Activist, 1927–1928"; and Samantha Rodriguez (University of Houston), "Waiting for No One: Tejana Interventionism Third Party Politics in the 1970s." The panel was chaired and commented by Sara Luna of the University of Houston.

The final Academic Panel was "Confronting Power Structure" from 3:30 to 5 p.m. The papers presented were authored by Mary Ellen Curtin (American University), "Barbara Jordan and Black Power"; and Becky Smith (University of Houston), "Houston's Feminists: Significant Gains as Political and Social Activism Increases (1971–1974)." The panel was chaired and commented by Nancy Sims of the University of Houston.

Following this was a one hour break. Guests could tour the Shuart Women's Archive a final time or relax before reconvening over at the University Student Center Ballroom next door to the Library. At 6 p.m. there was a catered reception open to top donors that have contributed to Houston Public Media; the Department of Women's Gender and Sexuality Studies; Department of History; and to the symposium panelists. The reception would also be an opportunity for the donors, panelists, and partners to meet with Tamara Keith.

The keynote address began at 7 p.m. in the University Center Theater with a welcome given by dean of libraries, Lisa German, thanking the sponsors for making the event possible and thanking the university partners for organizing the event. The welcome was followed by an introduction from former First Lady of Houston and *Houston Chronicle* editorial writer Andrea White, recapping Tamara Keith's career and aspirations of being a reporter for National Public Radio (NPR). Tamara Keith then took the stage with prepared remarks for her keynote address on her observations of the annual congressional women's softball game which she is a part of. It's a fundraiser for breast cancer charity and in her opinion is good for democracy because it's a microcosm that shows that women of both parties within Congress can reach across the aisles and work with one another to get things done through collaboration. To underscore this she notes that the Women of Congress softball team is bipartisan and bicameral. The keynote then concluded with a question and answer format with moderator Professor Leandra Zarnow, and then Keith took questions from the audience before the event concluded at 8 p.m.

Both the keynote and daytime panels were recorded. We were able to secure a videographer for both events through the University of Houston Jack J. Valenti School of Communications.

Lessons Learned

So we made it through the big day and were able to accomplish all that we had set out to do for the inaugural symposium. What did we learn besides what went well and the immense amount of stress that led up until that point? The first thing I think we learned was that we as a team needed to hold a post assessment meeting to debrief after the symposium. Unfortunately one never occurred, as our schedules from that point forward had moved on to other projects. The development director of CLASS did send a follow-up survey and feedback via email to all parties concerned, but we are not sure who responded if at all and there was no follow-up. A meeting would have brought everyone together and allowed participants to better articulate issues, problems, and successes so that we could further refine the process for future events.

Another thing we have learned through this process is that academics don't necessarily make good event planners. First and foremost, we are good at our respective jobs of teaching, managing a department, donor development, and managing an archives. Oftentimes, academics are recruited into doing event planning on top of their already full plate. In retrospect, perhaps using a portion of the funds provided to hire a professional event planner or one for consultation may have been a more prudent course of action. How an event planner approaches planning and logistics for an event such as a symposium may be totally opposite to what an academic may envision as being successful. The professional makes it their living and having done many events through the course of their career, have the critical elements down pat and streamlined. Parsons notes, "Academics that are recruited to plan and organize meetings often have not planned or held a meeting before (or perhaps only one of a small scale), and PhD programs typically do not have courses on event planning. Planning a meeting is a lot different from planning a class, a field trip, or a committee meeting, there are far more moving parts, and issues crop up that one could not even imagine" (Parson 2015).

Also, since we did choose to plan for the symposium ourselves we should have done a bit more research online to see what resources were available. We could have used an existing template with guidelines and processes compiled other academics entitled "Logistics of Organizing the FOR Symposium." Their premise was to document their own process so that in the future they wouldn't have to reinvent the wheel should they have to plan for another symposium. Had we found and located this template this may have saved us from reinventing the wheel, expending much time and anguish as we came up with our own elements and processes in putting together our own project plan for the symposium. Also many of the organizing tips found within the template are presented in topical chunks in chronological order. The best part of the template is that it allows the user to customize and implement the parts that are most useful to them while ignoring the rest (Mazilli et al. 2014).

Finally, the most important lesson we learned is when to hold a symposium. Symposiums by their very nature are very time intensive for everyone involved from the beginning of the planning phase to when the big day finally arrives. Having gone through this process, we decided that to be most effective future women's history symposiums at the University of Houston should be held every two years. For one, this signifies to attendees and panelists alike that this is a special and significant event to be appreciated when it occurs as opposed to annual event which may become monotonous if it were to happen each year. Also, holding a biennial symposium and spacing things out avoids burnout that occurs within the planning committee. This gives them more time to recover after the big event and the added benefit for time to reflect on the past proceedings before reconvening for future planning.

REFERENCES

Dowson, Ruth, and David Bassett. 2015. *Event Planning and Management: A Practical Handbook for PR and Events Professionals*. London: Kogan Page.

Mazzilli, Sarah A., T.W. Gunsalus, Gary S. McDowell, Kristin A. Krukenberg, and Jessica A. Polka. 2014. "Logistics of Organizing the FOR Symposium." thewinnower.com

McLoughlin, Andrew. 2015. *The Future of Events and Festivals*. London: Routledge.

Parsons, E.C.M. 2015. "So You Think You Want to Run an Environmental Conservation Meeting? Advice on the Slings and Arrows of Outrageous Fortune that Accompany Academic Conference Planning." *Journal of Environmental Studies and Sciences* 5(4):735–744. doi 10.1007/s13412-015-0327-8.

Roberts, Katherine E. 2013. "Fueling Dreams: How to Run a Symposium." https://info.aiaa.org/SC/YPC/Shared%20Documents/Fueling%20Dreams%20-%20How%20to%20Run%20a%20Symposium.pdf.

Graphic Activism
Lesbian Archival Library Display

SHAWN(TA) SMITH-CRUZ

The cover of the 1977 issue of *Sinister Wisdom, a Lesbian Literary and Art Journal*, frames a two-toned photographic-negative print of two nude women in an embrace: one woman reclining, held in the arms of her lover (Desmoines and Nicholson 1977). The lover cradles the reclined figure, one arm clutching around her neck to meet her lips, the other arm, an arrow between her lover's open thighs with the entirety of her hand, disappearing into the darkness of the horizontal negative exposure; wisps of layered cropped hair dance at the lightest sections of the image, exclaiming a paucity of stillness (Corrine 1977). As described during the panel to celebrate the exhibition of this and other lesbian graphic art, "Graphic Activism" exhibition curator, Flavia Rando introduced the Tee Corrine print is a "part of a series of prints on women with physical difficulties, making love" (CLAGS 2016).

As a timestamp throughout lesbian culture, this iconic Tee Corrine print and its 1977 *Sinister Wisdom* debut as cover image represented a quest for visibility. This same issue featured an article by legendary poet Adrienne Rich titled, "It is the lesbian in us…" which speaks to today's presumption by young scholars of a cohesive lesbian and lesbian-feminist past. "The word "lesbian" must be affirmed because to discard it is to collaborate with silence and lying about our very existence, the closet-game, the creation of the *unspeakable*" (Rich 1977). Both Corrine's photographic print, highlighting differently abled bodies, and Rich's essay on language, speak to a current divisiveness in the queer community, where politics of gender-identities or any claim to the term "lesbian" has as a whole silenced young and older people who claim lesbian and woman-centered identities.

This current state of temporal lesbian collective identity is the culture for which the "Graphic Activism" exhibition hit the walls of the City University of New York in the 2016 summer and fall semesters. Tee Corrine's image on the 1977 Sinister Wisdom cover was juxtaposed with forty-six additional images of lesbian graphics from the '70s to today. The framed posters were curated inside display cases that lined the passageway of the university center main lobby, and extended to the first floor of the library. This essay describes the process for mounting such an exhibition. It aims to serve a dual role of acting as a hands-on case study for librarians wishing to hold an archival exhibit in their library.

The Graduate Center Library

Location, Location, Location

Diagonally facing the Empire State Building, the Mina Rees Library at the Graduate Center is one of thirty-one libraries spanning across the City University of New York. The campus which supplies doctoral and master's degrees to under five thousand students, has its library space on the first floor of the single-building campus, nestled on the northeast corner of Fifth Avenue and Thirty-Fourth Street in Manhattan, one avenue east of Herald Square where the Macy's emblem boasts "The Largest Macy's in the World." With floor to ceiling windows, the library's first floor is arranged as a walk-through leading to the concourse level and second floor, allowing for only a few rows of computer desk kiosks, but with plenty of walking space complete with a window-sized, multi-colored, steel sculpture, and a large oval reference desk, housing student workers, security, reserve books, and equipment for loan behind locked cases.

Display cases line the walls like vertical glass tiles leading toward the original architecture of the original B. Altman the historic elevator. In years' past, the university's Department of Buildings had authority to place items inside of the display cases, as they would every case throughout the building. Library control and oversight meant strategic planning was required on behalf of librarians to maintain a high standard of visual allure. With the employment of the new Chief Librarian Polly Thistlethwaite, a former public services librarian in this same library, and caretaker at the Lesbian Herstory Archives in the '90s (a lifetime ago), themed displays responded to intersections of programming at the Graduate Center with faculty and student interests in mind. With a small print collection of only a single floor of books, and an archive of solely institutional materials, a small number of special collections were available to manufacture alluring displays.

Displays as Outreach

Lesbian graphic art works was not the first idea for an exhibition inside library display cases. It is likely that the idea would not have taken hold without the primer of two distinct displays, each with a political herstory, and female activism (which one could define as harboring lesbian connotation) as its core context.

Creation of the library blog using the intra-campus wordpress platform, CUNY Academic Commons, allowed for a publicly accessible website which included an event calendar, detailed posts on library happenings, and a mailing list. In the span of two years, the blog became the centerpiece of library activity. An adjunct librarian position was created as Digital Outreach and Reference librarian. With the new position, all social media was connected to library administered Facebook and Twitter accounts. A new audience from within and outside of the campus emerged. An outward facing library was now at the helm of outreach service. An outward facing blog also mirrored the outward-facing display cases with a new goal for pointing back to the function and goals of library service. With much deliberation put toward objects that could stand in as visual representation of library materials, prospective display materials were pulled from special collections and intra-campus collaborative relationships.

Library Displays from Collaborative Relationships

In summer 2012, the Activist Women's Voices special collection was displayed in the library cases. Material was gathered from the ephemera donated to the library by the Center for the Study of Women and Society at the Graduate Center. The project was committed to documenting the voices of unheralded activist women in community-based organizations in New York City. It was a manageable size of thirty-six activists and their corresponding organizations, many of whom were still alive, including the GC's very own chief librarian. The display featured clippings, images, and writings from activists and organizations, including the Lesbian Herstory Archives. Displayed women were honored to be exhibited, and students whose focus was women's studies found the display useful to their research. The library blog highlighted the display, memorializing the collection.

Following the AWV exhibition, in 2013, two student fellows approached the library to use the display cases for an exhibition of their own—one that also acknowledged activism and women in the academy and the community. They proposed use of a current professor's research project: The Madeline Gittell Archive. This project highlighted the life of a CUNY scholar and community activist, deeply committed to racial, gender and educational justice. Gittell's archival material was processed with the direction of acclaimed university professor Michelle Fine. A formal request was made to the chief librarian followed by an outline of additional components of the exhibition, including a blog post written as an authored article, use of library materials, and as a departure from the AWV exhibition, an event to highlight the exhibition's materials and project. The display included archival books stacked for a three-dimensional effect, photographs, hand-written letters, and original newspaper clippings highlighting the NYC landscape on "public education in New York City, with an emphasis on Ocean Hill Brownsville during the black resistance movements of the 1960s" (Liebert 2013). The final event was An Evening in Honor of the exhibition and included a tour of the display cases through the GC library, followed by a welcome from the university president and off-site reception.

These two outward facing displays since 2012 paved the way for a 2016 unveiling of a lesbian graphic activist exhibition. Without these two very outward facing events, it is likely that the lesbian graphic activism exhibition would have seemed ill-fitted to the GC library. In each iteration of the library displays, interestingly focused on gender, highlighting women's activism, a new addition to expand the exhibits occurred. During summer 2016 "Graphic Activism" was mounted in both the library display cases as well as display cases in the main university lobby. For the first time in the library's history, a joint exhibition with the building's larger display windows curated the entire first floor of the Graduate Center. An additional new element to the "Graphic Activism" exhibit was its pre-existing nature; none of its collection was pulled from library collections.

A Pre-Existing Collection

One challenge that librarians commonly face with visual displays is the curation of material. Where within the larger library collection will the exhibition's material be pulled? How will the exhibit effect circulation and use? For the Gittell exhibition, for example, select books were pulled from the collection which required an edit to individual item records in the Aleph catalog. A change in circulation procedures had to be implemented for when books were sought for check-out. In addition, reference staff had to receive training on a protocol for retrieving items when requested, which included retrieving keys from open display cases (a procedure that was not accessible to circulation staff, who were often student workers). Decisions for whether displayed books should remain in circulation for the duration of the display had to include input from the Head of Circulation, as well as from the Associate Librarian for Public Services and Scholarly Communication. This single example was largely trial by error and made the case for not including circulating materials into the next exhibition. An exhibit that relied solely on outside materials was favorable.

"Graphic Activism": Lesbian Art Displayed from the Lesbian Herstory Archives

Points of Connection

As a pre-existing exhibit, the "Graphic Activism" exhibition was solely comprised of material that did not belong to the library collection. Instead, material was from an outside institution—a non-profit, community-based, and volunteer-run archive: The Lesbian Herstory Archives. As the largest and oldest archive of lesbian materials in the world, located in the same city as the Graduate Center, LHA was an easy target. Yet, the serendipity of the collaborative relationship stemmed from beyond an easily replicable formula. Archival lesbian artwork on the walls of the Graduate Center was made possible because of pre-existing relationships from multiple angles.

1. The Graduate Center's Department of Buildings lead engineer was also a member of the Robert Blackburn printmaking workshop which sponsored the pre-existing "Graphic Activism" exhibition.
2. The head of reference at the Graduate Center is a volunteer coordinator of the Lesbian Herstory Archives and also has six framed stills of her hand-made zines dedicated to black lesbian herstory and queer of color housing in NYC as part of the exhibition.
3. One of the curators of the "Graphic Activism" exhibition, Flavia Rando, also led a "Seminar in the City" with CLAGS: The Center for LGBTQ studies, a center that co-sponsored the event. Flavia is also a long-standing CUNY professor.
4. The chief librarian is a previous caretaker and volunteer with the LHA.

The list of connecting points does not represent an exhaustive list. Instead it aims to outline the relationship between the library, university center, and the archival organization as a long-standing and pre-existing one. As a result, the outside archival organization trusted the institution to take good care of the archival materials. The material arrived as a collection of framed original artifacts from the gallery where the collection was previously hung. Framing service was donated by the gallerists of the Elizabeth Foundation for the Arts Robert Blackburn printmaking workshop, the sponsoring gallery whose labor hung the pieces alongside the university's Department of Buildings staff person. Hardware and labor from outside of the library allowed for flexibility in the display's presentation, long-term length of display time (two semesters), and librarian labor.

Placement of framed images was determined by the exhibition curators. Instead of doing the work of printing display headers or hanging frames, the librarian's sole responsibility was to interact with the pre-existing curators, the gallery that managed the exhibition, and the Department of Buildings who had oversight for the mounting of large objects.

Scheduled during regular library hours, the prompt two-day hanging did pose only a few minor issues for library operation. One being the need to measure distance between frames for each case. Accounting for three different frame sizes, and two distinct display case widths meant the measurements could be conducted only after frame placement was decided. The workflow entailed first, the arrival of the frames from the gallery. Second, the gallery interns had to unpack, and then delicately position all frames onto a viewable wall, upright from the floor, inside the university main lobby to be surveyed by the curators. Third, the curators determined the placement of the images in two venues, inside and outside of the library. Lastly, the frames were measured into their individual cases and mounted.

Time was split into the arduous task of deciding the placement of frames. The LHA curators were very intentional about the many considerations and risks associated with the placement of one image beside another. Appropriateness of images to go into the library compared to those for the main university lobby had everything to do with the striking image quality, the size, and the lesbian-specific content of the image. Should a line-drawing of a vagina be placed beside a photographic depiction of a snarling lesbian holding a gun? And should any vaginas be placed inside of the library? It became clear that the curation of hanging the material meant two separate shows were being exhibited. One for a library audience, scholars in mid-thought, about to tackle and articulate a research question, and one for a general public of staff, faculty, students, and visitors in a bustling main Graduate School lobby of midtown New York City. It was determined that large-scale frames with extremely solicitous content, such as the "Lesbians Who Kill" poster, or a print of two nude women in a sexual embrace, should go into the university's main lobby. Posters focused on the representation of archival collections, such as the Black lesbian zines, or those with smaller images, requiring a closer, more intimate look by the viewer, would display in the library.

Groupings of materials by theme or format or time period was key. In the main passageway, music festival posters were grouped to sit alongside AIDS activism images, while conceptual images, such as "The Future is Female"—an unsourced phrase hovering around a glove cupped by two hands, opened the exhibition and began the long-walkway of lesbian themes. When it came to placement of images inside of the library, the eleven zine prints by two black lesbian zine authors were grouped together, each author having her own display case, piling five frames side-by-side with six. The third and fourth display cases were chosen as four large stills, two in each, of colorful comic art, especially created for the exhibition, that narrated a journey of a young person entering the Lesbian Herstory Archives, and calling it home.

A Culminating Event

To commemorate the "Graphic Activism" exhibition, alongside the curators, the library co-sponsored with an on-campus center, CLAGS: The Center for LGBTQ studies a panel event titled, "'Graphic Activism' Panel: Lesbian Posters & Zines 1970–Today." The event took place on a Thursday evening in October. It was intended to be an overlapping event with the New York Archivist's Roundtable New York Archivists Week (NYAW) series of events. The Graduate Center has annually participated in this week-long series, which in the past equated an Introduction to Archives workshop and a subsequent collaborative event with a local archive such as NYPL or the New York Historical Society. Adding events to the NYAW calendar often led to a larger audience, specifically non–GC affiliates, thereby opening the doors to an audience of librarian colleagues. This year the Graphic Activism Panel did not make the NYAW calendar. This was seen as a true loss since the library was excited to add lesbian subjects to a field-specific week of programming. Nevertheless, the CLAGS partnership led to a sold-out event with a primarily lesbian (and not archival or librarian-specific) audience.

A Candid Conversation

As a result of the lesbian-specific audience of the panel, and its self-affirmative nature, the best way to describe the culminating event, is to switch to a first person narrative, which I believe is best suited to finalize this essay.

The "Graphic Activism" panel included three of the five curators of the "Graphic Activism" exhibit: zinester, Elvis Wolf, art historian and founder of the Lesbian Studies Institute at the Lesbian Herstory Archives, Flavia Rando, and master printer, sculptor, and graphic artist, Ann Pachner. As the librarian and moderator, I steered the conversation, first outlining the multiple long-standing collaborations of the exhibition, then by supplying a brief chronological history of art programming at the Lesbian Herstory Archives.

Before the audience arrived, Elvis, Flavia, Ann and I queued the slideshow of images from the exhibition, and then with a bookcart, transported ten hand-selected framed images to decorate the room, placing the frames alongside the walls of the otherwise sterile classroom. To our good fortune, the room's original construction had blackboards on the two larger walls. The frames sat nicely upright with the base set inside the metal chalk holders, and the frame top, leaning against the cleaned black board surface. People arrived five minutes to the start. The room filled rather quickly with an intergenerational group of lesbian scholars, students, artists, and community members. There were no empty seats, and a few folks had to stand cradling the door. We asked the audience to help themselves to the library-sponsored coffee, sweet tarts, and contraband wine.

The liveliest part of the evening was the robust discussion. Each panelist was reflective of the pieces in the exhibition that spoke to them specifically. It was acknowledged that since none of the framed images held any attribution, it was up to the women in the room to take a trip to the Archive or inquire about images individually. The collection was meant to act as a representation of lesbian iconography, ideals, and activism over a period of time, not highlight individual artists. It was soon discovered that a handful of the artists happened to be in room. One audience member acknowledged that she "was probably the only one in the room who was not an academic" but wanted to state her claim on the material anyhow (CLAGS 2016). Others conferred that they too did not identify as academics, and still found impact from the work.

A final take-away from the event was the intergenerational nature of the group discussion. One older woman asked how we could use materials such as art and archives to educate youth in schools, where a younger woman who self-identified as a millennial asked, instead, what one was to do with archival images in today's world besides putting them on T-shirts of sharing them via social media. To find the answers, the panelists reverted the conversation to the lesbian theorists of the 1970s imploring the audience to find the answers within themselves. If using the lesbian activist images as a guide, then the lessons would be to find community in lesbian identity, and from that place, create content, and with the development of community in mind, in as many physical spaces as possible, without time as a barrier, never forget to put that content up for display.

REFERENCES

CLAGS. 2016. *Graphic Activism Panel: Lesbian Posters & Zines 1970-Today*. Digital. http://videostreaming.gc.cuny.edu/videos/video/4544/.
Corrine, Tee. 1977. "Cover Photograph." *Sinister Wisdom* 1 (3): Cover.
Desmoines, Harriet, and Catherine Nicholson. 1977. *Sinister Wisdom*, vol. 1.
Liebert, Rachel Jane. 2013. "The Gittell Archive Project & Library Exhibition." *Graduate Center Library Blog*. November 25. http://gclibrary.commons.gc.cuny.edu/2013/11/25/the-gittell-archive-project-library-exhibition/.
Rich, Adrienne. 1977. "It Is the Lesbian in Us..." *Sinister Wisdom* 1 (3): 6–9.
Smith-Cruz, Shawn(ta), Flavia Rando, Rachel Corbman, Deborah Edel, Morgan Gwenwald, Joan Nestle, and Polly Thistlethwaite. 2016. "Getting from Then to Now: Sustaining the Lesbian Herstory Archives as a Lesbian Organization." *Journal of Lesbian Studies* 20 (2): 213–33.

Resources to Support Men and Masculinities Studies

Recommendations and Experiences

AMY HUGHES

When we think about gender studies we most often think about women. And it's no surprise, many academic departments across the United States combine women and gender studies into a single a program or department. In fact, according to Peterson's, an online college guide, there are 361 women's studies programs among over 4000 schools in the United States. Whereas a search for men's studies on the same platform produces zero results and, ironically, reverts to women's studies (Peterson's 2016). Albeit, Peterson's is only one source for information, a quick search using any search engine produces an overwhelming amount of information on programs that combine women's studies and gender studies. In an academic setting, this is understandable considering the history of the women's movement, as well as the limited resources that are available for such programs—often these are small programs. And yet, this coupling perpetuates the notion that gender studies is women's studies.

Recently however, efforts are being made to include men and masculinities studies alongside LGBT and women's studies in gender studies programs, although very few of these programs are easily found. In fact, I discovered only three programs, two undergraduate and one graduate program in a search conducted in the spring of 2016. While there are several programs that offer courses related to men and masculinities studies, the majority, according to their course descriptions, still rely heavily on feminist theory. Despite the fact that men and masculinities studies has not yet taken off as a college major, or even a minor, there is still a need to provide resources and support to those faculty and students who are interested in this broad and increasingly diverse area of research. Therefore, the intent of this essay is to outline the major areas of scholarship within men and masculinities studies and highlight key resources for academic library collections.

Background

The concept of social roles was a theory introduced by anthropologists in the 1930s, and later sociologists and psychologists transformed the idea by applying it to gender, resultantly introducing the concept of sex roles (Connell 2000). The 1950s popularized sex roles, oftentimes through sociological and psychological research. According to Connell, sex roles were, "patterns of social expectation, norms for the behavior of men and women, which were transmitted to youth in a process of 'socialization'" (2000, 7). As history has shown, many were opposed to this idea, and the women's liberation movement of the late 1960s and '70s helped to lay the groundwork for feminist researchers. Feminists' critique of sex roles peaked in the 1970s and women's studies programs soon followed. A men's movement also arose during this time, yet did not gain the same attention as the women's movement. However, by the 1990s, the men's movement resurged, and today there are several groups with a multitude of different agendas or research areas that constitute the men's movement (Smiler 2004), much in the same way as the women's movement is an umbrella term for different women's rights or women's liberation groups.

Scholarship in the areas of psychology and sociology dominate men and masculinities studies. Within these disciplines, there are endless areas of research concentrations including men's health, boyhood studies, fathering and family development, sports, body image and appearance, ethnicity, identity, social and cultural influences, as well as profeminist and anti-violence researchers and advocates. Men and masculinities studies is growing internationally too and significant research from culturally, ethnically, and geographically diverse scholars continue to contribute to the growing body of knowledge. Given the various specialties within men and masculinities studies, the resources listed within this essay are far from comprehensive. Instead, the brief list of resources included here were selected because they represent essential, foundational resources for an academic library collection. Furthermore, the aforementioned description of gender studies in academia is a mere skeleton. Several groups and movements have contributed to the contemporary analysis and critique of men and masculinities studies. For a deeper history, start with encyclopedias that include excerpts from men and women, white and non-white, and national and international authors. In addition, these resources offer suggested readings for each entry that is included.

RECOMMENDED ENCYCLOPEDIAS FOR ACADEMIC LIBRARIES

Carroll, Bret. 2003. *American Masculinities: A Historical Encyclopedia.* New York: Sage.
Flood, Michael, Judith K. Gardiner, Bob Pease and Keith Pringle. Eds. 2007. *International Encyclopedia of Men and Masculinities.* New York: Routledge.
Kimmel, Michael, and Amy Aronson. 2003. *Men and Masculinities: A Social, Cultural, and Historical Encyclopedia.* Santa Barbara, CA: ABC-CLIO.

Key Resources

In the past two decades there has been a surge in academic publications. Still, compared to many other disciplines, the number of academic resources to support men and masculinities studies are relatively few. Furthermore, several once-promising journals have ceased. Popular press books and online resources such as blogs are increasingly available and accessible, yet many fail to offer students the quality of scholarship that many professors require. This can often leave students feeling frustrated if they cannot easily locate relevant and credible research. Having familiarity with a few resources is a helpful start. Another useful tool is to create a LibGuide or use a similar tool, to assist students in their navigation of resources.

Online Databases

There are two primary gender studies databases and neither provide comprehensive coverage to support men and masculinities studies. EBSCOhost's Gender Studies Database includes the greatest number of peer-reviewed journals, including journals from Men's Studies Press and Sage Publications. ProQuest's GenderWatch includes a greater selection of magazines and other popular press resources. A better bet for resources is to consult subject specific databases for sociology and psychology, including SocINDEX and PsycARTICLES. In addition to database subscription options, some resources are available through open access venues, including journals such as *Journal of Men, Masculinities, and Spirituality*; *Masculinities & Social Change*; and, *New Male Studies*.

Books

An invaluable and freely accessible resource, which includes lists of books, is Michael Flood's *The Men's Bibliography*. In its 19th edition, this online resource was last updated in 2008, and is a useful starting point for anyone unfamiliar with the literature. In addition to the encyclopedias mentioned earlier, one of the more popular, and well researched books for studies on masculinities is *The Men and the Boys* by Raewyn Connell. Although published in 2000, it includes theoretical perspectives, case study examples, and discusses issues related to globalizing masculinities that are all still relevant and growing topics today.

More recently, in 2016 the American Psychological Association published the *APA Handbook of Men and Masculinities*. In the introduction of the handbook, the editors note that despite the growth in literature, much of this literature is not backed by scientific research. This sentiment is shared by other scholars who research men and masculinities studies, which is why it may be necessary to help direct students to appropriate resources required for class assignments.

The book recommendations included here represent a few of the more recent, relevant titles for academic libraries. Note that many of the following books were authored or edited by psychologists and sociologists.

RECOMMENDED BOOKS FOR ACADEMIC LIBRARIES

Adams, Rachel and David Savran. Eds. 2002. *The Masculinity Studies Reader*. Malden, MA: Wiley-Blackwell.
Blazina, Chris. 2003. *The Cultural Myth of Masculinity*. Praeger.
Blazina, Chris, and David Shen-Miller. Eds. 2010. *An International Psychology of Men: Clinical Implications and Case Studies*. New York: Routledge.
Connell, Raewyn. 2000. *The Men and the Boys*. University of California Press.
_____. 2005. *Masculinities*. University of California Press.
Innes, Robert Alexander, and Kim Anderson, Eds. 2015. *Indigenous Men and Masculinities: Legacies, Identities, Regeneration*. University of Manitoba Press.
Kahn, Jack. 2009. *An Introduction to Masculinities*. Malden, MA: Wiley-Blackwell.
Kimmel, Michael. 2000. *The Gendered Society*. New York and Oxford: Oxford University Press.
Kimmel, Michael, Jeff Hearn and Raewyn Connell. Eds. 2004. *Handbook of Studies on Men and Masculinities*. New York: Sage.
Milani, Tommaso. Ed. 2015. *Language and Masculinities: Performances, Intersections, Dislocations*. New York: Routledge.
Pease, Bob. 2000. *Recreating Men: Postmodern Masculinity Politics*. London: Sage.
_____. 2002 *Men and Gender Relations*. Melbourne: Tertiary.
Reeser, Todd. 2010. *Masculinities in Theory*. Malden, MA: Wylie-Blackwell.
Roberts, Steven. Ed. 2014. *Debating Modern Masculinities: Change, Continuity, Crisis?* Houndmills, Basingstoke, Hampshire: Palgrave Macmillan.

Seidler, Victor. 2005. *Transforming Masculinities: Men, Cultures, Bodies, Power, Sex and Love*. New York: Routledge.
Vasquez del Aguila, Ernesto. 2014. *Being a Man in a Transnational World: The Masculinity and Sexuality of Migration*. New York: Routledge.
Ward, Michael R.M. 2015. *From Labouring to Learning: Working-Class Masculinities, Education and De-Industrialization*. Houndmills, Basingstoke, Hampshire: Palgrave Macmillan.
Whitehead, Stephen M. 2002. *Men and Masculinities: Key Themes and New Directions*. Cambridge: Polity.
Whitehead, Stephen M., and Frank J Barrett, eds. 2001. *The Masculinities Reader*. Cambridge: Polity.
Wong, Y., and Stephen R. Wester. 2016. *APA Handbook of Men and Masculinities*. American Psychological Association.

Journals

There are fewer than a dozen prominent, peer-reviewed journals, and access to these resources varies according to the publisher or vendors, such as Sage Publications and EBSCOhost as well as journals available through the Directory of Open Access Journals (DOAJ). Novice library users may not know how to access a single journal or may not consider seeking out multiple databases in order to locate these key journals. Moreover, the randomness of where these journals can be accessed, which ones are active or ceased, print or online, and scholarly or popular, can be additional barriers for students seeking information about men and masculinities studies research. Included in this section is a list of scholarly (peer-reviewed) active journals.

The *American Journal of Men's Health*, published by Sage Publications, appropriately focuses on men's health issues, and is one of two scholarly journals related to men's health. The *American Journal of Men's Health* began in 2007 and produces bi-monthly publications. It is accessible through Medline in addition to several other vendors. Sage Publications publishes two other journals on Men's Studies, *The Journal of Men's Studies* which started in 1992 and publishes three issues a year, and *Men and Masculinities*, which began in 1998 and publishes five issues annually. All three journals are essential for a men and masculinities collection.

The second men's health journal is published by Men's Studies Press. The Men's Studies Press currently publishes two journals, *Culture, Society & Masculinities*, and the *International Journal of Men's Health*. The former focuses on globalization and sociopolitical aspects of gender and masculinities, among other similar themes and is indexed in sociological databases. The *International Journal of Men's Health* includes all aspects of men's health and is indexed in selected databases within the Centre for Agriculture and Biosciences International (CABI) and general databases such as Academic Search Complete.

The American Psychological Association (APA) publishes the *Psychology of Men & Masculinities*, which started in 2000 and publishes issues quarterly. The journal is affiliated with APA's Division 51, Society for the Psychological Study of Men and Masculinity. The Nordic Association for Research on Men and Masculinities in conjunction with Taylor and Francis Publishers, publishes *NORMA: International Journal for Masculinity Studies* four times a year. The scope of this journal is international and aims to present research on the study of men within social structures as well as providing a place for new theories and methods related to masculinities. This is an important journal and distinct from others due to its international scope. Finally, *Boyhood Studies: An Interdisciplinary Journal* focuses on young masculinities including every aspect of a boy's life. It was recently acquired, and is now published by Beghahn Journals.

Noteworthy ceased publications, whose archived issues hold value for Men's Studies include *Fathering*, the *Journal of Men's Health and Gender, Journal of Men, Masculinities and Spirituality*. The *Journal of Black Masculinity* is no longer available for free online, despite some web sites suggesting that it is freely accessible. Archived issues of the journal can be acquired as a one-time purchase without a subscription. Issues from the *Journal of Men, Masculinities and Spirituality*, which ceased publication in 2012, were compiled into a book and published by Georgas Publishers. Full text documents are also available online from the original editor's web site, which can be found by searching for the journal title and the editor's name: "Journal of Men, Masculinities and Spirituality" AND "Joseph Gelpher."

Online Resources

As expected, there are numerous online resources representing a spectrum of perspectives. In regards to academic library collections, however, a few sites stand out. For organizational ease, I've categorized the most valuable resources for academic research into two categories. The first category lists sites that are associated with academic departments or institutions, and represent either an academic program or a collaborative project or initiative between one or more academic institutions. The second category lists well known organizations and networks, which is helpful for staying abreast of new trends and topics.

Education or Academic Sites

- Center for the Study of Men & Masculinities (Stony Brook University)
- Changing Men Collection (Michigan State University, MSU Libraries, Special Collections)
- American Men's Studies Association (University of Michigan's School of Social Work)
- Mobilizing Men for Violence Prevention (University of Michigan, University of Kansas, and the University of Washington, Tacoma)
- Biidwewidam Indigenous Masculinities Project (Aboriginal organizations, Canadian Universities and Indigenous communities)

Organizations and Networks

- Men's Resources Center for Change
- Society for the Psychological Study of Men and Masculinities, APA
- National Organization for Men Against Sexism, NOMAS
- Voice Male Magazine
- Men's Health Network
- Scholars Network on Black Masculinity

People

Finally, it may be worthwhile to be familiar with a few scholars and their publications. Sociologists and psychologist remain the prominent voices within men and masculinities studies:

- Michael Kimmel, sociologist
- Michael Messner, sociologist

- Raewyn Connell, sociologist
- Andrew Smiler, psychologist
- Christopher Kilmartin, psychologist
- Jay C. Wade, psychologist

Student Examples

As the librarian for the College of Social and Behavioral Sciences, I support a number of departments within the college, including the Women's and Gender Studies program. To date, no one from this program has asked specifically for resources about men and masculinities. Instead, the questions arise most often from psychology and sociology departments. The following examples from past student interactions serve as reference case studies and may be helpful for future questions regarding men and masculinities studies.

Psychology

A psychology student, who was working on a research project with a faculty member, was struggling to find information on Latino masculinities among Latino populations in the United States. While there is plenty of information found in mainstream media outlets, locating evidence-based research was not as easy. Our first approach was to look at Latino/a databases, such as Chicano Database and Hispanic American Periodicals Index (HAPI). Neither offered any useful resources, and in fact, at the time that we conducted the search, searching the subject term masculinity produced only three results. Our next attempt was sociology databases, and indeed, the most useful information that we located came primarily from sociology and psychology disciplines. In fact, conference proceedings from sociology conferences proved to be the most helpful guides, leading to some highly relevant research that was otherwise buried within databases and obscure book titles. WorldCat© was another useful search tool for books, dissertations and theses, and, again, conference proceedings. Three journals were especially useful, *Psychology of Men and Masculinity, Hispanic Journal of Behavioral Sciences,* and *Cultural Diversity and Ethnic Minority Psychology.* Overall, in our experience, keyword combinations proved more fruitful than conducting subject searches. The student and their professor, used the research to co-publish a book chapter.

Sociology

A student enrolled in a 300 level sociology class requested help finding information on the role of fathers during pregnancy and infancy. The useful resources in this case included medical resources such as PubMed and psychology resources, such as PsycINFO and PsycARTICLES, particularly psychology journals related to family studies and human development. The PsycINFO thesaurus suggested the terms father and infant development. Keyword searches yielded a greater number of results, while using Thesaurus and MeSH terms produced few yet highly relevant resources. There was an abundance of research on the role of fathers in infant development and many articles discusses attachment theory. Overall there was very little research on fathers and pregnancy. According to publication dates of articles this area of research may soon be increasing.

Political Science

One of the more challenging questions came from a student studying the influence of gender on foreign policy. The crux of the question concerned the influence of male stereotypes in contemporary Russian culture and how those stereotypes influenced interactions with the United States. Since the inquiry was complex, we started with two broad keyword searches, one search aimed to collect information on male stereotypes in Russia and the second search related to Russia's foreign policy with the United States. In order to get an idea of which journals or other resources would best meet the needs of the research, we conducted searches in Google Scholar and a dissertations and theses database. Google Scholar provided results for books and journal articles, the majority of which were political science and psychology journals. Searching dissertations and theses enabled us to use the references that the authors' had consulted. Starting with these two resources also provided additional keywords for a more focused search in the databases. For example, the most relevant term for this search was not "male stereotypes" but rather masculinity. The search strategies used required several tweaks, such as subtracting terms like feminism. Ultimately, however, the student was able to collect journal articles and book chapters that discussed at least one aspect of the original research question. Distinguishing the history of political control in Russia was key to conducting this search, as we learned, research on gender roles in Russia is still a new area of research.

Similar to the previous two examples, men and masculinities studies' research requires navigating and consulting literature in multiple disciplines.

Conclusion

Men and masculinities studies is emerging and developing as a new interdisciplinary field of research, as scholars challenge previous conceptions of men and masculinities. Research in this area has steadily increased over the past two decades and the need for varied scholarly resources is important to support the growing interest. Academic libraries can best prepare for research needs and requests by building and maintaining a robust collection of print and online resources.

REFERENCES

Connell, Raewyn. 2000. *The Men and the Boys*. University of California Press.
Peterson's. https://www.petersons.com/ (accessed May 23, 2016).
Smiler, Andrew. 2004. "Thirty Years After the Discovery of Gender: Psychological Concepts and Measures of Masculinity." *Sex Roles* 50, no. 1–2: 15–26.

About the Contributors

Laurel **Bliss** is a librarian at San Diego State University. Her research includes diversity and inclusion in libraries and publishing trends in art librarianship. She is chair of ALA's Membership Committee and is active in Art Libraries Society of North America.

Kristen L. **Chinery**, a reference archivist at the Walter P. Reuther Library, Wayne State University. She is a member of the Regional Archival Associations Consortium Steering Committee, chairs the Grant Development Committee, and is the organization's co-chair. Her research includes women's labor history and industrial organizational psychology as it relates to archivists.

Elizabeth **Clemens** is an archivist at the Walter P. Reuther Library, Wayne State University. She is the author of *The Works Progress Administration in Detroit* and *The First World War in Detroit*, is an editor for the Society of American Archivists Visual Materials Section and is a steering committee member of the group's Women's Archivists Roundtable.

Anna W. **Culbertson** is a special collections librarian at San Diego State University. She provides primary source research instruction, collaborates with teaching faculty, and curates the library's speculative fiction and comics arts collections. Her research includes feminist science fiction and comics, the gray literature of the women's movement, and ideas of utopia in speculative fiction and alternative religious movements.

Karl **Ericson** is a reference librarian at the University of Detroit Mercy and is responsible for liaison duties in addiction studies, African American studies, social work, sociology and women's and gender studies. His research includes assessment, information literacy instruction, critical pedagogy (as it applies to library instruction) and critical librarianship.

Karen **Evans**, an instruction and reference public services librarian at Indiana State University in Terre Haute, is a member of the American Library Association and Indiana Library Federation. Her writings have appeared in *College and Research Libraries News, Indiana Libraries, Choice, Journal of Consumer Health on the Internet*, and *Reference Reviews*. She is the recipient of two Carnegie-Whitney Grants from the American Library Association.

Barbara **Fiehn** is an associate professor for library media education at Western Kentucky University. Her interests are in school library administration, intellectual freedom, and LGBTQ materials for elementary children. She has served on intellectual freedom committees at state and national levels and has published articles in *Children and Libraries* and *Knowledge Quest*.

M'issa **Fleming** is a young adult librarian at the main branch of the New Orleans Public Library. They are a member of the American Library Association's Gay Lesbian Bisexual Transgender Round Table and the Young Adult Library Services Association, and volunteers for the Iron Rail Book Collective.

Linda **Garrison**, librarian at Canterbury School of Florida in St. Petersburg, is working toward her Ph.D. in texts and technology at the University of Central Florida. She has presented at Florida Council of Independent Schools and the Timucuan Science and History Symposium in Jacksonville, Florida, and she coauthored a paper that won third place in the IEEE Global Humanitarian Technology Conference, Seattle 2015.

Morna **Gerrard** is the Women and Gender Collections Archivist at Georgia State University. She serves on the boards of the Georgia Archives Institute and the Georgia LGBTQ Archives Project, and the Programming Board of the National Center for Civil and Human Rights' LGBT Institute. She has written about oral history and public programming the Georgia LGBTQ Archives Project.

Darcy I. **Gervasio** is the coordinator of reference services at Purchase College Library, State University of New York. She serves as liaison librarian for anthropology, gender studies, language and culture, and sociology. She has published in *Urban Library Journal* and *International Journal of Digital Library Systems* and presented on slow assessment at the ACRL 2015 National Conference.

Kimberley M. **Henze** is a dual-degree master's student in art history and library science at the University of North Carolina–Chapel Hill. She is a Learning from Artists' Archives IMLS fellow and research and design graduate assistant at the R.B. House Undergraduate Library. Her interests include visual and digital literacy, social media theory, critical museum studies, and early twentieth century women artists.

Jamie L. **Huber**, a staff member at the St. Charles City-County Library District and an adjunct instructor of gender studies for Lindenwood University in St. Charles, Missouri, is in an MLIS program at Valdosta State University. She is a member of the American Library Association, the Missouri Library Association, the Organization for the Study of Communication Language and Gender, and the National Women's Studies Association, among others.

Amy **Hughes** is an academic librarian for the College of Social and Behavioral Sciences at Northern Arizona University in Flagstaff. With expertise in faculty-librarian collaborations, her work has focused on information literacies and curriculum integration. Her interests include research methods in the social sciences, ethics in research, copyright and academic integrity, and information access in rural communities.

Jeanine M. **Huss** is an associate professor of education at Western Kentucky University. Her memberships include National Science Teachers Association and the North American Association for Environmental Education. She is a contributor to *How to STEM,* and the author of "Playgrounds for the Mind" in *Children and Libraries* and "Realities of War" in *Multicultural Education.*

Ellen E. **Jarosz** is head of Special Collections and Archives at the Oviatt Library at California State University Northridge. She is a member of the American Library Association, Society of American Archivists, and Society of California Archivists. She serves the Western Archives Institute as associate administrator and adjunct faculty member and is a past president of the Society of California Archivists.

Maggie Gallup **Kopp** is curator of rare books at L. Tom Perry Special Collections in Brigham Young University's Harold B. Lee Library in Provo, Utah. She has taught a course on women's book history at BYU since 2014. Her work appears in *Reference Services Review* and *The Journal of Library Innovation.*

Lynn D. **Lampert**, coordinator of information literacy and instruction at California State University Northridge's Oviatt Library, is the subject specialist librarian for gender and women's studies, queer studies, history and Jewish studies. She has written on information literacy, outreach and other areas of academic librarianship including her book, *Combating Student Plagiarism.*

Kendall **Larson** is the acquisitions, collection development, and digital collections librarian at Winona State University in Winona, Minnesota. She is involved in architectual history projects and was formerly the liaison to WSU's gender studies program. She has taught library instruction and been involved in a variety of technology projects and digital collections.

Tara Zachary **Laver** is curator of manuscripts in the Louisiana State University Libraries' Special Collections. She has published articles on archival topics and works of historical documentary editing in *American Archivist*, *Southeastern Librarian*, and *Louisiana History*, and presented on these and historical topics of local and regional interest.

Vince **Lee** is the archivist for the Carey C. Shuart Women's Archive and Research Collection at the University of Houston Libraries–Special Collections. He collaborates with the Friends of Women's Studies, the Department of Women, Gender and Sexuality Studies, UH Center for Public History and non-university partners such as Houston Area Rainbow Collective History and the Archivists of the History Area.

Coleen **Meyers-Martin** is coordinator of outreach services and a librarian at California State University Northridge's Oviatt Library and is the liaison to K–12 schools. She coauthored with Lynn Lampert "If You Build It Will They Come" in *Creative Library Marketing and Publicity Best Practices*. Her work has also appeared in *Reference Services Review*, *College & Research Libraries News*, and other publications.

Carrie E. **Moran** is the user engagement librarian at the University of Central Florida. She is the liaison to the Psychology, Social Work, and Women's & Gender Studies departments. Her role also includes user research, outreach, event planning, and library instruction. She is an active member of ALA and ACRL. She is also a passionate advocate for LGBTQ+ issues, and is president of UCF's Pride Faculty & Staff Association.

Lisa **Morgan** is a public services librarian at New River Public Library, Zephyrhills, Florida. She is a member of the Young Adult Library Services Association and the American Library Association and is a social sciences and cultural studies reviewer for *American Reference Books Annual*. She is pursuing a graduate certificate in women's and gender studies at the University of South Florida.

Megan **Novell** works in public services at the McNichols Campus Library at the University of Detroit Mercy, where she has worked with digital special collections of archival materials and displays for Women's History Month. She teaches writing and literature part-time in the English Department and the Women's and Gender Studies Program.

Rebecca **Oling** is the coordinator of instruction at the Purchase College Library, State University of New York, where she also serves as liaison librarian for literature, drama, and film. She manages the streaming collection and often works in an instructional design capacity to help instructors translate the goals of a course into the realities of the teaching environment. Her interests center on the assessment of information communication.

Leandra **Preston-Sidler** is an associate lecturer in women's and gender studies at the University of Central Florida. She has developed and teaches courses including girls' studies, virtual girls, girls and the body, third wave feminisms, theories of masculinities, and gender and technology. Her interests include biotechnologies, gender in social networks, and violence and masculinity.

Patricia **Rind** is an adjunct professor of gender studies, women's studies, and psychology at Purchase College, State University of New York. She is the author of *Women's Best Friendships* and a chapter for *The International Encyclopedia of Human Sexuality*. She is writing a book on talking to children about sex and sexuality.

Lura **Sanborn** is the research and instruction librarian at St. Paul's School in Concord, New Hampshire, and is the architect for the digital library. She also teaches research skills and sources. Her writing has appeared in *The Journal of Academic Librarianship*, *Reference and User Services Quarterly*, *Teacher Librarian*, *Against the Grain*, *School Library Monthly* and *Library Journal*.

Carol **Smallwood** has a MLS and MA in history, is a school, public, and special librarian, and has edited a number of books on librarianship topics. Her *Women on Poetry: Writing, Revising, Publishing and Teaching* is on *Poets & Writers Magazine* list of Best Books for Writers.

Shawn(ta) **Smith-Cruz** is an assistant professor and head of reference at the Graduate Center of the City University of New York. Her work has appeared in *Sinister Wisdom*, *Journal of Lesbian*

Studies, Frontiers, and other publications. She is on the advisory board for Gale Primary Resources' Sexuality and Gender database and speaks internationally on lesbian archival narrative sourcing the work of the Lesbian Herstory Archives.

Michael **Taylor** is curator of books in the Louisiana State University Libraries' Special Collections. He has received additional training in special collections librarianship at the Rare Book School (University of Virginia) and California Rare Book School (UCLA). His work has appeared in *Louisiana Libraries, Manuscripts,* and various historical publications.

Therese F. **Triumph** is a science liaison librarian for the Kenan Science Library at the University of North Carolina–Chapel Hill. She is a member of the Special Libraries Association and the North Carolina Library Association. She is interested in student outreach, especially outreach to the women in the sciences. Her writings appear in *College & Research Libraries,* and the *Journal of Librarianship and Scholarly Communication.*

Stewart **Van Cleve** is the web and digital services librarian at Winona State University in Winona, Minnesota, where he is the liaison to the Women's, Gender, and Sexuality Studies Program. He is the author of *Land of 10,000 Loves: A History of Queer Minnesota.*

Rosemary **Weatherston** is an associate professor of English and director of the Women's and Gender Studies Program at the University of Detroit Mercy. Her publications on gender and queer studies have appeared in *The Americanist, ARIEL, Discourse, Theatre Journal,* and *Post Identity,* and in anthologies including *Body Politics and the Fictional Double* and *Queer Frontiers.*

Callan **Wells** works for Georgia Legal Services Program, a nonprofit law firm that provides civil legal services to rural residents. She runs a hotline that helps connect low-income people with public benefits and focuses on ensuring survivors of domestic violence can gain financial independence from their abusers to maintain their safety.

Stephanie H. **Wical**, periodicals and electronic resources librarian and women's studies affiliate at the University of Wisconsin–Eau Claire, works with publishers and providers of journals and databases to ensure that faculty members have the resources they need. She completed her MLS degree in Library and Information Studies at SUNY Buffalo and her MA degree in Women's Studies at the University of Alabama in Tuscaloosa.

Samantha R. **Winn**, collections archivist for Virginia Tech, works to document traditionally marginalized communities in Southwest Virginia and Southern Appalachia. Her memberships include the Society of American Archivists, Art Libraries Society of North America, Visual Resources Association, and the Association for Women in Science. She has written for *Provenance* and the Hack School library blog.

Joy **Worland** is director of the Kellogg-Hubbard Library in Montpelier, Vermont. A member of the American Library Association's Alex Award Committee, she also cochaired ALA's Amelia Bloomer Project. She has presented at ALA, Vermont Library Association Conferences, and has published locally and nationally.

Anthony **Wright de Hernandez** is the first resident librarian at Virginia Tech, the librarian for the Intercultural Engagement Center and a facilitator for the SafeZone program.. He is a member of the American Library Association, Theatre Library Association, Virginia Library Association, and the Association of College & Research Libraries. He is on the ALA GLBT Round Table and ACRL Residency Interest Group Web Committees.

Jessica **Zellers** worked for ten years in public libraries small, medium, and large, before becoming the collection development librarian at Western Carolina University in Cullowhee, North Carolina. She is the author of *Women's Nonfiction* and is a frequent contributor to NoveList. She is interested in readers' advisory, collection development, and book deselection.

Index